Best of the Best from INDIANA Cookbook

Selected Recipes from Indiana's
FAVORITE COOKBOOKS

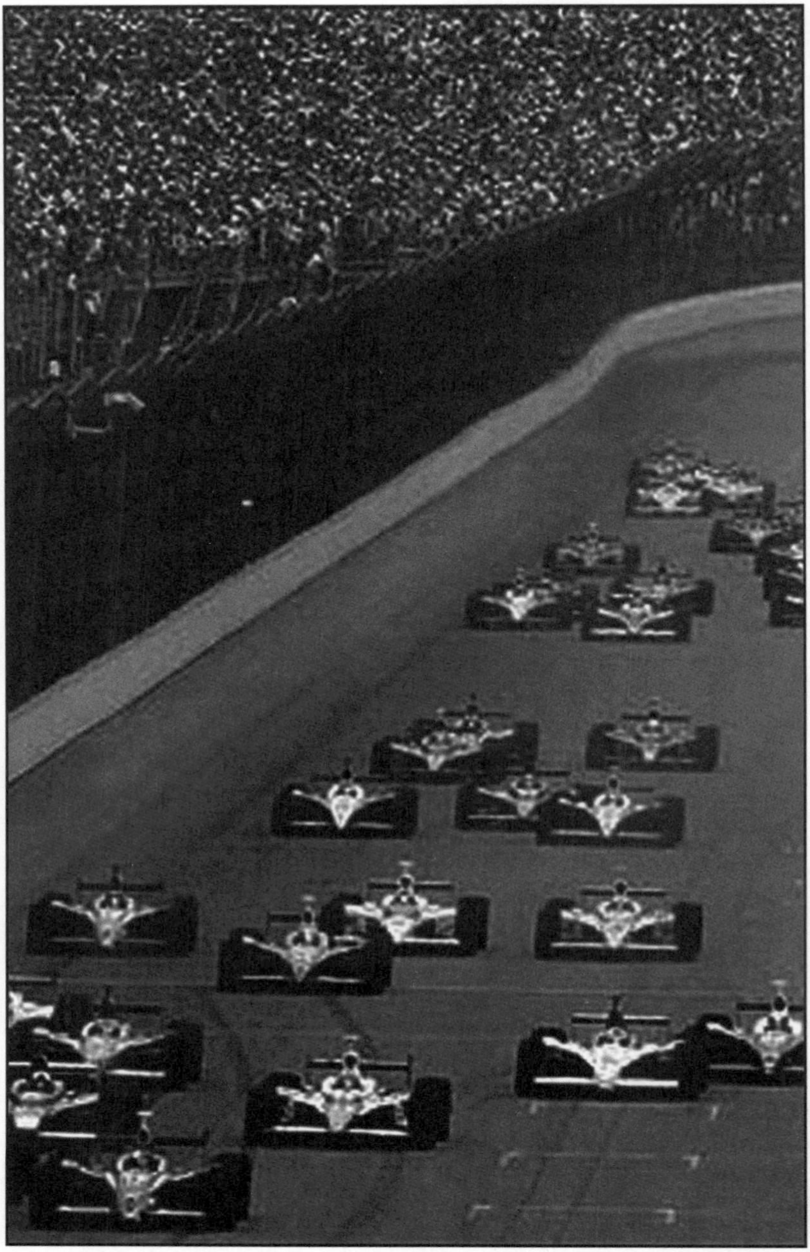

AUTORACINGSPORT.COM

"The Greatest Spectacle in Racing," the Indianapolis 500
is one of the oldest motor sport events.
Indianapolis Motor Speedway near Indianapolis.

Best of the Best from INDIANA Cookbook

Selected Recipes from Indiana's FAVORITE COOKBOOKS

EDITED BY
Gwen McKee
AND
Barbara Moseley

Illustrated by Tupper England

QUAIL RIDGE PRESS
Preserving America's Food Heritage

Library of Congress Cataloging-in-Publication Data

Best of the best from Indiana; selected recipes from Indiana's favorite cookbooks/edited by Gwen McKee and Barbara Moseley;illustrated by Tupper Jones
p. cm.
Includes index.
ISBN-13: 978-0-937552-57-5
ISBN-10: 0-937552-57-7
1. Cookery-Indiana. 1. McKee, Gwen. II. Moseley, Barbara.
TX715.B485637371995
641.59772-dc20 95-24447 CIP

ISBN-13: 978-0-937552-57-5 • ISBN-10: 0-937552-57-7

First printing, September 1995 • Second, September 1996 • Third, November 1997
Fourth, November 1998 • Fifth, September 2001 • Seventh, November 2004
Eighth, September 2009

Designed by Barney and Gwen McKee
Printed by Tara TPS in South Korea

Cover photo courtesy of Indiana Department of Commerce

QUAIL RIDGE PRESS

P. O. Box 123 • Brandon, MS 39043 • 1-800-343-1583
info@quailridge.com • www.quailridge.com

CONTENTS

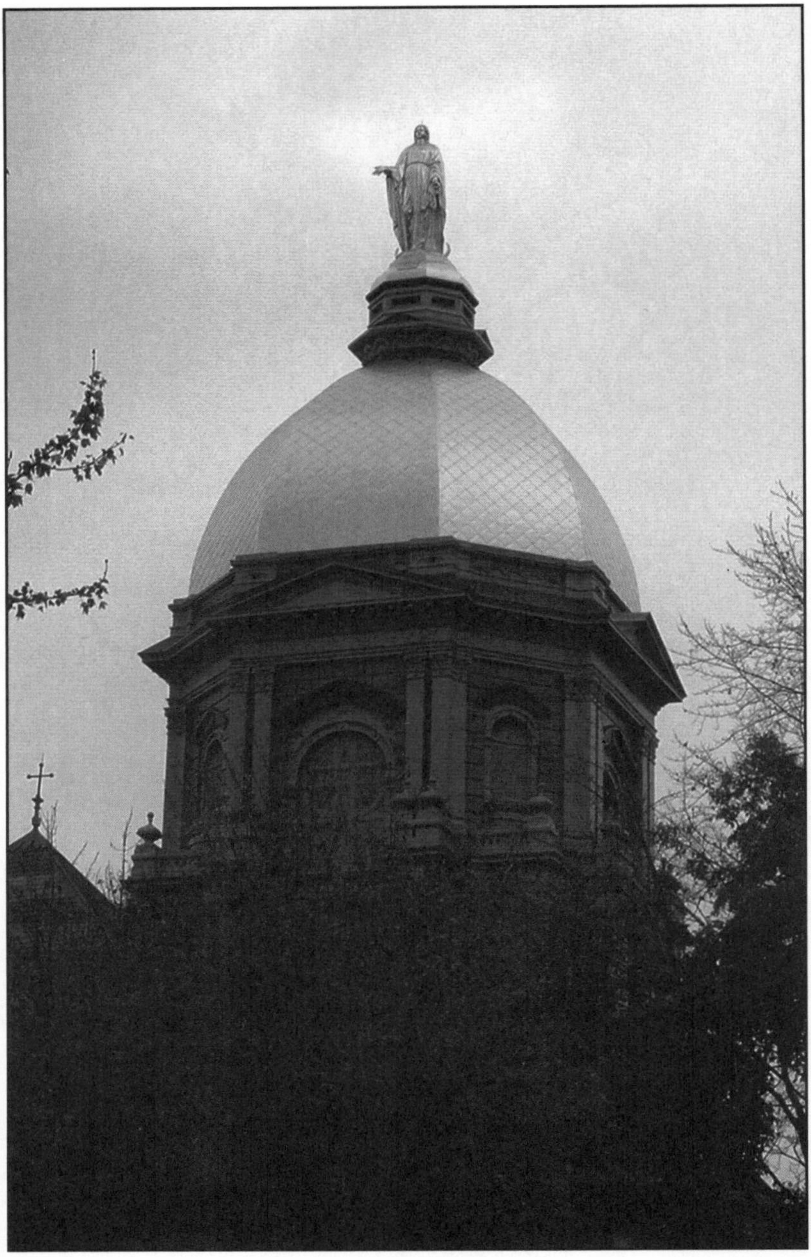

The Golden Dome on the Notre Dame Campus. South Bend.

Preface

Indiana . . . a land of farms and fields and colorful trees, of sandy dunes and rocky caves, of sandy car races and sports hall-of-famers . . . a state that is a continuous network of charming towns and old-fashioned Hoosier hospitality.

Hoosier! What's a Hoosier? Well, there are many theories as to the origin of the name (see page 60), so we cannot tell you for sure which is correct. But what we most certainly can tell you is that Hoosiers are proud to be Hoosiers, however they got the name! And they are also proud to tell you about their food and some of the history connected to it.

Indiana cooking is literally the backbone of their heritage, and German, Italian, and Polish influences are strong among them. Basically, though, Indiana cooking began back on the farm, and there are many handed-down treasures like Aunt Sally's blue-ribbon winning recipes . . . Marge's home-grown herb creations . . . James Whitcomb Riley's Favorite Bean Soup . . . mmmmm, such delicious pride. Asked what they eat, Hoosiers are quick to tell you: Beef and Noodles, Sugar Cream Pie, Funnel Cakes, German Potato Salad, Friendship Cake . . . but they will also expound on their own particular creations: "You haven't tasted anything till you've tried . . . Grandpa Pastura's Grilled Swordfish, Annie's Apple Pudding, Mt. Mama's Mudslide Cake, a Super Sullivan Taco, Mom Unser's Indy Chili, Maybe-the-Best Yeast Rolls, etc., etc., etc."

In our search for cookbooks and Indiana cuisine, we came across the phrase "tavern- food." Indeed, taverns serve food that locals like. In Evansville, food editor Sara Corrigan took us to one of their local taverns where we ordered the Batter-fried Pork Brain Sandwich, and a regional Barbeque Soak. (We have made some tasty discoveries in the name of research!) We learned it can't be called a tavern if it doesn't serve food, and you don't have to be 21 to eat there as long as you're with Mom or Dad.

Fiddlers (small fried catfish) and fried chicken are often served at an all-you-can-eat price; the pork chops are thick, sometimes smoked and often stuffed, and the Dutch fries are always on the menu; Southern Indiana tomatoes on a summer salad are the tastiest you'll ever find, and a big bowl of burgoo is guaranteed to warm up a chilly day. Sampling favorite Hoosier dishes in places we visited around the state was always a delicious treat.

We found so many fine cookbooks, probably missed a few, and regret we could not utilize all we came across. Thank you, thank you, thank you to all who created these wonderful recipes, including the authors, editors, chairpersons, and publishers for their cooperation in making this book possible. It is our hope that people will be encouraged to order these delightful books from the complete catalog beginning on page 267.

We owe many thanks—to dear friend Paula who welcomed us in Fort Wayne, and to Chris and Mike for giving us the royal treatment in South Bend . . . how wonderful to experience Hoosier hospitality first-hand! We are indebted to the food editors from newspapers across Indiana who helped us with our research, as well as book and gift store, tourism, and home extension personnel, and all the lovely people who took the time to talk to us along the way. And always our thanks to Tupper, for the 17th time, for her right-on-target artwork that lends so much to this book.

Indiana was fun! We hope this book will take you—like it did us—back to the farm, back to dinner-table meals, exemplifying the pioneer spirit of welcoming food and warm hospitality.

Gwen McKee and Barbara Moseley

CONTRIBUTING COOKBOOKS

Amish Country Cookbook I
Amish Country Cookbook II
Amish Country Cookbook III
Aspic and Old Lace
Back Home Again
The Brown County Cookbook
Champions: Favorite Foods of Indy Car Racing
Christmas Thyme at Oak Hill Farm
The Conner Prairie Cookbook
The Cookery Collection
Cookin' to Beat the Band
Cooking with Herbs
Cooking with the Warriors
Country Cooking
Festival Foods and Family Favorites
For Crying Out Loud
Great Beginnings, Grand Finales
The Guild Cookbook I
The Guild Cookbook II
The Guild Cookbook III
The Guild Cookbook IV
Guten Appetit
The Heart of Cooking
The Heart of Cooking II
Home Cooking
Home Cooking II
The Hoosier Cookbook
Hoosier Heritage Cookbook
Hopewell's Hoosier Harvest II
The IU Cookbook
The Indiana Bed & Breakfast Cookbook

CONTRIBUTING COOKBOOKS

The Indiana Kid's Cookbook
Indiana's Finest Recipes
It's About Thyme
The James Whitcomb Riley Cookbook
Jasper County Extension Homemakers Cookbook
Love Cookin'
The Midwestern Country Cookbook
Mincemeat and Memories
More Hoosier Cooking
New-Fangled, Old-Fashioned Bread Puddings
Nutbread and Nostalgia
Our Best Recipes to You, Again
Our Favorite Recipes
Our Favorite Recipes II
Our Italian Family Cookbook
Recipes from Jan's Cake & Candy Crafts
Recipes of the Durbin
Service League's Favorites
Sharing Our Best
Specialties of Indianapolis II
Taste & See
A Taste of Fishers
A Taste of Twin Pines
White Feather Farms Saturday Secrets
The Wild Flavor
Winners

BEVERAGES & APPETIZERS

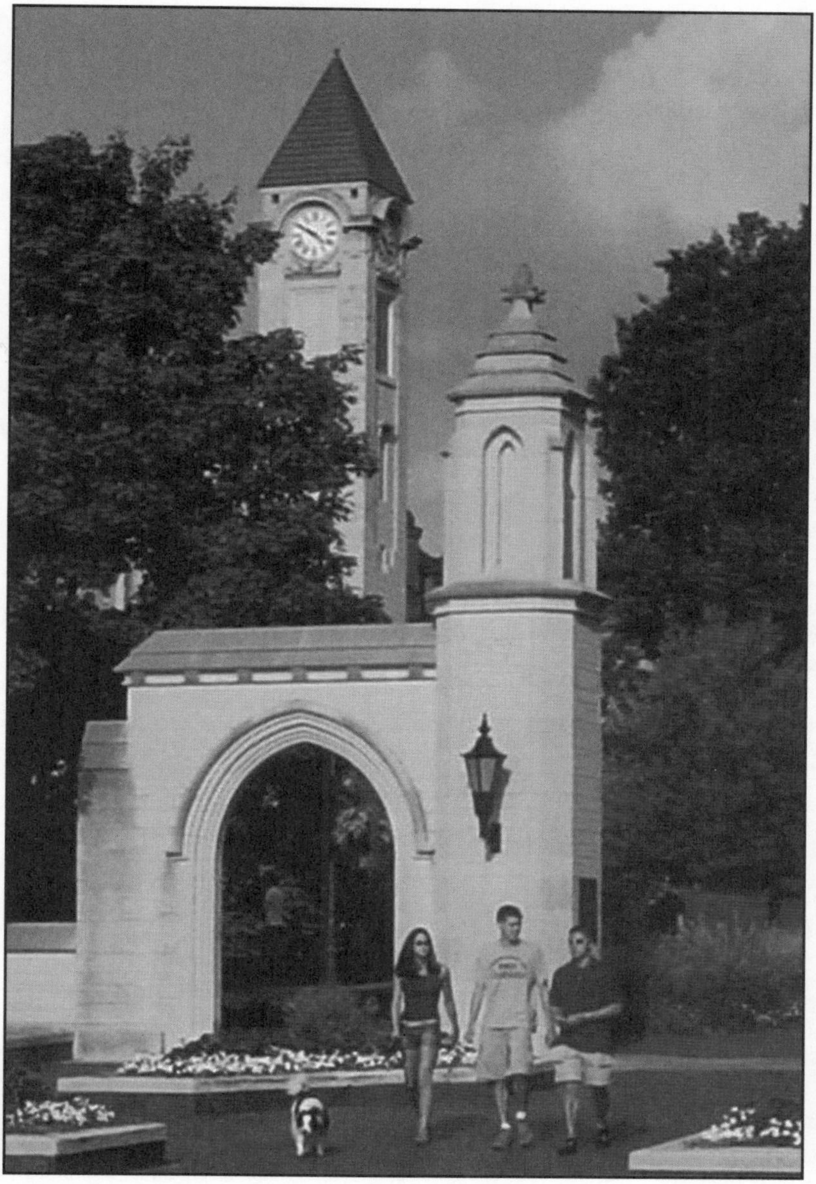

WIKIPEDIA.COM

The Clock Tower entrance to the University of Indiana. Bloomington.

Friendship Tea

A hot drink especially for holidays.

FOR 30-CUP PERCOLATOR:

9 cups unsweetened pineapple juice
9 cups cranberry juice cocktail
4½ cups water
1 cup brown sugar
4¼ teaspoons whole cloves
4 broken cinnamon sticks
¼ teaspoon salt

FOR 10-CUP PERCOLATOR:

3 cups unsweetened pineapple juice
3 cups cranberry juice cocktail
1½ cups water
⅓ cup brown sugar
1½ teaspoons whole cloves
1 broken cinnamon stick
⅛ teaspoon salt

Combine pineapple juice, cranberry juice and water in an automatic percolator. Combine remaining ingredients in basket. Allow to go through perk cycle. Remove basket and stem from coffee maker. Serve piping hot.

Taste & See

Cranberry Tea

1 pint cranberry juice
3 pints water
1½ cups sugar
1 (12-ounce) can frozen orange juice concentrate
2 cans water (total of 24 ounces)
1 (12-ounce) can frozen grapefruit juice concentrate
Dash each of cinnamon, nutmeg, and cloves

Mix all together and simmer 10 minutes. Makes 14 (6-ounce) servings.

The Cookery Collection

Yuletide Punch Bowl

2 pints raspberry sherbet
1 cup lemon juice
1 cup orange juice
¾ cup sugar
1 large bottle cranberry juice cocktail
2 bottles ginger ale

Soften 1 pint sherbet in punch bowl. Combine softened sherbet, lemon juice, orange juice, and sugar; stir to dissolve sugar. Add cranberry juice and ginger ale, all of which have been chilled. With ice cream scoop, float remaining 1 pint sherbet over top of punch. Makes about 15-20 (6-ounce) servings.

Jasper County Extension Homemakers Cookbook

Parisian Mocha

2 cups water
3 (1-ounce) packages instant cocoa mix
2 tablespoons instant coffee
½ teaspoon cinnamon
Whipped cream
Shaved chocolate curls
2 cinnamon sticks

Measure water into 1-quart measure. Microwave 4-5 minutes on HIGH or until almost boiling. Combine cocoa mix, instant coffee and cinnamon. Add to water. Stir. Pour into cups. Garnish with whipped cream and chocolate curls. Add cinnamon sticks and serve immediately. Serves 2. If recipe is doubled, use only 5 packages cocoa mix.

Mincemeat and Memories

Shipshewana is home to one of the largest flea markets in the United States. The Shipshewana Auction is held every Wednesday year round. They often have up to twelve rings of auctioneers, all selling at once.

Bailey's Nog

6 eggs, beaten until foamy
½ cup sugar
3 cups milk
1½ cups Bailey's Irish Cream
½ teaspoon ground nutmeg
½ cup whipping cream, whipped
Ground nutmeg

Gradually add sugar to beaten eggs. Beat 5 minutes, until thick and lemony. Reduce speed on mixer to low; gradually add milk, Bailey's, and nutmeg. Beat until combined. Chill thoroughly.

Stir whipped cream into chilled mixture until thoroughly combined. Sprinkle with nutmeg. Yield: 2 quarts.

Champions: Favorite Foods of Indy Car Racing

Perfect Eggnog

2 quarts milk
4 cups sugar
12 egg yolks, beaten
1 cup brandy
2 cups rum
3 cups bourbon*
12 egg whites, beaten stiff
3 (½-pint) cartons whipped cream (sweetened with 3 teaspoons sugar)
Freshly grated nutmeg

Combine in a large punch bowl the milk and sugar. Add egg yolks; slowly add the brandy, rum, and bourbon. To this mixture, fold in stiffly beaten egg whites and whipped cream. Sprinkle with nutmeg and chill overnight.

*If you want to make Rudolph's nose glow a little brighter this holiday season, double the brandy, rum, and bourbon.

Aspic and Old Lace

"The Crossroads of America" was the slogan adopted for Indiana by the General Assembly in 1937.

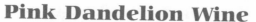

Pink Dandelion Wine

2 quarts dandelion blossoms
2 quarts boiling water
Juice of 3 lemons
1 (10-ounce) package frozen red raspberries
3½ cups sugar
1 cake of yeast

Gather the dandelion blossoms early in the morning while they are still fresh. Prepare the blossoms for the wine as soon as you return to the house, as they soon wilt. Snip off the end of each dandelion blossom to remove any remaining bitter stem particles as well as the little collar of leaves at the base of the blossom. Do not wash the flowers. Put the petals in a l-gallon stoneware crock and pour the boiling water over them. Let stand overnight. In the morning, strain the liquid from the flowers, squeezing all of the juice out of them.

Combine the dandelion juice, lemon juice, raspberries, and sugar. Boil gently for 20 minutes. Pour back into the crock, cook to lukewarm, and add the yeast. Cover the crock and let ferment for about 10 days, or until it stops hissing. Using filter paper or a double layer of cheesecloth, strain the liquid into a scalded cider jug and let stand for about 3 days to settle. Then strain again into clean quart wine bottles with screw-on caps, but do not tighten the caps. Let stand until the wine is still before corking or capping the bottles tightly. Age in the cellar until Christmas time. Fills 3 (5-quart) wine bottles.

The Wild Flavor

Fresh Fruit Dip

Tasty, pretty and delicious summer dip.

½ cup (1 stick) butter
1 cup firmly packed brown sugar
1 cup sour cream
3 teaspoons vanilla

Melt butter in small saucepan over medium heat. Add brown sugar; stir until smooth. Remove from heat and cool. Add sour cream and vanilla to cooled mixture. Serve with fresh fruit. Serves 8-10.

Winners

Easy Party Dip

Sure to be one of your favorite dips. You will be surprised.

1 cup Hellmann's mayonnaise
1 cup chopped onion
8 ounces Swiss cheese, shredded
2 artificial lobster tails or 3 sea legs or 12 cooked shrimp
1 box Ritz crackers

Simply mix first three ingredients in a small casserole dish. For color and added taste, shred one or a combination of seafood mentioned above. Mix well. Cover casserole dish. Bake at 350° until cheese is melted, approximately 15-20 minutes. Serve warm on a Ritz cracker.

Indiana's Finest Recipes

Yummy Veggie Dip

- ¾ cup mayonnaise
- ⅓ cup sour cream
- 1 tablespoon minced onion
- 1 tablespoon parsley
- 1 teaspoon Lawry's Seasoned Salt
- ½ teaspoon Accent
- 1 teaspoon dill weed
- ½ teaspoon Worcestershire sauce
- 2 drops Tabasco sauce

Combine all of the above ingredients. (Serve with veggies of your choice).

White Feather Farms Saturday Secrets

Curry Dip

- 1 cup mayonnaise
- 1 teaspoon horseradish
- 1 tablespoon curry powder
- 1 teaspoon grated onion
- 1 teaspoon lemon juice

Mix ingredients and chill. Serve with chilled raw vegetables.

Recipes of the Durbin

Mexican Party Dip

- 1 (8-ounce) can bean dip
- 1 cup guacamole
- 2 cups sour cream
- Dry taco seasoning
- 2 tablespoons chopped onions
- 2 tablespoons chopped green chiles
- ½ cup chopped tomatoes
- Salt and pepper
- 1 cup shredded Monterey Jack or Colby cheese
- Sliced black or green olives
- Taco chips

Spread bean dip on a large serving platter. Add guacamole and sour cream in layers. Sprinkle with taco seasoning, onions, green chiles, tomatoes, and salt and pepper. Top with shredded cheese and olives. Chill and serve with taco chips.

Aspic and Old Lace

Mexican Cheesecake

What a combination! Mexican and cheesecake!!

1 pound cream cheese, softened
2 cups (8 ounces) shredded sharp Cheddar cheese
2 cups sour cream, divided
1½ packages taco seasoning mix
3 eggs, room temperature
1 (4-ounce) can green chiles, drained and chopped
⅔ cup salsa

Preheat oven to 350°. In large bowl, combine cheeses. Beat until fluffy. Stir in 1 cup sour cream and taco seasoning. Beat in eggs, one at a time, mixing well after each addition. Fold in chiles. Pour into 9-inch spring-form pan. Bake 35-40 minutes or until center is firm. Remove from oven. Cool 10 minutes. Spoon remaining 1 cup sour cream over cheesecake. Bake 5 minutes longer. Cool completely. Cover and refrigerate several hours. Before serving, remove sides of spring-form pan and top with salsa. Serve with plain taco chips. Yield: 10 servings.

Great Beginnings*, *Grand Finales

Bar Cheese

2 pounds pasteurized processed cheese
1 cup (8 ounces) horseradish
10 dashes hot sauce
1 cup plus 2 tablespoons mayonnaise

In a 2-quart saucepan, over low heat, melt cheese, stirring frequently. Add remaining ingredients. While warm, pour into 4-serving containers. (Soup or cereal-size bowls are perfect, as the bowls may be placed in several areas around the room for easy access.) Cover the warm dip with plastic wrap and store in refrigerator. If served cold, serve with crackers. Or if served warm, serve with chips. Makes about 1½ quarts, and serves approximately 50 persons.

Specialties of Indianapolis II

Jezebel

Great for parties!

1 (9-ounce) jar pineapple or apricot preserves
1 (9-ounce) jar apple jelly
2½ ounces horseradish
1 tablespoon dry mustard
½ teaspoon ground black pepper
2 (8-ounce) packages cream cheese

Mix first 5 ingredients together. Spread mixture over bricks of cream cheese. Serve with crackers. There is enough glaze to spread over 2 (8-ounce) packages cream cheese.

A Taste of Fishers

Tapenade

A spicy black Provencal olive paste.

1 cup pitted black olives
¼ cup chopped fresh or frozen basil
3 cloves garlic, peeled
1 (2-ounce) can anchovies, drained and rinsed
½ cup olive oil

Place all ingredients, except for oil, in food processor. Process until smooth, then slowly add oil as machine is running. Put tapenade in a bowl. Serve with crisp crackers, Melba toast or on a pasta. It will keep for a month in the refrigerator. Makes 1 cup.

Cooking with Herbs

Gouda Wellington

Makes a great accompaniment to a soup supper.

1 (8-ounce) package refrigerated crescent rolls
1 (7-ounce) Gouda cheese
⅓ cup apricot preserves or jam
1 egg white, beaten
Sesame seeds for garnish

Preheat oven to 350°. Using fingers, firmly press perforations on dough to seal and form a solid rectangle. Remove casing from Gouda cheese. Place in center of dough. Cover cheese with preserves or jam. Fold dough around cheese, sealing tightly to avoid leaking. Brush top with beaten egg white. Garnish with sesame seeds. Bake 30 minutes or until brown. Allow to set a few minutes. Cut into wedges and serve warm with French bread or crackers.

Great Beginnings, Grand Finales

Boursin

This is the real thing. A purist will tell you one can't make boursin with dried herbs—only fresh ones. Well, maybe he's right.

1 (8-ounce) package cream cheese, softened
1 tablespoon fresh lemon juice
1 clove garlic, minced
½ teaspoon Worcestershire sauce
½ teaspoon dry mustard
1 tablespoon finely chopped fresh parsley
1 tablespoon finely chopped fresh chives
4 tablespoons minced fresh herbs*

Combine all ingredients, but don't beat—just mix gently and thoroughly. Cover tightly and refrigerate. When ready to serve, bring to room temperature. Makes about 1 cup.

*Use at least four of the following herbs—the more, the better! Rosemary, thyme, dill, Greek oregano, marjoram, summer savory, basil, sage.

It's About Thyme

Jerry's Cheese Cubes

1 (8-ounce) package cream cheese
½ pound sharp Cheddar cheese
½ pound butter
2 egg whites, stiffly beaten
1 loaf unsliced white bread

Melt first 3 ingredients together in top of double boiler. Fold in egg whites. Cut unsliced bread into 1-inch cubes. Dip cubes into cheese mixture. Freeze on cookie sheet. Just before serving, bake at 400° for 10 minutes or until puffy and brown.

Note: For a different taste, try using light or dark rye bread for cubes.

Our Italian Family Cookbook

Cheese Torte

1 (10-ounce) package grated sharp Cheddar cheese
1 cup chopped pecans
1 medium onion, finely chopped
2 (8-ounce) packages cream cheese, softened
⅓ cup chutney
⅓ cup frozen chopped spinach, well drained
⅛ teaspoon oregano
Dash of pepper, celery seed, cumin, and nutmeg
1 tablespoon beef granules
¼ teaspoon garlic salt or powder
⅛ teaspoon basil

Pan or pans should be lined with plastic wrap so torte can be inverted to serve. Combine Cheddar cheese, pecans, and onion. Put ½ in 8-inch pie plate or 9-inch cake pan.

Combine 8 ounces cream cheese and chutney. Blend well and spread on Cheddar mix. Combine spinach, remaining 8 ounces cream cheese and seasonings. Blend well and spread on chutney mix. Top with remaining Cheddar mix. Serve with crackers. May be frozen.

Cooking with Herbs

Angel of Death Cheese

1 head garlic, separated into cloves
8 ounces ricotta cheese
4 ounces gorgonzola cheese
1 cup heavy cream
½ teaspoon salt
4 fresh sage leaves
Chopped walnuts

Cook garlic in microwave until tender (about 15 seconds). Mince in garlic press and measure 2 tablespoons.

Beat ricotta in medium-size bowl until softened. Add gorgonzola and mix until smooth. Beat in cream, salt, and minced garlic.

Dampen 18-inch square piece of cheesecloth and place sage leaves bottom-side-up in a pattern in center of square. Spoon cheese mixture over leaves. Tie ends of cloth together to form a ball shape. Place in cheesecloth-lined strainer and allow to drain for 24 hours in the refrigerator. Unmold cheese on serving platter. Decorate with chopped walnuts if desired. Serve at room temperature with an assortment of crackers.

White Feather Farms Saturday Secrets

Seafood Appetizers

1 package Hidden Valley Ranch Italian dry mix
6 ounces Kraft fat-free Swiss cheese slices, chopped
8 ounces nonfat sour cream
¾ cup nonfat mayonnaise
8 ounces imitation crab-meat, finely chopped
1 (1-pound) loaf of cocktail rye bread

Preheat oven to 350°. Combine all ingredients in a medium bowl. Spread mixture evenly on individual rye slices. Place on ungreased baking sheet. Bake for 10-15 minutes or until lightly browned. Makes 40 servings.

Nutrition Analysis Per Serving: (1 slice) Calories 47; Fat .2g; Cal from fat 0; Chol 1.4mg; Sod 339mg; Fiber .3g; Exchanges ½ starch.

The Heart of Cooking II

Sassy Shrimp

A savory attraction for any gathering.

2 pounds raw shrimp, cooked, peeled, deveined
¼ cup vegetable oil
2 cloves garlic, crushed
1 tablespoon dry mustard
2 teaspoons salt
½ cup lemon juice
1 tablespoon red wine vinegar
1 bay leaf, crumbled
½ teaspoon paprika
Dash of ground red pepper
1 lemon, very thinly sliced
1 medium red onion, very thinly sliced
1 (4-ounce) can whole ripe olives, drained, pitted
2 tablespoons chopped pimiento
2 tablespoons chopped parsley

Place shrimp in a large container with tight-fitting lid. Blend oil, garlic, dry mustard, salt, lemon juice, vinegar, bay leaf, paprika, and red pepper in a medium glass bowl. Stir in lemon slices, onion, olives, pimiento, and parsley. Add shrimp; toss well to coat. Marinate in refrigerator at least 1 hour or up to 4 hours. Serves 6-8.

Back Home Again

Crab Stuffed Mushroom Caps

- 1 tablespoon butter
- ¼ cup finely diced onion
- ¼ cup finely diced celery
- 1 ounce white wine
- 1 teaspoon salt
- ¼ teaspoon white pepper
- ½ teaspoon thyme
- 1 teaspoon lemon juice
- 4 ounces king, snow or lump crabmeat
- 1 ounce heavy cream or half-and-half
- ¼ cup shredded baby Swiss cheese
- ½ cup bread crumbs
- 16 large mushrooms, stems removed
- 16 small thin slices baby Swiss cheese

Preheat oven to 375°. Melt butter in medium skillet. Sauté onions and celery in butter until tender. Add wine, seasonings, lemon juice, and crabmeat; simmer 3 minutes. Add cream and shredded cheese; cook until cheese melts. Add bread crumbs. Spoon crab mixture into mushroom caps. Top with slices of baby Swiss cheese. Bake 12-15 minutes or until cheese is lightly browned.

The Matterhorn Restaurant Elkhart, Indiana.
Great Beginnings Grand Finales

Picnic Sandwich

1 (1-pound) loaf frozen bread dough
4 ounces each: cooked ham, cotto salami, pickle and pimiento loaf or your favorite luncheon meats, sliced thin
6 ounces provolone cheese or Monterey Jack cheese, coarsely shredded
8 ounces ricotta cheese
1 medium onion, chopped
½ cup chopped green bell pepper
½ cup chopped red bell pepper
1 teaspoon oregano

Let frozen dough thaw to room temperature. Preheat oven to 350°. Cut meats into ¼-inch wide strips. Mix meats, cheeses, onion, chopped peppers, and oregano. On lightly floured surface, roll dough to 10x14-inch rectangle. Place dough on lightly greased baking sheet. Spread meat filling in center of dough. Bring edges to center and seal. Turn over to hide seam. Make slits on top of loaf. (If desired, brush with egg wash and sprinkle with sesame or poppy seeds.) Bake immediately for 25 minutes or until golden brown. Cool on rack to ensure crispy bottom. Yield: 16 appetizer servings.

Variation: 2-3 ounces sliced olives may be added.

Great Beginnings, Grand Finales

Tortilla Roll-Ups

1 (4-ounce) can Old El Paso Green Chili Peppers
3 green onions, chopped
1 (8-ounce) package cream cheese, room temperature
½ teaspoon garlic salt
3-4 large flour tortillas
1 jar Chi-Chi's Salsa

Mix peppers, onions, cream cheese, and garlic salt together. Spread this on the tortillas, roll up, and refrigerate until chilled. Cut into bite-size pieces. Serve salsa on the side.

Hopewell's Hoosier Harvest II

Pepperoni Pinwheels

1 cup (3½ ounces) pepperoni, chopped
4 ounces shredded Mozzarella cheese
½ teaspoon oregano
1 egg, beaten
2 (8-ounce) packages crescent rolls

Mix first 4 ingredients together. Unroll crescent rolls onto wax paper. Pinch triangles together to form rectangles. Spoon pepperoni-cheese mixture evenly onto rectangles. Roll up and place in the freezer until firm enough to slice. Slice each roll into 8 slices. Bake at 375° for 10-12 minutes, until lightly browned. Makes 64.

Hopewell's Hoosier Harvest II

Crockpot Hors D'Oeuvres

1 (10-ounce) jar chili sauce
1 (10-ounce) jar grape jelly
1 package sausage links (can be cut in half)

Melt chili sauce and jelly in saucepan. Brown sausage links. Put everything in crockpot on LOW for full flavor. Use toothpicks to spear.

Home Cooking II

Polish Mistakes

1 pound ground beef
1 pound hot sausage
1 pound sharp cheese
1 tablespoon Worcestershire sauce
1 tablespoon oregano
2 loaves party rye bread
Mozzarella cheese for topping

Brown meat and drain. Add cheese, Worcestershire, and oregano and cook until cheese is melted. Spread on rye bread. (Could be frozen at this point.) Sprinkle mozzarella on top. Bake at 400° for 15 minutes.

Taste & See

Reuben Snacks

- 4 cups rye bread crumbs
- 1 cup shredded Swiss cheese
- 1 cup shredded corned beef
- 1 cup drained chopped sauerkraut
- ½ cup melted butter

Combine crumbs, cheese, and corned beef. Add kraut, mixing well. Pour melted butter over mixture and mix again. Press mixture together and let stand a short time. Form into balls (golf size or smaller). Bake at 375° for 20 minutes. Makes about 3 dozen.

Guten Appetit

Laura's Marinated Vegetables

Everyone will ask for the recipe!

MARINADE:

1⅓ cups vinegar
⅔ cup vegetable oil
3 tablespoons lemon juice
½ cup sugar
2 teaspoons oregano
1 teaspoon salt
½ teaspoon pepper
Dash Tabasco

In a large bowl, combine ingredients. Stir to dissolve the sugar.

2 medium red onions, thinly sliced
1 pound fresh mushroom caps, cleaned
1 large head broccoli, cut into flowerets
1 head cauliflower, cut into flowerets
1 (6-ounce) can large, pitted black olives, drained

Add vegetables to Marinade and stir gently to coat well. Refrigerate for several hours, or overnight, stirring occasionally. At serving time, drain and arrange on a plate with the broccoli forming a "wreath" around the other vegetables. Serve with toothpicks.

Variation: You may substitute or add 1 pound fresh or frozen shrimp and cherry tomatoes. Add tomatoes at serving time. Serve as a luncheon salad. Serves 8-10.

Nutbread and Nostalgia

Cucumber Appetizers

So simple, yet so good!

1 package dry Italian dressing mix
1 (8-ounce) package cream cheese, softened
1 loaf party rye bread
2 large cucumbers, sliced

Blend dressing mix with cream cheese. Spread mixture on rye bread slices and top with a cucumber slice. Yield: about 30 appetizers.

Great Beginnings, Grand Finales

Artichoke Nibbles

- 2 (6-ounce) jars marinated artichoke hearts
- 1 small onion, finely chopped
- 1 clove garlic, minced
- 4 eggs, beaten
- ¼ cup fine bread crumbs
- ¼ teaspoon salt
- ⅛ teaspoon pepper
- ⅛ teaspoon oregano
- ⅛ teaspoon hot pepper seasoning
- 2 cups shredded sharp Cheddar cheese
- 2 tablespoons minced parsley

Preheat oven to 325°. Drain marinade from 1 jar of artichoke hearts into medium skillet. Drain second jar and discard marinade. Chop artichokes and set aside.

Heat marinade. Add onion and garlic and sauté until onion is limp, about 5 minutes. Combine eggs, bread crumbs, salt, pepper, oregano, and hot pepper seasoning. Fold in cheese and parsley. Add artichokes and sautéed onion mixture, blending well.

Pour into 9-inch square glass baking dish. Bake about 30 minutes. Allow to cool briefly before cutting into l-inch squares. (Can also be served cold.) May be prepared a day or 2 ahead and reheated 10-12 minutes.

Our Best Recipes to You, Again

Vegetable Bar

2 packages crescent rolls
1 (8-ounce) cream cheese, softened
½ cup sour cream
½ cup Kraft Mayonnaise
1 envelope Hidden Valley Ranch Dressing
1 cup chopped cauliflower
¾ cup canned mushrooms
½ cup diced tomatoes (optional)
½ cup diced green peppers
1 cup finely chopped broccoli
½ cup ham bits
1 cup grated cheese

Spread rolls out and press on a pizza pan. Bake at 375° for 8 minutes, and let cool. Mix together cream cheese, sour cream, mayonnaise, and Hidden Valley Ranch Dressing with a beater. Spread over crescent rolls. Then add vegetables in layers. Put ham bits on top of vegetables. Top with grated cheese. Makes 12 servings.

The Indiana Bed & Breakfast Cookbook

Orange Crisps

1 (1-pound) loaf thinly sliced white bakery bread
½ cup butter
½ cup sugar
Grated rind from 1 large orange

Remove all crust from bread. Melt butter; add sugar and heat until sugar is dissolved. Add orange rind. Brush butter mixture over one side of each slice of bread. Cut bread slices into halves or fourths and place on an ungreased cookie sheet. Bake in a 300° oven for 25-30 minutes. Watch last 5 minutes. Crisps should be golden brown. When cut into fourths, this makes about 100 pieces.

Note: Can be made ahead. Product stores nicely in a tightly covered container.

Specialties of Indianapolis II

Apricot Nibbles

A healthy snack to serve family and guests instead of candy.

1 cup dried apricots, coarsely chopped
1 cup banana chips
½ cup raisins
½ cup dried apple slices, coarsely chopped
½ cup pitted dates, chopped
½ cup peanuts
½ cup sunflower seeds

Combine all ingredients in bowl; stir until mixed. Makes about 1½ quarts.

The Cookery Collection

Frosted Pecans

1 egg white
1 tablespoon water
1 cup sugar
1 tablespoon cinnamon
1 teaspoon salt
1 pound pecan halves

Beat egg white and water until white and foamy. Mix sugar, cinnamon, and salt. Fold pecans into first mixture until covered. Repeat in second mixture. Spread on large cookie sheet. Bake 45 minutes in 265° oven. Stir every 15 minutes.

Indiana's Finest Recipes

Chocolate Chip Cheese Ball

3 (8-ounce) packages cream cheese
2 teaspoons vanilla
1-2 teaspoons cinnamon
1 cup powdered sugar
1 bag mini chocolate chips
½ cup chopped pecans

Soften cream cheese and mix with vanilla, cinnamon, sugar, and chips. Form into 1 very large or 2 medium-size cheese balls. Roll in pecans. Refrigerate overnight. Serve with ginger snaps and/or vanilla wafers.

Hopewell's Hoosier Harvest II

Crunchy Munchies

Tastes great when made with Cajun seasonings also!

1 cup Cheerios
1 cup Wheat Chex
1 cup Corn Chex
2 cups Rice Chex
2 cups pretzel sticks
⅓ cup apple juice
4 teaspoons Worcestershire sauce
½ teaspoon garlic powder
1 teaspoon onion powder

Combine dry cereals to make 5 cups and add pretzel sticks. Combine apple juice, Worcestershire sauce, and seasonings. Toss with the cereals. Place in a shallow nonstick baking pan. Bake at 275° for 50 minutes. Stir every 10 minutes. Cool before serving.

For spicy version, use 1½ teaspoons of Cajun seasonings in place of onion and garlic powder.

Microwave instructions: Place mixture in microwave oven at FULL power for 6 minutes. Stir every 2 minutes. Serves 8.

Nutrition Analysis Per Serving: Calories 123; Fat 0.88; Cal from fat 596; Chol 0; Sod 364mg.

The Heart of Cooking

Microwave Caramel Corn

4 quarts popped corn
1 cup brown sugar
¼ cup lite Karo syrup
½ cup margarine
½ teaspoon salt
½ teaspoon baking soda

Spray large grocery bag well with "Pam" or other nonstick vegetable spray. Pour in popped corn. Cook brown sugar, syrup, margarine, and salt on medium-high for 5 minutes after it comes to a boil. Then add baking soda and stir well. Pour syrup over corn in bag. Fold down top and shake well. Microwave on HIGH for 1½ minutes. Shake bag well. Microwave for 1 minute. Shake bag well. Microwave 45 seconds. Shake bag well. Microwave 35 seconds. Shake bag well. Spread corn on wax paper to cool.

Our Favorite Recipes

BREAD & BREAKFAST

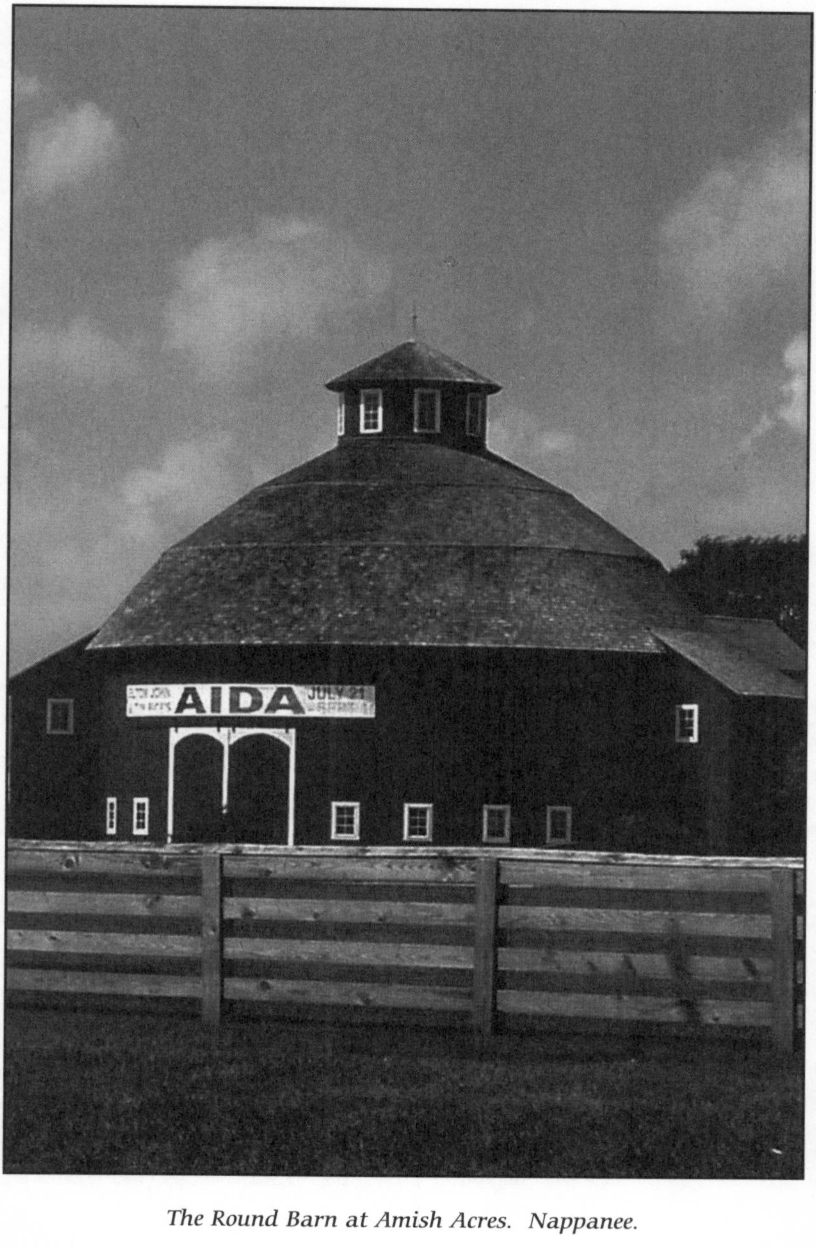

WIKIPEDIA.COM

The Round Barn at Amish Acres. Nappanee.

Sourdough Starter

2½ cups warm water
1 package dry yeast
2 cups flour
1 tablespoon salt
1 tablespoon sugar

Measure warm water into glass bowl or crock. Add yeast; let set a few minutes until yeast dissolves. Stir mixture well with wooden spoon. Add flour, salt, and sugar; stir again. Cover bowl and let stand 3 days, stirring every day. Refrigerate. When ready to make biscuits, etc., take out starter to make recipe.

2 cups warm water
2 cups flour

To replenish starter, stir warm water and flour into remaining starter. Let ripen 12 hours or more; refrigerate.

The Guild Cookbook III

Sourdough Biscuits

Biscuits are light and fluffy with marvelous tangy taste!

1½ cups sifted flour
¼ teaspoon baking soda (½ teaspoon if starter is quite sour)
2 teaspoons baking powder
½ teaspoon salt
¼ cup butter or margarine
1 cup sourdough starter

Sift dry ingredients together. Cut in butter with pastry blender. Add starter and mix.

Turn dough out on lightly floured board. Knead lightly until satiny. Roll dough ½-inch thick. Cut with floured 2½-inch cutter. Place biscuits in well greased 9x9x2-inch pan. Brush with melted butter and let rise in warm place for about 1 hour. Bake in hot oven 425° for 20 minutes. Yield: 12 biscuits.

The Guild Cookbook III

Country Apple Biscuits

If you like something sweet at coffee time, try making this easy biscuit recipe. It has that taste-tempting look.

1½ cups chopped, peeled apples, divided
1 (10-ounce) can Hungry Jack Flaky Biscuits
1 tablespoon margarine
⅓ cup firmly packed brown sugar
¼ teaspoon cinnamon
⅓ cup light corn syrup
1 large egg
½ cup pecan halves and pieces

GLAZE:
⅓ cup powdered sugar
1-2 teaspoons milk
¼ teaspoon vanilla

Generously grease bottom and sides of 9-inch round cake pan. Spread 1 cup chopped, peeled apples in bottom. Separate 1 can Hungry Jack Flaky biscuits into 10 biscuits, cutting each into 4 pieces. Arrange over apples, point sides up. Top with another ½ cup apples.

In small bowl, combine margarine, brown sugar, cinnamon, light corn syrup, and egg. Beat until sugar is partially dissolved. Stir in ½ cup pecan halves and pieces. Spoon over biscuit pieces. Bake in 350° oven for 35-45 minutes or until deep golden brown. Cool 5 minutes. Mix Glaze ingredients and drizzle over biscuits while warm. Store leftovers in refrigerator.

Sharing Our Best

Maybe-The-Best-Yeast Rolls

Not only the best, but easy too!

½ cup butter or margarine, softened
⅓ cup sugar
1½ teaspoons salt
2 tablespoons instant potato flakes
1 cup hot water
2 envelopes active dry yeast
½ cup lukewarm water
4½ cups flour, divided
Melted butter or margarine

Combine butter, sugar, salt, potato flakes, and hot water in a bowl. Stir and let cool to lukewarm. Sprinkle yeast on the ½ cup lukewarm water and stir to dissolve. Add yeast and 1 cup of flour to the potato mixture. Beat with an electric mixer at medium speed until smooth, about 2 minutes. Scrape bowl occasionally. Gradually add the rest of the flour to make a soft dough. Place dough in a large greased bowl; turn to grease the top. Cover and let rise in a warm place until doubled, about 1¼ hours.

Turn dough out onto lightly floured surface and knead 6 or 8 turns. Divide dough into 24 smooth balls. Put balls in a large greased pan, or into 2 smaller pans. Brush tops carefully with melted butter. Let rise about 45 minutes. Bake at 375° for 20 minutes. Watch carefully—do not overbake. As soon as rolls come out of oven, brush tops again with melted butter. Makes 24 rolls.

It's About Thyme

Indiana is the birthplace of many entertainers who have gained fame around the world. To name a few: Steve McQueen; Carole Lombard; Shelly Long; Anne Baxter; Chad Everett; James Dean; Red Skelton; Janie Fricke; David Letterman; John Cougar Mellencamp; Herb Shriner; Karl Malden; Florence Henderson; Michael Jackson; Phil Harris; James Best; Leon Ames; Alex Karras; Ron Glass; Jo Anne Worley; Dick York; Forrest Tucker; Sydney Pollack; Betsy Palmer; Will Geer; Hoagy Carmichael; and Cole Porter.

Hoosier Biscuits

1 teaspoon salt
1 pint milk
3-4 cups flour
2 tablespoons hot water
1 teaspoon cream of tartar
2 tablespoons yeast
2-3 eggs

Add a teaspoon of salt to a pint of new milk, warm from the cow. Stir in flour until it becomes a stiff batter, add great spoonfuls of lively brewer's yeast, put it in a warm place and let it rise as much as it will. When well raised, stir in a teaspoon of saleratus (cream of tartar) dissolved in the hot water. Beat up 3 eggs (2 will answer), stir with the batter, and add flour until it becomes a tolerable stiff dough. Knead it thoroughly, set it by the fire until it begins to rise, and then roll out, cut to biscuit form, put it in pans, cover it over with a thick cloth, set by the fire until it rises again, then bake in a quick oven (400°) for about 30 minutes, or until golden brown.

The Conner Prairie Cookbook

Quick and Easy Yeast Rolls

1½ cups warm water
2 packages yeast
¼ cup sugar
1½ teaspoons salt
⅓ cup soft shortening
2 eggs
4-5 cups flour, divided

Pour warm water in large bowl; add yeast. Let sit until dissolved; stir. Add sugar, salt, shortening, eggs, and half of flour. Beat 1½-2 minutes. Add remaining flour and stir. Cover bowl and let set until about double in size (approximately 30 minutes). Stir 20-25 strokes. Form into rolls and let rise 30 minutes. Bake at 425° until light brown.

Our Favorite Recipes

Butter Crust Rolls

1 package yeast
¼ cup warm water
½ cup shortening
¾ cup milk
½ cup sugar
3 eggs, slightly beaten
1 teaspoon salt
4½ cups flour

Dissolve yeast in warm water. Melt shortening in milk over low heat. Combine all ingredients and mix well. Let dough rise until double in bulk. Divide the dough into thirds. Roll each third out on floured board into a circle. Spread melted butter or margarine on each circle and then cut into 12 pie-shaped pieces. Starting at the big end, roll each piece. Place in greased pan and let rise for 1 hour. Bake at 375° for about 15 minutes. Makes 3 dozen rolls.

Home Cooking

Onion Bread

½ cup milk
½ cup water
3 tablespoons butter
1 tablespoon minced onion
1½ tablespoons sugar
½ teaspoon rosemary
½ teaspoon salt
2¼ cups flour
1 package dry yeast

Combine all ingredients except flour and yeast in a saucepan until warm (120°-130°). In the meantime, combine 1 cup flour and yeast in a large bowl. Add warm milk mixture to flour and yeast and mix at slow speed of mixer 30 seconds, then at HIGH speed for 3 minutes. Add remaining flour by hand, beating well after each addition.

Cover with a damp towel and let rise in a warm place for 20-30 minutes or until doubled in bulk. Beat 25 strokes. Spread in an 8-inch round layer cake pan and let rise 20-30 minutes, until doubled. Bake in a preheated oven at 375° for 35 minutes. Remove from pan immediately and cool. Brush with butter if a soft crust is desired.

Hopewell's Hoosier Harvest II

Zesty Lemon Tea Bread

½ pound unsalted butter, softened
3 cups sugar, divided
4 eggs
3 cups flour
½ teaspoon salt
2 teaspoons baking powder
2½ tablespoons grated lemon rind
½ cup milk
½ cup half-and-half
Juice of 3 lemons

In large bowl, cream butter and 2 cups sugar. Add eggs, one at a time, beating after each addition. Sift together flour, salt, and baking powder. Combine with rind. Add to butter mixture, alternating with combined milk and half and-half. Mix well.

Pour into 2 greased 9x5- or 8x4-inch bread pans. Bake at 350° for 50 minutes or until tester comes out clean. While bread is baking, combine 1 cup sugar and lemon juice. Mix until sugar is dissolved. Pierce top of hot baked bread with fork in 10 or 20 places. Loosen sides from pan. Spoon juice mixture over top and sides.

Cool in pan 30 minutes. Remove from pan and finish cooling on rack.

Dan Quayle—JD'74 (Former Vice-President of the United States)

The IU Cookbook

Herb Bread

1 teaspoon oregano
1 teaspoon garlic salt
3 tablespoons grated Parmesan cheese
2 teaspoons parsley flakes
½ pound soft butter
1 loaf French bread

Mix first 5 ingredients well. Slice bread. Butter generously on both sides. Wrap in foil and bake at 350° for 15-20 minutes. (Any extra butter is great on popcorn.)

The Guild Cookbook II

Mrs. Rockne's Swedish Coffee Cake

For over half a century, Knute Rockne was one of the most dominant figures in college football. During his 13 years as head coach, Rockne transformed the University of Notre Dame from an unheralded Midwestern school into a national institution.

½ pound butter, softened
2 cups sugar
3 eggs
3 teaspoons baking powder
3 cups flour
1 large can evaporated milk

TOPPING:
¾ cup brown sugar
¾ cup flaked coconut
4 tablespoons flour
4 tablespoons melted butter

Cream butter with sugar; add eggs and beat well. Combine baking powder with flour; sift. Add milk alternately with the sifted flour mixture. Pour the batter into 2 greased pans: one 13x9 inches and one 9x9 inches*. (Or use an 8x8-inch pan for the small cake; it makes it a little higher.) Mix Topping and sprinkle over batter. Bake for 30-35 minutes at 350°. This Coffee Cake freezes well.

*This coffee cake (a 1920s recipe from Mrs. Knute (Bonnie) Rockne can also be baked in three 8-inch round pans. It probably serves 12-18 people.

Aspic and Old Lace

Knute Rockne's coaching career record was 105 wins, 12 losses, and 5 ties. Notre Dame has won eight national football championships.

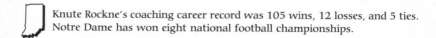

Raspberry Cream Cheese Coffee Cake

Probably one of the best coffee cakes I have ever eaten! Very rich and absolutely wonderful.

2½ cups flour
1 cup sugar, divided
¾ cup margarine
½ teaspoon baking powder
½ teaspoon baking soda
¼ teaspoon salt
¾ cup sour cream
1 teaspoon almond extract
2 eggs
1 (8-ounce) package cream cheese, softened
½ cup best quality red raspberry preserves
½ cup sliced almonds

Preheat oven to 350°. Grease and flour a 9- or 10-inch spring-form pan with a solid bottom (not a tube pan). In a large bowl, combine flour and ¾ cup sugar. Cut margarine into flour mixture with a pastry blender to make coarse crumbs. Reserve 1 cup of this crumb mixture. To remaining crumb mixture, add baking powder, baking soda, salt, sour cream, almond extract and 1 egg. Blend well. Batter will be stiff. Spread batter over bottom and 2 inches up sides of the prepared pan. Batter should be about ¼ inch thick on sides.

In a small bowl, combine cream cheese, ¼ cup sugar, and 1 egg. Blend well. Pour into batter-lined pan. Carefully spoon preserves evenly over cheese mixture.

In another small bowl, combine the reserved 1 cup crumb mixture and the almonds. Sprinkle over preserves. Bake for 45-55 minutes, or until cream cheese is set and crust is golden brown. Check after 45 minutes. Cool 15 minutes. Carefully remove sides of pan. Let cake cool completely while it's still on the spring-form pan bottom. When cool, run knife around bottom of pan (between the cake and the pan) to loosen the cake. Place cake on serving plate.

If you wish to freeze the cake, wrap it well and freeze up to 2 weeks. Thaw, wrapped, when ready to serve. Refrigerate any leftover cake. Very rich, so cut into small servings. Will serve 16-20.

Christmas Thyme at Oak Hill Farm

Blueberry Coffee Cake

Prepare for the raves.

TOPPING:

½ cup granulated sugar
1 teaspoon ground cinnamon
4 tablespoons butter (½ stick)
¼ cup chopped pecans (optional)

Combine sugar and cinnamon in small bowl. Cut in butter until mixture is crumbly. Refrigerate for 30 minutes.

CAKE:

2 cups all-purpose flour
1 teaspoon baking powder
1 teaspoon baking soda
Dash of salt
½ cup (1 stick) margarine
1 cup granulated sugar
2 eggs
1 cup sour cream
1 teaspoon vanilla
2 cups fresh blueberries (may substitute frozen blueberries)

Preheat oven to 350°. Grease a 9x13-inch baking pan. Sift together flour, baking powder, baking soda, and salt. Set aside. Beat together margarine and sugar in large bowl. Add eggs, sour cream, and vanilla. Mix well. Add dry ingredients; mix well. Fold in blueberries. Pour into prepared pan. Sprinkle Topping mixture over batter. Bake at 350° for 40-45 minutes. Serves 8-10.

Winners

Cinnamon Cheese Coffee Cake

1 tube of crescent rolls
1 (8-ounce) package cream cheese
½ teaspoon vanilla
½ cup sugar
1 egg yolk
¼ cup sugar
½ teaspoon cinnamon
¼ cup chopped nuts

Lay ½ of crescent rolls flat in 8x8-inch pan. Soften cream cheese. Mix vanilla, ½ cup sugar, and egg yolk into cream cheese. Spoon this mixture over dough. Lay remaining ½ of crescent rolls on top. Mix ¼ cup sugar, cinnamon, and nuts and sprinkle over mixture. Bake at 350° for 30-35 minutes. Makes 8 slices.

The Indiana Bed & Breakfast Cookbook

Favorite Carrot Muffins

1¼ cups oil
2 cups sugar
4 eggs
3 cups flour
2 teaspoons baking powder
1 teaspoon baking soda
½ teaspoon salt
1 teaspoon cinnamon
½ teaspoon nutmeg
2¼ cups grated carrots
1 cup coarsely chopped walnuts
1 cup raisins

Preheat oven to 350°. Mix oil, sugar, and eggs in mixer for about 2 minutes at medium speed. In another bowl sift dry ingredients and add gradually to sugar mixture. Add carrots, walnuts, and raisins. Blend dough until no flour is seen. Fill muffin cups (either paper-lined or greased) ⅔ full. Bake 35-40 minutes or until a toothpick inserted in center comes out clean. Serve either warm or at room temperature.

Recipe submitted by Governor and Mrs. Evan Bayh.

Indiana's Finest Recipes

Pecan Rolls

1 package regular butterscotch pudding
⅔ cup sugar
1 teaspoon cinnamon
1 package Rich's frozen roll dough
1 cup chopped pecans
1 stick margarine, melted

Mix pudding with sugar and cinnamon. Spray Bundt pan with Pam. Arrange frozen rolls in pan. Cover with pecans. Sprinkle pudding mixture over rolls. Pour melted butter over all. Let rise overnight. Bake in preheated 350° oven for 25 minutes. Makes 24 rolls.

The Indiana Bed & Breakfast Cookbook

Jiffy Cinnamon Rolls

4-5 cups all-purpose flour
1 (9-ounce) box Jiffy White Cake Mix (1 layer)
2 (¼-ounce) packages quick-rise yeast
1 teaspoon salt
2 cups warm water (120°-130°)
2 tablespoons butter or margarine
½ cup sugar
1 tablespoon cinnamon

In large mixing bowl combine 3 cups flour, cake mix, yeast, salt, and warm water; mix until smooth. Add enough remaining flour to form soft dough. Turn out onto a lightly floured surface. Knead until smooth, about 6-8 minutes. Roll dough into a 9x18-inch rectangle. Spread with butter and sprinkle with sugar and cinnamon. Roll dough jelly-roll style, starting with long end. Slice the rolls into 1-inch circles. Place on greased cookie sheet. Cover and let rise for 15 minutes. Bake at 350° for 15 minutes. Frost. Makes 18 rolls.

Taste & See

Quick Cinnamon Rolls

Make a pie dough mixture. Roll out and cut in squares. Sprinkle each square with sugar, cinnamon, and a slice of butter. Roll up and bake until brown.

Our Favorite Recipes II

Rum Rolls

½ cup sugar
¼ cup butter
¼ cup light rum
1 tray Pepperidge Farm party rolls

Boil first 3 ingredients for 1 minute. Pour over tray of Pepperidge Farm party rolls. Follow directions on rolls to heat.

For Crying Out Loud...Let's Eat!

Danish Roll

Rich and good!

1 cake yeast
1 cup milk, warmed
3 eggs
½ teaspoon salt
4 tablespoons sugar
4 tablespoons shortening
4 tablespoons butter
4 cups flour
Butter, melted
Brown sugar
Nut meats
Dates
Confectioners' sugar icing

Mix yeast, warm milk, and eggs together. Add salt, sugar, shortening, butter, and flour (mix as pie dough). Put in refrigerator overnight. Next day, divide dough in half. Roll out; spread with melted butter, brown sugar, nut meats, and dates. Roll (like jelly roll) and shape in crescent on greased cookie sheet. Repeat with other ½ of dough. Let rise 2½-3 hours. Bake in 325° oven 20-30 minutes. Ice while hot with confectioners' sugar icing. Yield: 2 large crescents.

The Guild Cookbook III

In Ferdinand, the Monastery Immaculate Conception, known as the "Castle on the Hill," is home to one of the largest communities of Benedictine Women in the United States. Visitors of all beliefs are welcome to tour the majestic domed church, outdoor Stations of the Cross, rosary steps and a Lourdes grotto.

Refrigerator Bran Muffins

1 (15-ounce) box raisin bran cereal
5 cups flour
3 cups sugar
5 teaspoons baking soda
2 teaspoons salt
1 tablespoon pumpkin pie spice (optional)
1 cup vegetable oil (or melted shortening)
4 cups buttermilk
4 eggs, beaten

Mix dry ingredients together in a large bowl. Add eggs, shortening, and buttermilk; mix until dry ingredients are moistened. Store in covered container in refrigerator. For muffins, fill greased muffin pans ⅔ full and bake at 400° for 15-20 minutes. Batter keeps for 6 weeks.

More Hoosier Cooking

Maids of Honor

½ cup butter
½ teaspoon salt
1 cup sugar
2 eggs
1 teaspoon vanilla
2 teaspoons baking powder
1½ cups flour
⅔ cup milk
Pie pastry
Apple jelly

Make a cake batter. First, mix the butter, salt, and sugar until fluffy, then add the eggs and vanilla. Mix the baking powder with the flour and add to the butter mixture every other time with the milk. Beat very well. Line muffin tins with the pastry; put drop of jelly in; drop in cake batter to make it about ¾ full. Bake in a moderate (350°) oven for about 20 minutes or until cake tests done.

The Conner Prairie Cookbook

The International Violin Competition of Indianapolis is held every four years and attracts the finest young violinists in the world.

Little Applesauce Muffins

You can't eat just one!

½ cup (1 stick) butter, softened
1 cup granulated sugar, divided
2 eggs
¾ cup applesauce
1¾ cups all-purpose flour
1 tablespoon baking powder
½ teaspoon salt
¼ teaspoon ground cinnamon
4 tablespoons (½ stick) butter, melted

Preheat oven to 425°. Grease one or more mini-muffin tins. Beat together ½ cup butter and ½ cup sugar in large bowl. Beat in eggs, one at a time, until light and fluffy. Beat in applesauce. Stir together flour, baking powder and salt. Add to butter mixture.

Stir just to moisten. Fill prepared muffin tins ⅔ full. Bake at 425° for 15 minutes or until golden.

Combine remaining ½ cup sugar and cinnamon. Dip tops of warm muffins into melted butter and then into the cinnamon-sugar. Serve warm. Yield: 36 muffins.

Winners

Pancake Mix

This mixture makes light and fluffy pancakes, easy to prepare. It keeps well for months on your kitchen shelf—it doesn't have to be refrigerated.

12 cups flour
4 cups dry instant powdered milk
¾ cup baking powder
¾ cup sugar
2 tablespoons salt

Combine flour, powdered milk, baking powder, sugar, and salt. Sift several times. Be sure it is mixed well.

TO MAKE PANCAKES:
1½ cups mix
1 cup water
1 egg
2 tablespoons oil

Beat until smooth and fry cakes on hot griddle.

Sharing Our Best

Breakfast Cookie

1½ cups flour
⅔ cup sugar
½ cup grapenuts
1 teaspoon baking powder
½ cup crumbled cooked bacon
½ cup soft butter
1 egg
2 tablespoons frozen orange juice concentrate
¼ cup raisins

Combine the first 4 ingredients. Then add the remaining ingredients. Mix well. Drop on ungreased baking sheet and bake for 12–14 minutes in a preheated 350° oven. Makes 2 dozen.

Mincemeat and Memories

Apple Pancake Puff

Great to serve for weekend or overnight guests.

6 eggs
1½ cups milk
1 cup all-purpose flour
2 tablespoons granulated sugar
1 teaspoon vanilla
¼ teaspoon salt
¼ teaspoon cinnamon
⅛ teaspoon nutmeg
½ cup (1 stick) butter or margarine
2 tart green apples, peeled, cored, thinly sliced
2 tablespoons brown sugar
¼ cup chopped walnuts or pecans

Preheat oven to 425°. In a blender or processor, mix eggs, milk, flour, sugar, vanilla, salt, cinnamon, and nutmeg. Place butter in a 13x9-inch baking dish; heat in oven until butter is melted but not brown. Add apple slices and heat in oven several minutes until they begin to sizzle. Quickly remove from oven and pour batter over apples all at once; sprinkle with brown sugar and nuts. Return to oven; bake approximately 20 minutes, or until puffed and golden. Cut in squares. Serve immediately. Serves 6–8.

Back Home Again

Funnel Cakes

A real festival favorite.

2½ cups sifted flour
1 teaspoon baking powder
¼ teaspoon salt
¼ teaspoon cinnamon
2 eggs
2 cups milk
Shortening for frying
Powdered sugar

Sift dry ingredients together. Beat eggs and milk together. Gradually add dry ingredients to egg and milk mixture, beating until smooth.

Heat shortening in a large heavy skillet at a ¼-inch depth to 375°.

Pour ⅓-½ cup batter into a wide-spout funnel, holding your finger over the opening. Allow batter to flow through opening of funnel into the hot fat in a tight coil pattern. Fry 2 minutes on each side, or until cakes are golden brown. Drain on absorbent towels. Repeat procedure until all batter is used. Sprinkle cooling funnel cakes with powdered sugar. Serve warm. Yield: 6-9 cakes.

Festival Foods and Family Favorites

Breakfast Puff

Light cooking; low cholesterol.

Egg substitute equivalent to 3 eggs (i.e. Eggbeaters)
½ cup enriched, all-purpose flour
½ teaspoon salt
½ cup skim milk
3 tablespoons tub margarine, melted

Chill 8-inch iron skillet in freezer. Preheat oven to 450°. Place egg substitute and flour in blender and blend at LOW speed. Add salt and milk and blend again. Coat cold iron skillet with margarine and add batter. Bake until the crust is brown, about 30 minutes. Serve immediately. Top with stewed fruit, jam or maple syrup, if desired. If doubling recipe, use 12-inch skillet. Can also be served as a dessert. Yield: 4 servings.

For Crying Out Loud...Let's Eat!

Oven-Baked Amaretto French Toast

2 egg whites
1/3 cup skim milk
2 tablespoons brown sugar
3 tablespoons frozen egg substitute, thawed
2 tablespoons amaretto
1/2 teaspoon ground cinnamon
8 slices (3/4-inch thick) French bread

Preheat oven to 425°. Beat egg whites at HIGH speed with electric mixer until stiff peaks form. Set aside.

Combine milk and next 4 ingredients in a medium bowl, beating at HIGH speed until sugar dissolves. Gently fold 1/3 of egg whites into milk mixture; fold in remaining egg whites.

Dip bread slices in milk mixture, coating well. Place in a 9x13-inch pan which has been prayed with vegetable cooking spray. Bake for 7 minutes; turn and bake 3 minutes more or until golden. Serve immediately with maple syrup or powdered sugar if desired. Serves 8.

Nutritional Analysis Per Serving: (1 slice) Calories 123; Fat 1.5g; Cal from fat 12%; Chol 1mg; Sod 223mg; Fiber .8g; Exchanges 1½ starch.

The Heart of Cooking II

Breakfast Burritos

1 pound pork sausage
1/4 cup chopped onion
1/4 cup chopped red or green pepper
1½ cups frozen hash brown potatoes
4 eggs, beaten
12 (8-inch) flour tortillas
1/2 cup grated Cheddar cheese
Picante sauce
Sour cream

Brown sausage; add onion and pepper. Cook until tender. Drain. Add potatoes, cook 6-8 minutes. Add eggs. Stir. Cook until set. Brown tortillas in hot oil in skillet 5 seconds on each side, or microwave for 45-60 seconds. Divide filling among 12 tortillas; sprinkle with cheese. Fold sides, then bottom up. Serve with picante sauce and sour cream. May be prepared ahead and frozen. Reheat in microwave.

The Indiana Bed & Breakfast Cookbook

Cheese Blintzes

What a winner! Surprising that such a treat can come out of a loaf of white bread!

1 (2-pound) loaf Pepperidge Farm bread
2 (8-ounce) packages cream cheese, softened
½ cup sugar
2 egg yolks
½ cup butter, melted
1 cup sugar
1 tablespoon cinnamon
Sour cream

Cut crust off bread; roll flat with a rolling pin. Cream together cream cheese, sugar, and egg yolks. Spread on flattened bread and roll tightly. Brush with melted butter and sprinkle with mixture of sugar and cinnamon. Cut rolls in half. Bake in 375° oven 15-20 minutes on cookie sheet or freeze for future use. Serve with sour cream. Yield: 60-64 blintzes.

Variation: Cheesy Cinnamon Roll-ups: Use 1 loaf white sandwich bread (30-40 slices). Use only 1 egg yolk in filling. Dip rolls in 1 cup melted butter; roll in mixture of 2 cups sugar and 4 teaspoons cinnamon. After freezing on cookie sheet, store in plastic bags. When ready to use, bake 10-15 minutes at 400°. Do not thaw.

The Guild Cookbook IV

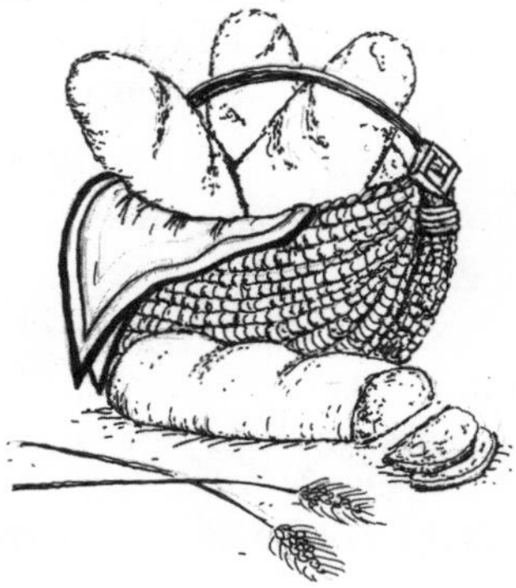

Night Before the Race Egg Casserole

1 pound sausage (regular or hot)
2 slices bread
6 eggs
2 cups milk
1 teaspoon salt
1 teaspoon dry mustard (if regular sausage is used)
1 (8-ounce) can mushrooms, drained
1¼ cups grated Cheddar cheese

Grease a 10x10x2½-inch casserole. Cook sausage well and drain off grease thoroughly. Cut bread into cubes and cover bottom of casserole. Beat eggs, milk, salt, dry mustard (if used), sausage, mushrooms, and grated cheese. Pour this over bread cubes. Cover and leave in refrigerator overnight. Bake at 325° for 40-45 minutes. Leave covered until last 10 minutes. Serves 6-8.

Champions: Favorite Foods of Indy Car Racing

Wake Up Casserole

2 cups seasoned croutons
1 cup shredded Cheddar cheese
1 (4-ounce) can mushroom pieces, drained
1½ pounds country-fresh sausage, browned and crumbled
½ cup chopped onion
6 eggs
2½ cups milk
½ teaspoon salt
½ teaspoon pepper
½ teaspoon dry mustard
1 (10¾-ounce) can cream of mushroom soup

Place croutons in greased 9x13x2-inch pan. Top with cheese and mushrooms. Brown sausage and onion; drain and spread over cheese. Beat eggs with 2 cups of milk and seasonings; pour over sausage. Cover and refrigerate overnight. (May be frozen at this point.) Mix soup with ½ cup milk and spread on top. Bake at 325° for 1 hour. Serves 8.

The Indiana Bed & Breakfast Cookbook

One-Egg Omelet

Separate 1 large egg (at room temperature). Place the white on a sturdy dinner plate and the yolk in a small bowl. Beat the egg white with a pinch of salt on the plate, using a flat wire whisk, until soft peaks form. Add 2 teaspoons cold water to the egg yolk in the bowl and beat it vigorously with a fork. Pour the beaten egg yolk over the beaten egg white on the plate and fold the two together, using the whisk. Pour the egg mixture into a heated skillet containing a small amount of sizzling fat (1 teaspoon of bacon grease or butter), and fry the egg in one piece over medium heat, tilting the pan or lifting the edges of the egg to allow the uncooked egg to spread over the pan. Do not overcook, and turn the heat down if the skillet is holding too much heat. Turn the egg once with a spatula. Season with salt and pepper. The omelet cooks very quickly, in only a minute or so.

For a sandwich, place the egg between two slices of homemade bread, with or without butter. A leaf of lettuce may be placed in the sandwich, along with a bit of chopped green onion.

For a special touch, you can also add a few chopped raw or lightly sautéed mushrooms, a sprinkling of lemon pepper, and some alfalfa sprouts. And lightly toast the bread. This makes a perfect meatless sandwich.

The Midwestern Country Cookbook

Creamed Eggs on Toast

¼ cup margarine
¼ cup flour
2 cups milk
½ teaspoon salt
4 eggs, hard boiled
6 slices bacon, fried

Melt margarine and blend in flour. Add milk (gradually) and salt, stirring continuously. Slice eggs and crumble in bacon. Serve with or over toast.

Amish Country Cookbook II

Apple Raisin Quiche

A favorite bed and breakfast recipe.

Pastry for 9-inch pie (1-crust)
3¾ cups peeled, cored and thinly sliced Granny Smith apples (about 3 medium)
½ cup raisins
¼ cup packed light brown sugar
2 teaspoons cinnamon
3 cups (12 ounces) shredded Monterey Jack cheese
3 eggs
1 cup whipping cream

Preheat oven to 400°. Line 9-inch pie plate with pastry. Crimp edge and prick bottom and sides with fork at ½ inch intervals. To prevent shrinkage, bake only 6 minutes with pie shell covered snugly with aluminum foil. Remove foil and bake about 10 minutes until shell is lightly browned. Layer ½ the apples, raisins, sugar, and cinnamon in pie shell; repeat layers. Cover completely with cheese.

Beat eggs with cream. Make a small hole in cheese; pour egg mixture into cheese. Cover hole with cheese. Bake until top is browned and apples are tender when tested with pick. Cool 10-15 minutes before cutting into wedges. Serve with sausage or Canadian bacon.

A Taste of Twin Pines

Granola Cereal

7 cups old-fashioned oatmeal
1 cup wheat germ
1 cup powdered milk
1 cup whole-wheat flour
1 cup brown sugar
Sunflower seeds
Sesame seeds
Almonds
Chopped dates
Raisins
Coconut
¾ cup honey
¾ cup oil

Mix the first 5 ingredients well and add any amount of any or all of the next 6 ingredients. Mix well. In blender, mix the honey and oil. Pour over mixture and stir well. Spread on shallow pans (cookie sheets) and bake at 250° for 30 minutes or until slightly brown. Store in covered container. Yield: approximately 1 gallon.

The Hoosier Cookbook

The Best Fresh Herb Butter I Know Of!

Keep this butter in the refrigerator and bring to room temperature to use. The title tells you my opinion of it!

2 sticks unsalted butter, room temperature
1 tablespoon chopped fresh green basil
1 tablespoon chopped fresh marjoram
1 tablespoon chopped fresh chives
1 teaspoon chopped fresh rosemary
1 teaspoon fresh lemon juice

Use your kitchen scissors and chop the herbs fairly fine. Blend all herbs and the lemon juice into the butter with a wooden spoon. Don't use your electric mixer, food processor or blender unless you like your butter to be green. Make this butter a day of two before using it so flavors will blend. Makes about 1 cup.

It's About Thyme

Almost-A-Meal Breakfast Drink

2 (5¼-ounce) cans pineapple tidbits
2 medium bananas
½ cup milk
16 ounces pineapple sherbet or low-fat yogurt
2-4 tablespoons orange juice

In food processor, combine all ingredients. Blend until smooth. Makes 4 servings. Recipe may be doubled for more servings.

The Indiana Bed & Breakfast Cookbook

Sassafras Jelly

4 cups sassafras tea
5 cups sugar
¾ teaspoon citric acid or sour salt
1 package dry pectin

Brew strong tea. Add sugar and citric acid; stir until boiling point is reached. Add pectin and continue to boil, stirring constantly until jelly forms in drops on tip of raised spoon. Ladle into sterilized glasses and seal with paraffin.

The Brown County Cookbook

Parke County is home to 30 covered bridges, one more than Lancaster, Pennsylvania, making it the "Covered Bridge Capital of the World."

SOUPS

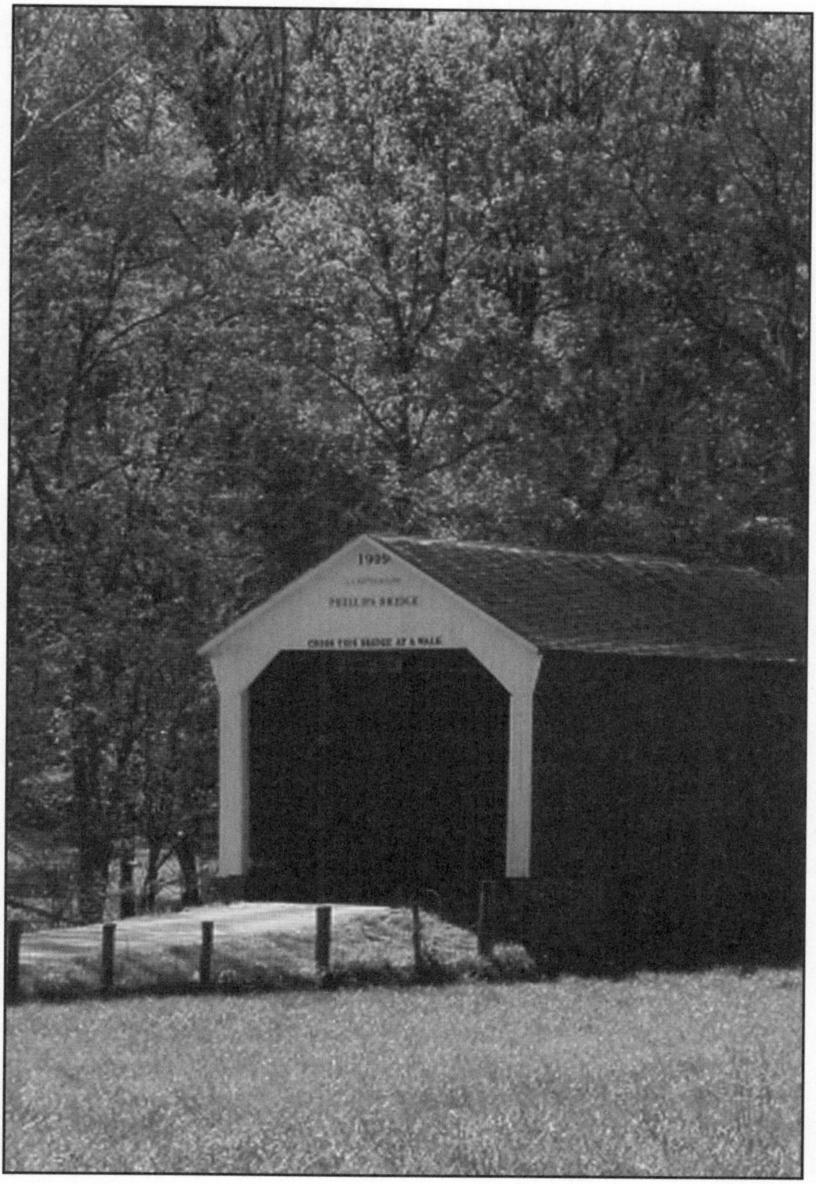

WIKIPEDIA.COM

The Phillips Bridge, built in 1909, crosses Big Pond Creek in Parke County. Near Montezuma.

Lou Holtz Chili

1 (28-ounce) can tomatoes
1 (15-ounce) can tomato sauce
8 ounces V-8 juice
2 tablespoons chili powder
½ cup water
1½ pounds lean ground beef
2 cloves garlic, crushed
Olive oil
1 (15-ounce) can kidney beans

Blend together tomatoes, tomato sauce, V-8 juice, chili powder, and water. Sauté lean ground beef and garlic in olive oil. Combine ingredients and simmer over low heat for 1-1½ hours. Stir often. For last 20-30 minutes, add kidney beans. Serve with grated cheese, chopped onions, chips, etc.

Indiana's Finest Recipes

White Chili

1 pound navy or Great Northern beans (dried)
6 cups chicken broth
2 cloves garlic, minced
2 medium onions, chopped
1 tablespoon oil
2 (4-ounce) cans mild green chiles, chopped
2 teaspoons ground cumin
¼ teaspoon cayenne pepper (optional)
4 cups diced, cooked chicken breasts
Monterey Jack cheese
Sour cream
Salsa

Combine beans, broth, garlic, and half the onions in a large stock pot. Bring to a boil. Reduce heat and simmer until beans are soft, adding more broth if necessary. In a skillet, sauté the remaining onions in oil until tender. Add chiles, cumin, and cayenne pepper to the onions, and mix thoroughly. Add to bean mixture. Add chicken, and simmer 1 hour. Top with cheese, sour cream, or salsa.

Hopewell's Hoosier Harvest II

Mom Unser's "Indy" Chili

- 1 pound lean pork (tenderloin or chops)
- 1 medium onion, chopped
- 1 clove fresh garlic, chopped
- 1 (#2) can of tomatoes
- 1 shake oregano
- 3 cans mild or medium green chiles
- Salt to taste

Remove all fat from pork and cube it. Sauté pork, onion, and garlic together. Squeeze tomatoes through fingers and add to skillet with tomato juice. Add 1 shake of oregano and salt to taste. Add green chiles and simmer approximately 35 minutes. Add water if necessary. Pinto beans may be added, if desired, or served as a side dish. Serves 4.

Note: Mary "Mom" Unser is mother of Al, Bobby, Louie, and Jerry Unser.

Champions: Favorite Foods of Indy Car Racing

James Whitcomb Riley's Favorite Bean Soup

2 cups nine bean soup mix (below)
1 pound ham, diced
1 clove garlic, minced
1 (16-ounce) can tomatoes, undrained and chopped
2 quarts water
1 large onion, chopped
½ teaspoon salt
1 (10-ounce) can tomatoes and green chiles, undrained

Sort and wash 2 cups Bean Mix; place in a Dutch oven. Cover with water 2 inches above beans. Let soak overnight. Drain beans; add next 5 ingredients. Cover and bring to a boil. Reduce heat and simmer 1½ hours or until beans are tender. Add remaining ingredients and simmer 30 minutes, stirring occasionally. Yield: 8 cups soup.

BEAN MIX:
Lima beans
Black beans
Red beans
Black-eyed peas
Lentils
Pinto beans
Navy beans
Great Northern beans
Split peas

Mix 1 pound of each of these 9 beans.

Hoosier Heritage Cookbook

The origin of the word Hoosier is mixed. One is that a man named Hoosier had workers he called his Hoosiers. Another is that two men had a barroom brawl: one got his ear cut off and someone round it and asked "Who's ear?" Another is that when a guest comes to the door, Indianians holler, "Who's 'ere?" Many say curiosity is how it got started—"Who's, your mom? Who's your dad?" Who knows?

Lentil Soup

1 (8-ounce) package lentils
2 or 3 smoked ham hocks
4-6 cups water (depending on amount and size of hocks)
2 tablespoons instant beef bouillon or to taste
1 teaspoon salt
2-3 carrots, diced
1 cup diced celery with greens
1 cup pickled small onions
2 tablespoons vinegar

Put all ingredients in crockpot; simmer on LOW heat overnight or 8 hours. Take meat out and cut from bone. Taste soup now—has delicious sweet-sour flavor. Put meat back and serve. This is a high-protein, hearty meal; color is a dark brown; favored in Europe. Yields 4-6 servings.

The Guild Cookbook II

Spinach-Lentil Soup

This one hit the top of the scale

1 pound lentils, washed
10 cups chicken broth or stock
2 tablespoons olive oil
1 tablespoon butter
1 large onion
4 cloves garlic, crushed
2 stalks celery, finely chopped
2 pounds fresh spinach, chopped, or 2 (10-ounce) packages frozen chopped spinach, unthawed
¾ cup fresh lemon juice
Salt and freshly ground pepper to taste

Combine lentils and broth in a large kettle. Simmer for 3-4 hours.

Heat oil and butter in a medium-size skillet. Add onion, garlic, and celery; sauté over medium heat until tender. Add to cooked lentils. Add spinach, lemon juice, salt, and pepper. Cook gently for 30 minutes or more to blend flavors. Serves 10-12.

Note: Even better the next day.

Winners

Soupe Au Pistou

A delicious meatless main dish containing complete protein.

2 quarts chicken broth*
3 medium potatoes, peeled and diced
½ pound fresh green beans, cut up
3 carrots, sliced
1 medium onion, chopped
1 tablespoon salt
¼ teaspoon pepper
½ pound zucchini, sliced
1 (16-ounce) can kidney beans

Combine chicken broth, potatoes, green beans (unless canned), carrots, onion, salt, and pepper in a large soup kettle. Bring to a boil and simmer covered for 10 minutes. Add squash and kidney beans (also green beans, if canned beans are used) and simmer another 10 minutes longer or until vegetables are tender.

*Eight bouillon cubes in 2 quarts water may be substituted for the chicken stock.

SAUCE:
4 cloves garlic, mashed (or ½ teaspoon garlic powder)
1 (6-ounce) can tomato paste
1 tablespoon dried basil
½ cup grated Parmesan cheese
½ cup chopped parsley
¼ cup olive or vegetable oil

Mix together garlic, tomato paste, basil, Parmesan cheese, and parsley. Gradually beat in the oil. Just before serving, stir sauce into hot soup. When serving, pass extra Parmesan cheese to sprinkle over top of soup. Serve with crusty, buttered rolls. Yield: 8-10 servings.

The Guild Cookbook III

Columbus is known as "America's architectural showplace," with more than 50 buildings by some of the world's top architects (I. M. Pei, the Saarinens, Richard Meier, Robert A. M. Sterrn) dotting its skyline.

French Vegetable Beef Soup

A real "knife and fork" soup. Almost like a stew.

2 pounds beef stew meat, cut in ½-inch cubes
¼ cup oil
1 (10½-ounce) can condensed onion soup
6 cans water
1 (6-ounce) can tomato paste
1½ teaspoons salt
¼ teaspoon pepper
1 tablespoon basil
1 (16-ounce) can wax beans, drained
1 (16-ounce) can kidney beans, drained
8 carrots, sliced
2 cups sliced celery
½ cup grated Parmesan

Brown meat in oil. Reduce heat and stir in soup and water. Add tomato paste, salt, pepper, and basil. Simmer covered, 1½ hours.

Add all vegetables. Reheat to boiling, then simmer covered for 30 minutes, or until meat and vegetables are tender. Stir in cheese. Yield: 8 servings.

For Crying Out Loud...Let's Eat!

Mulligatawny Soup

This soup is a second cousin to Indian Curry. While not so hot as a curry, it does have the distinctive taste.

¼ cup butter
1 medium onion, sliced
1 medium carrot, sliced
1 stalk celery, diced
1 green pepper, diced coarsely
1 medium apple, pared, cored, sliced
1 cup cooked chicken, cut up
⅓ cup flour
1 teaspoon curry powder
⅛ teaspoon mace
2 whole cloves
1 sprig parsley
2 cups white stock (chicken broth)
1 cup tomatoes, cooked
Salt and pepper to taste

In deep kettle, in ¼ cup butter, sauté onion, carrot, celery, green pepper, apple, and chicken. Stir frequently until onions are tender. Gradually stir in remaining ingredients. Simmer, covered, ½ hour. Serve. Makes about 6 servings.

The Cookery Collection

Asparagus Soup

30 stalks asparagus (2 pounds)
4 quarts water
1 tablespoon salt
¼ cup minced onion
¼ cup minced parsley
1 teaspoon ground coriander
2 tablespoons butter
1 tablespoon flour
2 cups chicken broth, heated
½ cup heavy cream
1 tablespoon lemon juice
½ teaspoon salt
¼ teaspoon white pepper

Trim tough ends and peel asparagus stems with potato peeler. Tie together in 3 bunches; simmer in large pot of salted water until just tender. Lift bundles out; place in sink of cold water. When cool, drain on paper towels. Cut tips from stalks and reserve. Cut stalks into 1-inch pieces; reserve.

In medium saucepan, sauté onion and parsley with coriander and butter until soft. Stir in flour; cook for 3 minutes. Remove pan from heat; stir in heated broth. Simmer mixture 5 minutes. Add reserved asparagus stalks. Purée mixture in blender or food processor until smooth. (Do in batches.) Return purée to saucepan; stir in cream and reserved tips. Heat. Do not boil. Stir in lemon juice. Add salt and pepper. Serve hot or chilled. Makes 6 servings.

Our Best Recipes to You, Again

Cream of Broccoli Soup

1 pound broccoli (fresh or frozen)
½ pound butter
1 cup flour, sifted
1 quart chicken stock*
1 quart half-and-half cream (may use part milk)
1 teaspoon salt
¼ teaspoon white pepper

Clean broccoli; remove stems. Cut into ½-inch pieces. Steam in ½ cup water until tender. Do not drain. Set aside. Melt butter in saucepan over medium heat. Add flour to make a roux. Cook for 2-4 minutes. Add chicken stock, stirring with a wire whip and bringing to a boil; turn heat to low. Add broccoli, half-and-half, and salt and pepper. Heat, but do not boil. Serves 8-10.

*Homemade, canned, or 4 bouillon cubes dissolved in a quart of hot water.

Love Cookin'

Parmesan Corn Chowder

2 cups boiling water
2 cups chopped potatoes
½ cup carrot slices
½ cup celery slices
¼ cup chopped onion
1½ teaspoons salt
¼ teaspoon pepper
¼ margarine
¼ cup flour
2 cups milk
1 cup (4 ounces) grated Parmesan cheese
1 (17-ounce) can cream-style corn

Add water to potatoes, carrots, celery, onion, salt, and pepper. Cover and simmer 10 minutes. Do not drain. Make a white sauce with margarine, flour, and milk. Add cheese, stirring until melted. Add can of corn and undrained vegetables. Heat—do not boil. Garnish with chopped parsley if desired. Serves 6-8.

Hoosier Heritage Cookbook

Chicken Velvet Soup

This recipe is a standard at the famous Tea Room of L. S. Ayres' Department Store in Indianapolis. Ayers' opened for business in 1907, and Riley probably shopped there. In the store's early years, it was thought that food was served from informal food stands before the Tea Room opened in 1929.

6 tablespoons butter or margarine
6 tablespoons flour
½ cup milk
½ cup light cream
3 cups chicken broth
1 cup finely chopped cooked chicken
Dash of pepper

In saucepan, melt butter or margarine. Blend in flour, then stir in milk, light cream, and chicken broth. Cook over medium heat, stirring constantly, till mixture thickens and comes to a boil. Reduce heat. Stir in finely chopped cooked chicken and pepper. Return soup to boiling and serve immediately. Makes about 5 cups soup.

The James Whitcomb Riley Cookbook

Nancy Marie's Italian Market Soup

(Zuppa di Mercato Italiano)

1 package dried 13-15 variety beans
2 chicken breasts
4 thick slices ham
2 (4-inch) pieces smoked sausage
2 carrots, sliced
2 stalks chopped celery (leafy part included)
1 medium onion, chopped
1 large can tomatoes (including juice)
¼ teaspoon salt
½ teaspoon pepper

Soak beans overnight. Cube or slice, brown, drain, and set aside chicken, ham, and sausage. Drain and wash beans. Refill large pot with water. Add beans and cook over medium heat. Add meats and remaining ingredients. Cook over low heat until beans are tender. Stir soup occasionally to keep from sticking. Serve with hard crusty Italian bread or rolls. This is a meal in itself.

Our Italian Family Cookbook

Midwest Minestrone Soup

1 pound Italian sweet sausage
1 tablespoon olive or vegetable oil
1 cup diced onion
1 clove garlic, finely minced
1 cup sliced carrots
1 teaspoon crumbled basil
2 small zucchini, sliced
1 (16-ounce) can Italian pear tomatoes, undrained, chopped
2 (10¾-ounce) cans beef bouillon
2 cups finely shredded cabbage
1 teaspoon salt
¼ teaspoon pepper
1 (16-ounce) can Great Northern beans, undrained
Chopped fresh parsley

Slice sausage crosswise about ½-inch thick; brown in oil in a deep saucepan or Dutch oven. Add onion, garlic, carrots and basil; cook for 5 minutes. Add zucchini, tomatoes with liquid, bouillon, cabbage, salt and pepper. Bring soup to a boil; reduce heat and simmer, covered, for 1 hour. Add beans with liquid; cook another 20 minutes. Garnish with parsley. (Soup is even better the second day!) Makes 8 servings.

Specialties of Indianapolis II

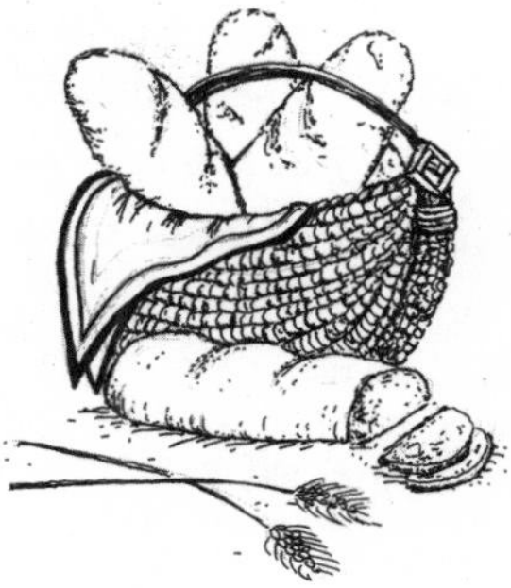

Burgoo

Every fall burgoo festivals in Southern Indiana serve as fund-raisers for area churches and schools whose volunteers make up hundreds of gallons at a time and cook it overnight in huge pots over slow fires. Legend has it that burgoo developed as a result of pioneer women wanting to clean out their pantries each year in order to have canning jars for the new crops coming in; the thick, chowdery potage was what resulted from dumping last year's harvest into a community pot with whatever meat (including wild game) was available. A party always ensued. Nowadays, burgoo is available year around at several area taverns.

3 pounds cheap beef roast
2 pounds pork roast
4 cups dry Great Northern beans
1 bunch celery
6 medium turnips
8 medium potatoes
8 medium onions
½ pound fresh green beans
3 pounds carrots
1 small head green cabbage
3 cans corn
3 cans hominy
3 quarts tomatoes, canned or peeled fresh
1 large can chicken broth
½ lemon, chopped (rind and all)
3 tablespoons mixed pickling spice, tied up in a cheesecloth bag
6-8 ounces ketchup
Salt and pepper to taste

Precook meats and dry beans. Grind meats and vegetables in a food chopper or food processor (do not purée).

Combine all ingredients in a pot. If using more than 1 pot, blend burgoo back and forth between pots as it cooks. Cook 5 hours over low heat, stirring often and on a regular basis to prevent sticking on bottom. Season with salt and pepper to taste. Yield: 10 gallons.

Note: Recipe may be halved. Burgoo freezes well.

Festival Foods and Family Favorites

The Indiana Dunes provide a rich habitat for plant, animal, and bird life. Carl Sandburg said they are a "signature of time and eternity every bit as moving as the Grand Canyon or Yosemite National Park." And moving they are: Mt. Baldy, Indiana's largest "live" dune, moves a short distance away from the lake each year. Mt. Tom is the tallest sand dune at 192 feet.

SALADS

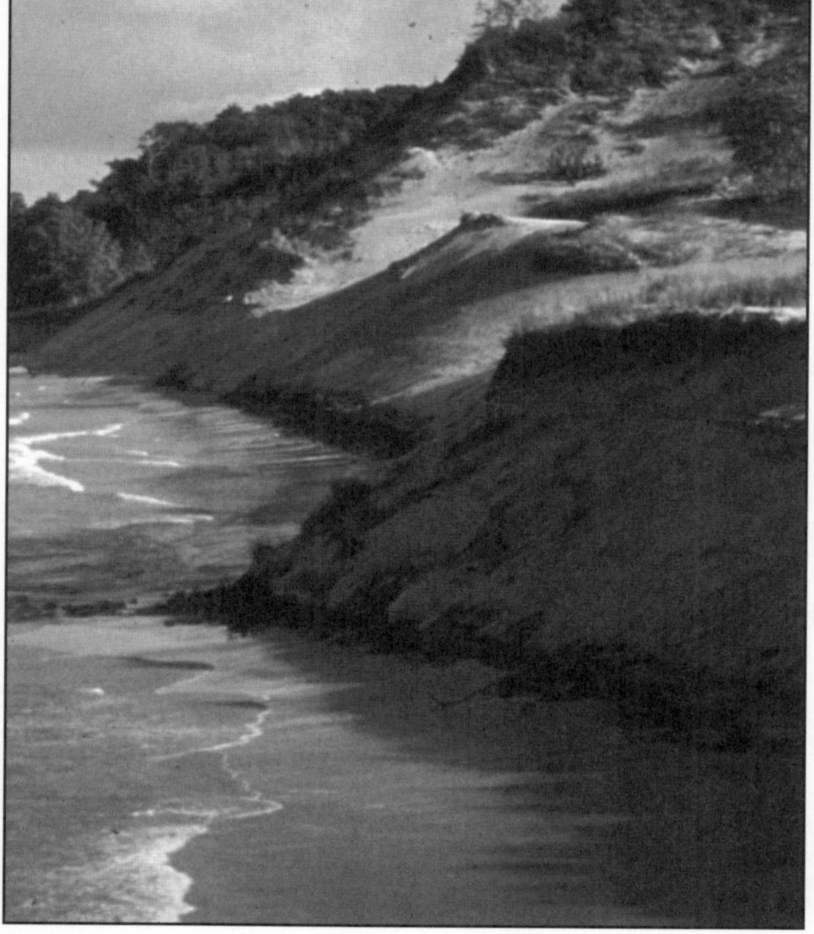

*Mount Baldy is a living, moving mountain. Indiana Dunes.
On Lake Michigan. Porter County.*

Back Home in Indiana Potato Salad

2 pounds potatoes
6 slices bacon, chopped
½ cup minced onions
⅓ cup vinegar
⅓ cup water
1 tablespoon chopped parsley
Salt and pepper to taste

Boil potatoes with skins until slightly tender. Remove from water and slice while still hot into Pyrex dish. Sauté chopped bacon and onions, only until onions are almost, but not quite, brown. Stir in vinegar, water, parsley, salt and pepper to taste. Pour over potatoes and warm in oven to serve. Sprinkle additional parsley for decoration before serving.

Indiana's Finest Recipes

Best Ever German Potato Salad

5 pounds potatoes
1 onion
½ pound bacon
1 cup sugar, well rounded
2 teaspoons salt
3 tablespoons flour
2 cups vinegar (diluted with water, depending on strength of vinegar)
8 tablespoons bacon grease (approximately)
5 hard-cooked eggs

Cook potatoes with skins on. Peel and slice medium size. Chop onion fine and mix with potatoes. Combine potatoes and onions and mix well. Cut bacon fine and fry crisp. Set frying pan aside. In a saucepan, mix sugar, salt, and flour. Add vinegar and stir until well blended. Add this mixture to the bacon bits and grease. Cook sauce until thick, stirring constantly. Pour sauce over potatoes and mix well. Chop hard-cooked eggs and gently mix with ingredients. Serve warm. If desired, slice 2 hard-boiled eggs and use on top for garnish.

Guten Appetit

Marj's Mustaccioli Salad

Great with all barbecued meat.

1 (16-ounce) package mustaccioli noodles
12 slices bacon (sliced in 1-inch pieces)
1 teaspoon garlic salt
½ cup sugar
5 carrots, finely grated
2 large green peppers, chopped
1 large onion, chopped
2½ cups salad dressing (not mayonnaise)
Salt and pepper to taste

Cook noodles 20–25 minutes. Slice bacon, fry until crisp, remove and drain on paper towel. When drippings are cool, mix all other ingredients together with drippings. Drain noodles, blanch with warm water, drain again. Mix noodles with dressing and sprinkle crisp bacon on top just before serving. Serve at room temperature. Yield 12–16 servings.

The Guild Cookbook II

Whole Meal Hawaiian Chicken Salad

4 cups diced, cooked chicken
1 (15-ounce) can pineapple chunks, drained
1 cup chopped celery
1 (11-ounce) can mandarin orange sections, drained
½ cup sliced pitted ripe olives
1 cup chopped bell pepper
2 tablespoons grated onion
1 cup mayonnaise or salad dressing
1 tablespoon prepared mustard
1 (5-ounce) can chow mein noodles
Lettuce leaves

In a large bowl, combine cooked chicken, pineapple, celery, oranges, olives, green pepper, and onion. Blend mayonnaise or salad dressing and mustard; toss gently with chicken mixture. Cover and chill several hours.

Just before serving, mix in chow mein noodles. Serve on lettuce leaves or turn into a lettuce-lined serving bowl. Makes 8 large servings.

Love Cookin'

Fruit Chicken Salad

6 cups cooked chicken
French dressing
1 cup celery
2 tablespoons lemon juice
½ cup pineapple tidbits
¼ cup whipped cream (or more)
3 teaspoons salt
Dash of white pepper
1 cup grapes
1 cup mayonnaise
½ cup slivered almonds
Olives for garnish

Dice chicken in ½-inch pieces and marinate in French dressing for 2 hours. Mix all other ingredients together (except almonds). Chill. When ready to serve, sprinkle almonds over top and garnish with olives.

Recipes of the Durbin

Chicken Salad with Dill

1 bottle dry white wine
8 cups (2 quarts) homemade chicken stock or canned broth
2 bay leaves
16 cups (4 quarts) water or
20 large chicken breasts, halved
4 cups (1 quart) mayonnaise
3 cups sour cream (or as needed)
¼ cup fresh lemon juice
4 cups thinly sliced celery
1 cup thinly sliced scallions
¾ cup chopped fresh dill, or ⅛ cup dry dill
½ cup chopped fresh parsley leaves
Salt and freshly ground black pepper to taste

Bring the wine, chicken broth, bay leaves, and water to a boil in a 12-quart pot. Lower the heat to a simmer and add the chicken breasts. If necessary, add boiling water to cover chicken. Simmer for 30 minutes, stirring occasionally.

Drain chicken breasts well. When cool enough to handle, skin and remove from bone. Shred the meat into bite-size pieces and put them into a large bowl.

Combine the mayonnaise, sour cream, and lemon juice in a separate large bowl. Add the remaining ingredients and mix thoroughly. Pour the mixture over the chicken and combine. Taste for seasoning. Chill well. Serve on a large platter. If desired, surround the salad with fresh dill sprig and cherry tomatoes. Serves 50.

Our Best Recipes to You, Again

Tarragon Chicken Salad

Serve this with raw vegetables and fruit slices and wait for the compliments!

8 ounces chicken breast, skinned and boned
2 tablespoons rice wine vinegar
1 tablespoon crushed tarragon
¼ teaspoon salt
¼ teaspoon white pepper
Fat-free mayonnaise to mix
½ cup sliced celery
½ cup red onion
½ cup red grapes
¼ cup toasted pecans (optional)

Boil or microwave chicken. Cut chicken into chunks. Mix vinegar, tarragon, salt, and white pepper in fat-free mayonnaise. Add chicken, celery, onion, and grapes. In a skillet over medium heat, toast the pecans and then mix into salad. Yield: 4 servings.

Nutrition Analysis Per Serving: Calories 225; Fat 7g; Cal from fat 28%; Chol 35mg; Sod 260mg. (Without Pecans) Cal 175; Fat 2g; Cal from fat 18%.

The Heart of Cooking

Hot Sauerkraut Salad with Knackwurst

2 pounds sauerkraut, drained
2 pared large carrots, grated
1 cup chopped celery
1 cup chopped onion
½ cup chopped green pepper
½ cup sugar
6 knackwurst

In large saucepan, combine first 6 ingredients. Toss to mix well. Heat, stirring occasionally, over low heat for 10 minutes or until heated through. Meanwhile, cook knackwursts. Bring water to boiling in large saucepan. Add knackwursts and bring to a boil again. Simmer gently, uncovered, for 10 minutes. Serve with sauerkraut salad and if desired, mustard and pumpernickel. Serves 6.

Guten Appetit

Fruited Pork Salad

DRESSING:
¼ cup grapefruit juice
2 tablespoons red wine vinegar
1 tablespoon vegetable oil
1 teaspoon poppy seed
2 teaspoons honey
½ teaspoon Dijon mustard

In a jar with tight-fitting lid, shake together Dressing ingredients; set aside.

1 pound boneless pork loin, sliced thinly
1 head green leaf lettuce
2 red grapefruit, peeled and sectioned
1½ cups seedless green grapes
1 cup fresh strawberries

Spray large nonstick skillet with vegetable cooking spray. Heat to medium hot. Stir-fry pork slices 3-4 minutes, just until done. Arrange lettuce on individual plates. Top with fruit and pork. Spoon Dressing over salads. Serves 4.

Calories: 267; protein 27g; fat 89g; cholesterol 67mg; sodium 81mg.

A Taste of Fishers

Broccoli Salad

1 stalk fresh broccoli, washed and chopped
1 small onion (red), chopped
1 pound bacon, fried crisp and chopped
1 cup sunflower kernels
1 cup golden raisins
1 cup mayonnaise
½ cup sugar
1 teaspoon salt
1 tablespoon vinegar

Layer first 5 ingredients in a bowl, cover and refrigerate. Mix mayonnaise, sugar, salt, and vinegar together and add to vegetables when ready to serve.

Note: Good to mix together and refrigerate overnight and add bacon before serving.

Cooking with the Warriors

Overnight Salad

1 medium tomato, chopped
1½ cups sliced lettuce
1 cup sliced carrots
1½ cups sliced mushrooms
1 cup shredded red or green cabbage
1 cup shredded Swiss cheese
½ cup mayonnaise
½ cup cottage cheese
¼ cup sour cream
2 tablespoons onion, chopped
1 small clove garlic, minced
1 teaspoon whole peppercorns, finely crushed
2 teaspoons cider vinegar
½ teaspoon lemon juice
½ teaspoon Worcestershire sauce

Layer vegetables and Swiss cheese in a 2-quart soufflé dish. Process remaining ingredients in blender until smooth. Spread over top of salad. Refrigerate, covered, overnight. Toss before serving. Serves 6-8.

Champions: Favorite Foods of Indy Car Racing

Pea Salad

1 (16-ounce) package frozen peas
½ cup diced celery
2 hard-boiled eggs, grated
1 small onion, diced
1 cup sweet red pepper, diced
1 cup diced American cheese
1½ cups mayonnaise
Salt and white pepper to taste

Blanch peas in boiling water for 30 seconds. Immediately plunge into ice water. Drain thoroughly. In a large bowl, combine peas with remaining ingredients, adding salt and pepper to taste. Chill before serving.

Our Favorite Recipes II

Greens and Red Cabbage Salad

2 pounds spinach, trimmed and washed
½ small head red cabbage, finely shredded (3 cups)
1 large white onion, cut into rings
½ pound small yellow squash, cut ¼ inch thick
1 (16-ounce) bottle creamy garlic and herb salad dressing

Tear spinach coarsely into large pieces. Line salad bowl with spinach. Arrange red cabbage, onion, and yellow squash in center. Cover and refrigerate. At serving time, pour dressing over vegetables and toss to mix well. Makes about 12 servings.

The James Whitcomb Riley Cookbook

The Crown Point Court House (called the "Grand Old Lady") served as a wedding chapel to Ronald Reagan, Rudolph Valentino, and Casius Clay. The historic building now features a collection of unique specialty and gift shops.

Hot Egg Salad in Tomatoes

Good even when tomatoes art not in season!

6 large tomatoes
8 hard-boiled eggs, chopped
¼ cup minced celery
2 tablespoons minced green pepper
1 tablespoon minced onion
1 teaspoon salt
¼ cup lemon juice
2 teaspoons mustard
¼ cup mayonnaise
Dash of cayenne pepper
⅓ cup soft bread crumbs
1 tablespoon margarine, melted

Preheat oven to 450°. Cut stem ends from tomatoes. Scoop out pulp. Turn upside down to drain. Combine remaining ingredients except crumbs and margarine. Fill tomatoes with egg mixture.

Toss crumbs in margarine; sprinkle over tops. Place tomatoes in a 10x6x1½-inch baking dish. Bake at 450° for 10 minutes. Yield: 6 servings.

Cookin' to Beat the Band

Apple Salad

Makes an appetizing and attractive salad.

DRESSING:
1 cup Miracle Whip Salad Dressing
2 tablespoons sugar
2 cups Cool Whip

SALAD:
3 large apples, chopped (leave skins on and use preferably red apples)
1 cup chopped celery
1 cup finely grated carrots
1 cup chopped nuts
1 cup raisins

Mix Dressing ingredients together. When mixed good, add and stir Salad ingredients.

Home Cooking II

Feta Cheese, Apple & Spiced Pecan Salad

2 tablespoons wine vinegar
1 tablespoon + 1 teaspoon Dijon mustard
½ cup olive oil
Salt and freshly ground pepper
1 head Boston lettuce or ½ romaine, torn in pieces
1 head red leaf lettuce, torn into pieces
Spiced Pecans
1 red Delicious apple, finely chopped
½ pound feta cheese, crumbled

Mix vinegar and mustard in large bowl. Gradually whisk in oil. Season with salt and pepper. Add lettuce and toss to coat. Sprinkle pecans, apple, and cheese over salad and serve. Serves 8.

SPICED PECANS:
3 tablespoons unsalted Butter
1 teaspoon salt
1 teaspoon cinnamon
¼ teaspoon cayenne pepper
Dash of hot pepper sauce (like Tabasco)
1⅔ cups pecans (6 ounces)

Melt butter; mix in seasonings. Pour butter mixture over pecans; toss. Spread on heavy cookie sheet. Bake until crisp, about 15 minutes at 300°. Cool completely.

A Taste of Twin Pines

Pear and Brie Salad

RASPBERRY PURÉE:

¼ cup raspberry vinegar
¾ cup sour cream
1 cup raspberries

Mix vinegar, sour cream, and raspberries in a blender or food processor. Process to blend. Strain through fine mesh colander if you wish to remove seeds. Set aside.

1 head Bibb lettuce, washed, dried and chilled
1 small head romaine lettuce, washed, dried and chilled
4 pears
Juice of 1 lemon
¼-½ pound Brie, thinly sliced, bite-sized
¼ cup raspberries, washed, drained

Arrange chilled greens on serving plates. Peel, quarter, core and slice pears. Brush lightly with lemon juice. Arrange pears on greens in a decorative pattern. Top with 3-4 bite-size Brie pieces. Drizzle with Raspberry Purée and accent with whole berries to serve. Serves 4-6.

Back Home Again

Mandarin Orange and Avocado Salad

DRESSING:

½ cup vegetable oil
¼ cup vinegar
½ cup sugar
2 teaspoons minced onion
½ teaspoon salt
Dash of paprika

Six hours or more before serving, put all ingredients into a blender. Blend well and refrigerate. Just before serving, blend again.

8–10 cups Bibb and leaf lettuce, torn into pieces
1 avocado, peeled, sliced and tossed lightly in lemon juice
1 (11-ounce) can mandarin oranges, drained
1 (3-ounce) can French-fried onion rings

In a large salad bowl, combine lettuce, avocado, oranges, and onion rings. Toss lightly with dressing and serve. This is especially nice with chicken. Serves 8–10.

Nutbread and Nostalgia

Mary E.'s Grape Salad

A summertime favorite.

1 (#2) can pineapple chunks, drain well, reserve juice
½ cup sugar
1 egg, beaten
2 tablespoons flour
Pinch of salt
1 cup miniature marshmallows
1 cup whole seedless green grapes
Lemon juice (optional)

Combine reserved juice, sugar, egg, flour, and salt in saucepan. Cook fast, stirring constantly, until thick. Cool. Fold in pineapple chunks, marshmallows, and grapes. Refrigerate overnight. Taste, and if the salad lacks "zing" add a little lemon juice. Serves about 8.

Home Cooking

Orange-Almond Salad

The glazed almonds add a crunch and flavor that takes this salad out of the ordinary and makes it something special!

½ cup slivered almonds
¼ cup sugar
1 head iceberg lettuce
½ bunch romaine lettuce
3 green onions, sliced
2 cups chopped celery
2 (8-ounce) cans mandarin oranges, drained

In heavy skillet, cook and stir almonds and sugar until golden. Watch carefully so that they don't get too brown. Set aside to cool. (This can also be made ahead and stored.) Tear iceberg and romaine lettuce into bite-size pieces. Add green onions, celery, and mandarin oranges.

DRESSING:
¼ cup white wine vinegar
¼ cup sugar
1 teaspoon salt
Dash of pepper
Dash of hot sauce
½ cup oil
2 teaspoons chopped fresh parsley

Whisk together wine vinegar, sugar, salt, pepper, and hot sauce. Add oil slowly. Stir in fresh parsley. Refrigerate 1 hour. To serve salad, toss greens with dressing. Top with almonds and additional oranges.

The Cookery Collection

Honey-Mustard Salad Dressing

¼ cup cider vinegar
¼ cup puréed onion
¼ cup sugar
1 cup honey
1 (6-ounce) jar Gulden's Spicy Brown Mustard
1½ cups mayonnaise
1¼ cups buttermilk

Combine all ingredients and mix well. Refrigerate between uses.

It's About Thyme

Strawberry and Spinach Salad

Strawberries and sweet-sour dressing make this a winner.

½ pound tender spinach
1 pint fresh strawberries, hulled and sliced
2 ounces slivered almonds, toasted

Wash and dry spinach. Arrange spinach and strawberries on individual plates or in clear glass salad bowl.

DRESSING:
½ cup granulated sugar
2 tablespoons sesame seed
1 tablespoon poppy seed
1½ teaspoons minced onion
¼ teaspoon Worcestershire sauce
¼ teaspoon paprika
¼ cup cider vinegar
½ cup oil

Place sugar, sesame seed, poppy seed, onion, Worcestershire, paprika, and vinegar in blender. Add oil in a steady stream with blender on LOW speed. Blend until dressing is creamy and thick. Drizzle dressing over salad. Garnish with toasted almonds. Serves 4.

Winners

Ruby Red Raspberry Salad

A beautiful salad to serve. Place a square on a lettuce leaf and garnish.

1 (3-ounce) package red raspberry gelatin
1 cup boiling water
1 (10-ounce) package frozen red raspberries, undrained
1½ cups sour cream
1 (3-ounce) package cherry gelatin
1 cup boiling water
1 (20-ounce) can crushed pineapple, drained
1 (1-pound) can whole cranberry sauce, or cranberry-raspberry sauce
Mayonnaise for garnish
Mint leaves for garnish, optional

Dissolve raspberry gelatin in hot water. Add red raspberries to gelatin and stir until berries are separated. Place in a 9x13-inch pan. Refrigerate to set.

Spread the sour cream over surface of the raspberry layer. Now dissolve cherry gelatin in hot water. Add the crushed pineapple and the cranberry sauce and stir to mix well. Let this mixture cool to room temperature, then spoon it over the sour cream layer. Cover and refrigerate until serving time. Cut into squares to serve. Put a teaspoon of mayonnaise on each square and stick a mint leaf in the mayonnaise, if desired. Serves 12-14.

Christmas Thyme at Oak Hill Farm

Favorite Cranberry Salad

After working on this recipe for years—it's finally just right!

1 (10-ounce) package fresh cranberries, picked over and washed
4 cups water
¼ teaspoon baking soda
2 cups sugar
3 (3-ounce) boxes strawberry gelatin
4 cups miniature marshmallows
2 cups apple, peeled and diced
1 cup chopped nuts (optional)
1 (9-ounce) can crushed pineapple, drained
2 navel oranges, peeled and sectioned
1 or 2 cups seedless green or red grapes, halved

Cook cranberries in the 4 cups water to a boil. Add soda and stir. Simmer 10 minutes. Stir in sugar, gelatin, and marshmallows. Stir until melted. Let mixture cool. Add apples, nuts, pineapple, orange sections, and grapes. Pour into one 9x13-inch pan and one 8x8-inch pan. Chill until firm. Will serve 20 or more.

It's About Thyme

Frozen Cherry Salad Loaf

A light and fresh salad to compliment any brunch or luncheon.

1 (16-ounce) can dark sweet cherries
1 (8-ounce) can crushed pineapple
1 (11-ounce) can mandarin oranges
1 (8-ounce) package cream cheese, softened
1 cup sour cream
¼ cup sugar
¼ teaspoon salt
2 cups mini marshmallows
½ cup chopped pecans

Drain fruit well. Reserve a few cherries and orange slices for garnish. Beat cream cheese until fluffy and blend in sour cream, sugar, and salt. Fold in fruits, marshmallows and nuts. Pour into loaf pans. Freeze 6 hours.

Remove ½ hour before serving; add garnish. Yield: 8-10 servings.

Cookin' to Beat the Band

Orange Sherbet Salad

2 (3-ounce) packages orange gelatin
1 cup boiling water
1 cup cold water
¼ cup lemon juice
1 pint orange sherbet
1 (11-ounce) can mandarin oranges

Dissolve gelatin in boiling water; add cold water, lemon juice, and sherbet. With mixer on LOW speed, blend until sherbet is melted and mixture is smooth. Add drained mandarin oranges. Pour into a 5-cup mold and chill until firm.

Variation: Dissolve gelatin in 1½ cups boiling water. Omit cold water and lemon juice. Add 1 (8-ounce) can well-drained crushed pineapple in addition to sherbet and mandarin oranges.

Variation #2: Dissolve gelatin in 1 cup boiling water. Add 1 cup mandarin orange juice instead of cold water. Omit lemon juice. Add 2 cups (2 cans) mandarin oranges and 1 can well-drained crushed pineapple to sherbet-gelatin mixture.

Mincemeat and Memories

Fairmount is the hometown of many distinguished people, including three college presidents, numerous authors, artists, scientists, inventors, etc. Notable among them are: movie legend, James Dean; "Garfield" creator, Jim Davis; Emmy Award winning journalist Phil Jones; and Director of the National Hurricane Center, Dr. Robert C. Sheets.

PASTA, ETC.

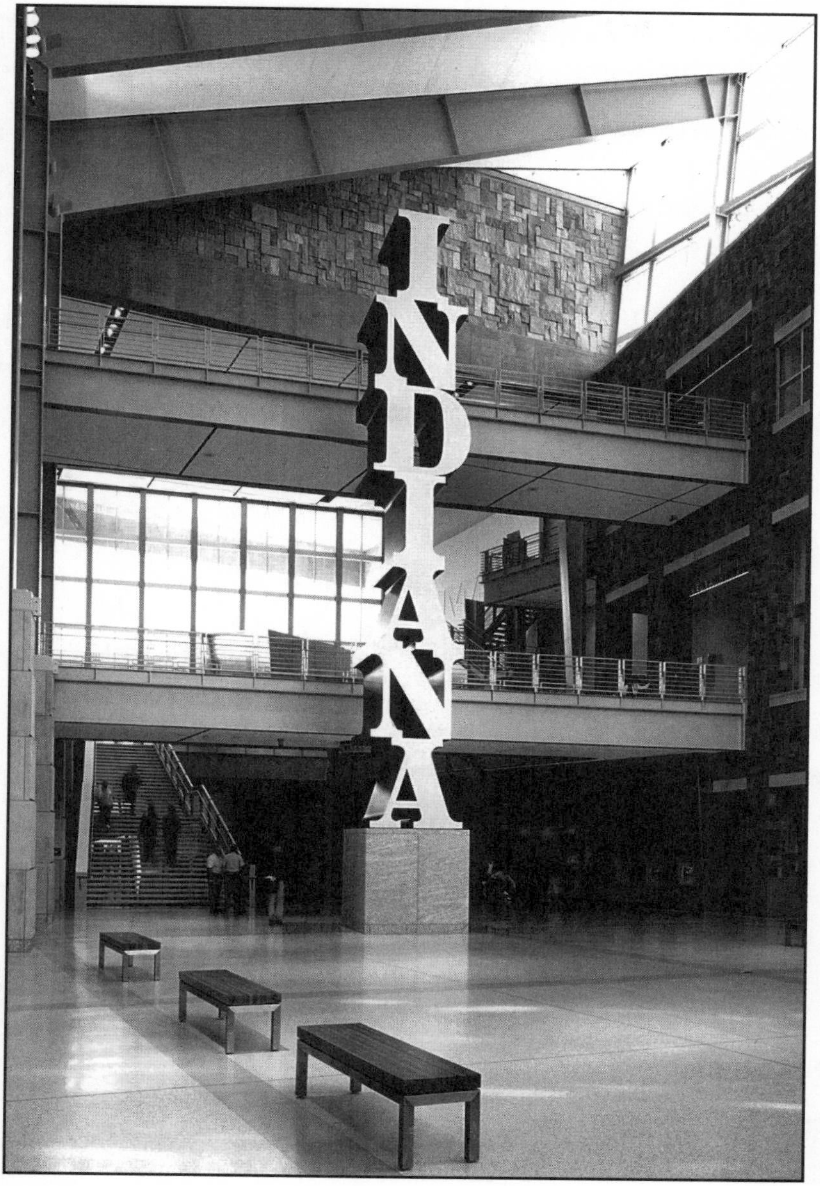

PHOTO ©JEFF GOLDBERG/EST

Visitors to the Indiana State Museum in Indianapolis are greeted by Robert, Indiana's 55-foot tall "INDIANA" Obelisk.

Beef or Chicken and Noodles

Of all dishes, beef and noodles or chicken and noodles seems to be a community favorite—truly, a typical Hoosier dish. Few cooks make their own noodles anymore, but we thought it might be fun to include detailed instructions for those of you who would like to try, and are trying for the first time.

1 (3-pound) chuck roast or 1 fat chicken

Place roast in roaster and nearly cover with water. Cover roaster and bake at 250° for 3-4 hours or until tender. Reserve broth. Cut off excess fat from meat, and tear meat into chunks.

If using chicken, cook, covered, in salted water for approximately 1 hour, or until tender. Reserve chicken broth. Skin, remove meat from bones and tear into chunks.

HOMEMADE NOODLES:
1 teaspoon salt
4 tablespoons milk
2 eggs
About 2 cups flour, more if needed

Add salt and milk to eggs and beat well with a fork. Add flour and stir into egg mixture until it sticks together enough to turn out on a well-floured bread board. Mix plenty of flour with it until it isn't sticky. Roll out very thin, keeping plenty of flour under and over egg dough. Don't be stingy with the flour, so put plenty over rolled out dough before rolling up into a log roll. Slice very thin with a sharp butcher knife. After slicing a few slices, pick up several with your fingers and drop them on the board so that extra flour drops off, also prevents them from sticking together. (A suggestion to help roll them thin: place fingers together on top of roll and guide your knife as you slice against fingernails.)

Sprinkle noodles in about 2 quarts of diluted chicken or beef broth (after it boils) until all noodles are added. Simmer slowly about 20 minutes. Stir occasionally and add

Continued

more water if needed to thin. When done, stir in beef or chicken meat.

Note: The secret of making noodles is in using plenty of flour. It will drop away from noodles after slicing—don't use this flour when cooking them.

Home Cooking

Pasta with Red Peppers and Ham

This is a perfect quick supper dish, special enough to serve for guests.

3 tablespoons butter
¼ cup olive oil
1 large sweet red pepper, cored, seeded, cubed
¼ pound baked Virginia ham, chopped
4 green onions, chopped
½ tablespoon basil leaves
4 tablespoons fresh, chopped parsley
½ teaspoon oregano
2 garlic cloves, minced
2 chicken bouillon cubes
1 cup hot water
1 tablespoon lemon juice
1 pound vermicelli pasta

Melt butter in a large skillet over medium heat; add oil. Stir in pepper, ham, and onions; sauté until pepper and onion are tender. Add basil, parsley, oregano, and garlic. Cook several minutes. Combine bouillon cubes, water, and lemon juice; stir to dissolve cubes. Add to ham and vegetable mixture. Bring to a boil; reduce heat and simmer until slightly thickened. Cook pasta following package directions until tender but firm. Drain and return to pan to keep warm. When ready to serve, pour pasta onto serving platter. Top with sauce; toss to combine. Serve immediately. Serves 4-6.

Back Home Again

From 1852, and for 114 years, Studebaker (in South Bend) shaped America's industrial age by producing rugged settlers' wagons, carriages, distinctive automobiles and trucks. Over 45,000 Studebaker automobiles were sold in 1915. The first ones were powered by electricity.

Spaghetti Bake

One of the best carry-in dishes. Everyone loves this.

2 pounds ground beef
1 cup chopped onion
1 clove garlic, minced
1 (28-ounce) can tomatoes, cut up
1 (16-ounce) can tomato sauce
1 (6-ounce) can tomato paste
1 (6 or 8-ounce) can mushroom pieces
2 teaspoons sugar
1½ teaspoons dried oregano
1 teaspoon salt
1 teaspoon dried basil
8 ounces spaghetti, cooked and drained
2-4 cups shredded Mozzarella cheese (depending on how cheesy you like it)
½ cup grated Parmesan cheese

In a large pan, cook ground beef, onion, and garlic until meat is browned. Drain off fat. Stir rest of ingredients into the pot except the spaghetti and the cheeses. Simmer, uncovered, for about 30 minutes. Stir in drained spaghetti. Put half of spaghetti mixture in a greased 9x13-inch pan. Cover with ½ the Mozzarella cheese. Add rest of spaghetti mixture. Top with other ½ of Mozzarella and sprinkle all over with the Parmesan cheese. Bake at 375° for about 30 minutes. Serves 10-12.

Note: You can make this dish ahead of time and either freeze or refrigerate it. It must, however, be at room temperature when you put it in the oven.

It's About Thyme

The Slippery Noodle Inn is a large blues bar and restaurant with two performance stages in downtown Indianapolis, Indiana. It also has the distinction of being the oldest continuously operating bar in the state of Indiana, having opened in 1850 as the Tremont House.

Spaghetti Pie

6 ounces spaghetti
2 tablespoons margarine
⅓ cup grated Parmesan cheese
2 eggs, well beaten
1 cup cottage cheese
1 pound ground beef or bulk pork sausage
½ cup chopped onion
¼ cup green peppers, chopped
1 (8-ounce) can tomatoes, cut up
6 ounces tomato paste
1 teaspoon sugar
1 teaspoon dried oregano, crushed
½ teaspoon garlic salt
½ cup shredded Mozzarella cheese

Cook spaghetti according to directions and drain. (Should have about 3 cups cooked spaghetti.) Stir in margarine until melted. Stir in Parmesan cheese and eggs. Form spaghetti mixture into a "crust" in a buttered 10-inch pie plate. Spread cottage cheese over the bottom of spaghetti crust.

In a skillet, cook meat, onion, and green pepper until cooked. Drain off fat. Stir in undrained tomatoes, tomato paste, sugar, oregano, and garlic salt. Heat through. Add meat mixture over cottage cheese in "crust." Bake uncovered at 350° for 20 minutes. Add Mozzarella cheese on top and bake for 5 minutes longer. Serves 6.

Amish Country Cookbook III

15-Minute Creamy Fettucine Alfredo

1 (8-ounce) package Philadelphia cream cheese, cubed
¾ cup Kraft 100% Parmesan cheese
½ cup margarine
½ cup milk
8 ounces fettucine, cooked, drained

In large saucepan, stir together cream cheese, Parmesan cheese, margarine, and milk over low heat until smooth. Add fettucine; toss lightly. Serves 4.

A Taste of Twin Pines

Spinach Lasagne

1 pound ricotta or small curd cottage cheese
1½ cups shredded Mozzarella cheese, divided
1 egg, beaten
1 (10-ounce) package frozen, chopped spinach, thawed and patted dry
½ teaspoon salt
⅛ teaspoon pepper
¾ teaspoon oregano
2 (15½ -ounce)jars spaghetti sauce
½ (8-ounce) package lasagne noodles, uncooked
1 cup water

In a large bowl, mix ricotta, 1 cup Mozzarella, egg, spinach, salt, pepper, and oregano. In a greased 13x9x2-inch baking dish, layer ½ cup of the spaghetti sauce, ⅓ of the uncooked noodles, and ½ of the cheese mixture. Repeat. Top with remaining noodles and sauce. Sprinkle reserved ½ cup of Mozzarella over the top. Pour water around edges. Cover tightly with foil. Bake at 350° for 1 hour and 15 minutes. Let stand 15 minutes to firm before serving. Nice with a large Italian salad.

Can be made ahead. Serves 8.

Nutbread and Nostalgia

Easy Lasagna

1 pound ground beef
1 (32-ounce) jar spaghetti sauce
½-¾ cup water
1 teaspoon salt
½ teaspoon sugar
1 (8-ounce) carton lasagna noodles
1 (16-ounce) carton cottage cheese
½ cup Parmesan cheese
3 cups Mozzarella cheese

Brown beef and drain fat. Add sauce, water, salt, and sugar. Simmer 5-10 minutes. In a 13¾x8½-inch casseroles, layer ⅓ of the sauce, ½ of the uncooked noodles, 1 cup cottage cheese, ¼ cup Parmesan cheese and 1 cup Mozzarella cheese. Repeat with rest of ingredients, ending with Mozzarella and Parmesan cheese. Cover with foil. Bake at 350° for 55-60 minutes. Remove foil and let stand 10 minutes before serving. Makes 12-14 servings.

Can be made in 2 lasagna pans. One for now, one frozen for later.

Jasper County Extension Homemakers Cookbook

Skillet Lasagna

1 pound ground beef
1 envelope spaghetti sauce mix
1 pound cream-style cottage cheese
3 cups noodles (uncooked)
1 (28-ounce) can tomatoes
1 cup water
1 (8-ounce) package shredded Mozzarella cheese

Lightly brown hamburger; sprinkle ½ of spaghetti mix over meat. Spread cottage cheese over meat. Next add noodles in layer. Sprinkle remaining spaghetti mix. Add tomatoes with liquid and water and continue cooking slowly for 30-35 minutes. Sprinkle cheese over top. Return cover and let stand 10-15 minutes before serving.

Amish Country Cookbook II

Church Supper Lasagna

1 (13-ounce) package lasagne noodles
2 tablespoons salad oil
1 pound ground beef
2 tablespoons instant minced onion
2 tablespoons chopped parsley
¼ cup chopped celery
¼ teaspoon garlic powder
1½ teaspoons salt
3 (8-ounce) cans tomato sauce
4 sliced boiled eggs
1 pound sliced Mozzarella cheese
1 pint large curd cottage cheese

Cook noodles; rinse under cold water and drain. Heat oil and brown beef in large skillet. Stir in onion, parsley, celery, garlic powder, salt, and tomato sauce. Cover and simmer 15 minutes. Reserve a few egg slices for garnish. In 13x9x2-inch oiled pan, layer about ⅓ each of the noodles, Mozzarella cheese, cottage cheese, eggs, and meat sauce. Repeat layers twice ending with meat sauce. Bake in 350° oven 30 minutes. Garnish with egg slices. Makes 10-12 servings.

Amish Country Cookbook I

Garlic Chicken Linguini

SEASONING MIX:

3 cups water
1½ tablespoons chicken base
1½ teaspoons Paul Prudhomme's Cajun Seafood Majic
½ tablespoon basil
1 tablespoon Italian seasoning
2½ tablespoons chopped garlic

Heat mixture once, then keep cool.

8 ounces sliced chicken breast
1 teaspoon margarine
¼ teaspoon chopped garlic
½ cup sliced mushrooms (broccoli florets may be substituted)
2 tablespoons chopped green onions
½ cup Seasoning Mix
¾ cup evaporated skim milk
2 tablespoons cornstarch and water, mixed
6 ounces cooked linguini

Sauté chicken in margarine and garlic over medium-high heat. When chicken is ¾-done, add mushrooms, green onions, Seasoning Mix, evaporated skim milk and sauté. When milk boils, add cornstarch mixture to thicken. Bring to boil again, add linguini, toss and serve. Chopped parsley may be sprinkled on top for color. Serves 2.

Nutrition Analysis Per Serving: Calories 485; Fat 6g; Cal from fat 11 %; Chol 180mg; Sod J 30mg.

Thirsty Camel, Fort Wayne.
The Heart of Cooking

Northern Indiana is home to a variety of classic car museums including the Studebaker National Museum in South Bend, the Antique Auto Museum In Elkhart, the Classic Car Museum in Warsaw, the Door Prairie Museum in LaPorte, and the Auburn-Cord Duesenberg Museum in Auburn. These museums show rare examples of legendary automobiles built in Indiana.

Pasta with Gorgonzola

2 cups heavy cream
10 ounces gorgonzola cheese
4 tablespoons grated Romano cheese
¾ teaspoon grated pepper
1 pound spinach fettucini
½ stick butter

Reduce cream to about 1½-1¾ cups (microwave HIGH, approximately 5 minutes or cook over medium-high heat for 8 minutes). Crumble gorgonzola cheese into hot cream and stir in. Add Romano cheese and pepper and stir until blended. Keep sauce warm while cooking pasta.

Cook pasta until al dente. Drain. Add butter to sauce and stir until melted. Mix pasta and sauce well in large bowl. Serve warm.

White Feather Farms Saturday Secrets

Gary's Broccoli and Mostaccioli

1 (10-ounce) package frozen broccoli spears
¼ stick butter
1 pound mostaccioli
1 toe minced garlic
½ cup olive oil
Parmesan cheese

Prepare and drain broccoli; add butter and set aside. Boil mostaccioli in salted water, al dente. While pasta is cooking, take a large skillet and brown garlic and oil. Add mostaccioli and broccoli, stirring lightly. Heat until mostaccioli and broccoli are well coated in oil. Pour into large bowl, sprinkle with 1 cup grated Parmesan cheese, toss lightly and serve.

Our Italian Family Cookbook

Manicotti with Green Chili

1 box manicotti shells
1½ cups shredded Mozzarella cheese, divided
1 cup cottage cheese
⅓ cup grated Parmesan cheese
2 eggs, beaten
¼ cup snipped parsley
1 teaspoon instant minced onion
1 small can chopped green chilies
1 (15-ounce) jar spaghetti sauce with mushrooms
⅓ cup water

Preheat oven to 350°. Cook manicotti shells and drain. Combine ¾ cup Mozzarella, cottage cheese, and Parmesan. Stir in eggs, parsley, onion, and green chilies. Set aside.

Combine spaghetti sauce and water in a separate bowl. Pour 1 cup of sauce into large baking dish. Fill manicotti shells with filling mixture and arrange in rows in baking dish. Pour remaining sauce over all and sprinkle remaining Mozzarella. Bake, uncovered, at 350° for 35 minutes. Serves 8.

Champions: Favorite Foods of Indy Car Racing

Rice Pilaf

½ stick butter
½ cup celery
½ cup green pepper
¼ cup onion
2 tablespoons sliced mushrooms
1 tablespoon diced pimento
3 cups chicken stock
½ teaspoon curry powder
1 cup long grain rice (not instant)
½ teaspoon salt
⅛ teaspoon pepper

Chop and sauté in butter the celery, green pepper, and onion. Brown lightly about 10 minutes. Then add mushrooms and pimento. Bring chicken stock and curry powder to boil; add rice and cook uncovered for 10 minutes. Add other ingredients. Cook until rice is tender, another 10 minutes. Season with salt and pepper.

Recipes of the Durbin

Caroline's Baked Rice Casserole

2 tablespoons butter
3 teaspoons chopped onion
2 cups chopped celery
1 (10¾-ounce) can cream of mushroom soup
1 (10¾-ounce) can cream of chicken soup
1 can beef consommé
¾ cup regular rice
1 teaspoon poultry seasoning
Salt to taste
1 (4-ounce) can chopped mushrooms with juice
1 cup slivered almonds

Sauté butter, onion, and celery. Mix together remaining ingredients except almonds in a 1½- or 2-quart casserole. Add the onions and celery to the mixture in the casserole. Bake covered for 30 minutes in a 350° oven. Add almonds (browned in butter).

Bake uncovered for 15 minutes longer. Let stand for 10-15 minutes to thicken before serving. Serves 6-8. This is good with any chicken recipe. (A 1960s recipe.)

Aspic and Old Lace

Joy Butler's Rice

6 tablespoons butter
1 can onion soup
1 can beef consommé
1 small can button mushrooms
1 cup uncooked long grain rice
¼ teaspoon Kitchen Bouquet

Chop butter and mix all the above ingredients in a 4-quart baking dish, as mixture swells during baking. Bake for about 1½ hours at 325°. Stir once after about ½ hour.

Mincemeat and Memories

Wan Q Chow Mein

2 tablespoons peanut oil
1 clove garlic minced
6 ounces thinly sliced beef, tenderloin, or chicken breast
1½ cups celery, sliced
½ cup water chestnuts, sliced thin
½ cup Chinese pea pods, sliced thin, lengthwise
½ cup carrots, shredded
1 cup bamboo shoots, shredded
1 teaspoon salt
2 tablespoons soy sauce
1 teaspoon sherry
1 cup chicken broth
1 tablespoon cornstarch
½ cup water
Hot cooked rice

Heat oil in skillet or wok. Add garlic and meat and quickly brown. Remove meat and set aside. Add celery, water chestnuts, pea pods, carrots, bamboo shoots, salt, and soy sauce. Cook and stir until vegetables are tender but crisp. Add sherry and broth. Cover and bring to a boil. Mix cornstarch with water and add to broth. Cook until slightly thickened. Serve with rice. Makes 4 servings.

Amish Country Cookbook III

Zucchini Pie

½ pound ground round
1 small onion, chopped
2 tablespoons garlic, minced
6 tablespoons bread crumbs
2 tablespoons Parmesan cheese
Pie crust (recipe follows)
1 tablespoon basil
1 tablespoon oregano
1 medium zucchini, shredded
2 tomatoes, sliced thin
1 (6-ounce) can tomato sauce (Italian style)
½ cup Mozzarella cheese (3g of fat/svg or fat-free)

Brown ground round in skillet with onion and minced garlic. Add ½ of bread crumbs and Parmesan cheese. Sprinkle ½ of bread crumbs on bottom of whole non-baked wheat pie crust. Top with meat mixture.

Mix spices with zucchini and place on top of meat. Cover zucchini with thinly layered sliced tomatoes. Pour sauce over mixture and top with shredded cheese. Bake at 350° for approximately 30 minutes. Serves 8.

Nutrition Analysis Per Serving: Calories 134; Fat 4g; Cal from fat 27%; Chol 28mg; Sod 202mg.

The Heart of Cooking

Pie Crust

¾ cup white flour
¼ cup wheat flour
¼ teaspoon salt
¼ cup margarine, low fat
1½ tablespoons cold water

Sift the flours and salt together. Cut in the margarine and add water to desired consistency. The dough should be crumbly. Form into a ball and roll to ⅛-inch thickness.

Place in a 9-inch pie pan and flute the edges. Bake at 400° for 10 minutes if recipe requires a pre-baked crust.

Nutrition Analysis Per Serving: Calories 75; Fat 2.9g; Cal from fat 35%; Chol 0mg; Sod 92mg.

The Heart of Cooking

Mushroom Sausage Pie

Savory meat pies were common in Riley's day—today we would call this a quiche.

Pastry for 9-inch single crust
1 pound hot pork sausage
¼ cup (½ stick) butter
¾ pound (12 ounces) fresh mushrooms
1 cup whipping cream, not whipped
2 egg yolks, beaten
1 tablespoon flour
1 tablespoon melted butter
1 tablespoon lemon juice
½ teaspoon salt
½ teaspoon pepper
½ cup freshly grated Parmesan cheese

Preheat oven to 450°. Roll out and fit pastry into 9-inch pie plate. Without pricking, bake the crust about 8–10 minutes, until lightly brown. As it bakes, air pockets underneath the pastry can cause it to puff up and crack, so check the pastry every 2–3 minutes, and push it down to fit the shape of the pie plate if this happens. Let stand while making filling.

In large skillet, fry the pork sausage and drain off fat well. In same skillet, melt the butter and add mushrooms and cook briefly. Spread the sausage and mushrooms evenly in the pastry.

Make rich custard; in medium mixing bowl, whisk together thoroughly the heavy cream, egg yolks, flour, melted butter, lemon juice, salt and pepper. Pour this mixture evenly over the pie filling. Bake the pie for 30–40 minutes at 375°, until rich brown and set. As you remove from the oven, sprinkle the Parmesan cheese over the top. Serve warm. Makes about 6–8 servings.

The James Whitcomb Riley Cookbook

Women were first admitted to Indiana University in 1867; not until 1972 did the University of Notre Dame admit women.

Swiss Alpine Quiche

2 cups shredded Swiss cheese
2 tablespoons flour
1 package chopped broccoli, thawed and drained
2 cups cooked, chopped ham
3 tablespoons chopped onion
1 unbaked pie shell (10-inch deep plate)
1¼ cups milk
3 eggs, slightly beaten
½ teaspoon salt
⅓ teaspoon pepper

Combine cheese and flour. Layer ½ of broccoli, ½ of ham, ½ of onion, and ½ of cheese mixture in pie shell. Repeat layers. Combine milk and eggs and seasonings. Pour over mixture in shell. Bake at 350° for 40-45 minutes until lightly browned. Let stand 5 minutes before slicing.

Recipes from Jan's Cake & Candy Crafts

Cranberry Chutney

This chutney is also great served over grilled chicken.

2 cups fresh or frozen cranberries
1 cup whole frozen unsweetened raspberries, thawed
1 cup honey
1 tart apple, peeled, cored and coarsely chopped
1 large orange, peeled, seeded and sliced
½ cup chopped celery
½ cup raspberry vinegar
2 tablespoons water
1½ teaspoons grated fresh ginger root
¼ teaspoon dry mustard
⅛ teaspoon ground cloves
2 (10-ounce) glass jelly jars

Combine cranberries, raspberries, honey, apple, orange, celery, vinegar, water, ginger, mustard, and cloves in a large, heavy saucepan. Bring to a boil, stirring frequently. Reduce heat; simmer 1 hour or until mixture thickens and liquid is syrupy, stirring occasionally.

Heat jars in boiling water; drain well. Ladle mixture into clean hot jars. Cover tightly and cool. Store in refrigerator up to 3 weeks. Yield: 2½ cups.

Back Home Again

Cranberry Conserve

This conserve can be used to accompany chicken, turkey or pork. Fill a peach or pear half with a tablespoonful. Glaze chicken breasts with it, then bake the breasts. Glaze pork roasts with it. Even brush on turkey the last few minutes of baking time for a beautiful finish to the bird. Enjoy!

4 cups raw cranberries, picked over and washed
1½ cups water
3 cups sugar
1 cup crushed pineapple, undrained
½ cup light raisins
1 seedless orange, chopped (including the rind)
½ cup walnuts or pecans, chopped

In a large, heavy saucepan, combine the cranberries and water. Bring to a boil over medium heat and simmer for 5-8 minutes, or until berries pop and are tender. Stir in the sugar, crushed pineapple, raisins, and chopped orange. Bring mixture to a boil, reduce heat and simmer for 20 minutes, stirring occasionally. Remove from heat and stir in the nuts. Can in hot, sterilized jars or cool and store in the refrigerator if conserve is to be used soon. Makes about 5 cups.

Christmas Thyme at Oak Hill Farm

Souper Meat & Potato Pie

1 can cream of mushroom soup
1 pound ground beef
¼ cup finely chopped onion
1 egg, slightly beaten
¼ cup fine dry bread crumbs
¼ teaspoon salt
Dash of pepper
2 cups mashed potatoes
¼ cup shredded milk cheese (Velveeta)

Mix thoroughly ½ can of soup and next 6 ingredients. Press firmly into 9-inch pie plate. Bake at 350° for 25 minutes; spoon off fat. Frost with potatoes; top with remaining soup. Place cheese on top. Bake 10 minutes more or until cheese melts. If desired, garnish with bacon slices. Makes 1 (9-inch) meat pie.

Our Favorite Recipes II

Potato Hot Dog Dish

3 tablespoons butter
3 tablespoons flour
¾ teaspoon mustard
1½ cups milk
1 teaspoon salt
1 teaspoon pepper
¾ cup mayonnaise
4 cups cooked, diced potatoes
1 pack hot dogs

Blend together butter, flour, mustard, milk, salt, and pepper. Mix well. Cook over medium heat, stirring constantly until mixture thickens. Remove from heat. Add mayonnaise, potatoes, and ½ of the hot dogs, sliced. Mix well. Spoon into 2½-quart dish. Cut remaining hot dogs in halves lengthwise. Arrange over potatoes. Bake at 350° for 30-35 minutes or until hot dogs are done.

Country Cooking

VEGETABLES

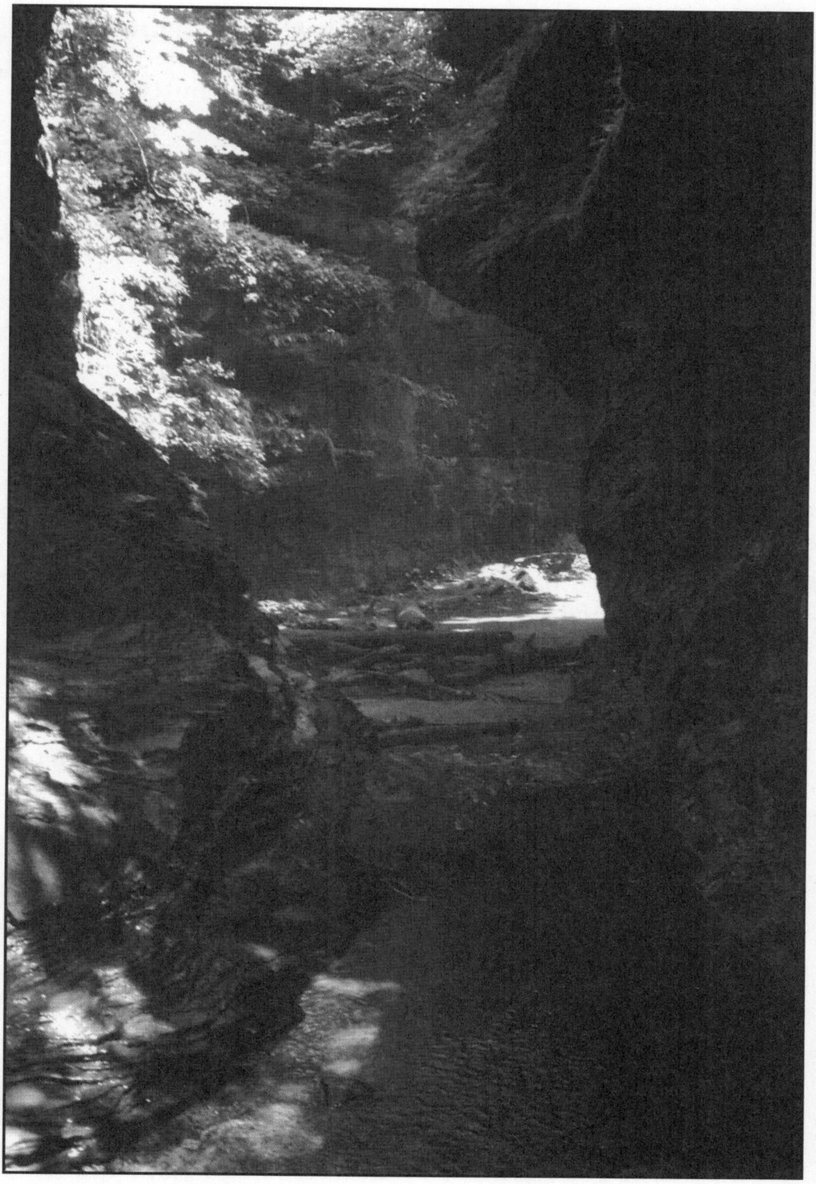

WIKIPEDIA.COM

Some of the natural geologic wonders along the trails of beautiful Turkey Run State Park. Marshall.

Zucchini Rounds

⅓ cup biscuit mix
¼ cup Parmesan cheese
⅛ teaspoon pepper
2 eggs, slightly beaten
2 cups shredded, unpared zucchini
2 tablespoons butter or margarine

Mix together first 3 ingredients. Stir in eggs, just until moistened. Fold in zucchini. Melt butter in skillet over low heat. Drop mixture (in 2-tablespoon amounts) into skillet, forming rounds. Cook for 2-3 minutes on each side, or until golden brown in color. Keep warm while cooking the remainder.

Jasper County Extension Homemakers Cookbook

Zucchini and Cheese

3 cups finely grated zucchini
1 cup cracker crumbs
1 cup grated Cheddar cheese
2 beaten eggs
2 tablespoons chopped onion

Combine all ingredients and put in a well-buttered 2-quart baking dish. Bake for 1 hour at 350°. Serves 6.

Mincemeat and Memories

Green Beans with Hot Bacon Dressing

1 (10-ounce) package frozen green beans
¼ cup mayonnaise
1 tablespoon sugar
¼ cup chopped onion
1 tablespoon melted butter
2 tablespoons vinegar
6 slices bacon, fried crisp and crumbled

Cook beans according to package directions. Drain and set aside. Combine mayonnaise, sugar, onion, butter, and vinegar in a small bowl. Microcook for 30 seconds, or combine these ingredients in a small saucepan and heat. Pour over hot cooked beans. Top with crumbled bacon and serve immediately. Serves 4.

Nutbread and Nostalgia

Green Bean Casserole

3 tablespoons butter
2 tablespoons flour
3 tablespoons grated onions
1 pint sour cream
Salt
Pepper
2 quarts green beans (or 3 cans)
1 package Swiss cheese

Make sauce by blending the melted butter and flour. Cook briefly. Remove from heat. Add onions, sour cream, salt and pepper. Add sauce mixture to the green beans. In casserole, alternate layers of green bean sauce with cheese slices. Cook in oven at 350° for 30 minutes.

Jasper County Extension Homemakers Cookbook

There are 32 covered bridges in Park County. In October, there is a 10-day festival that brings over one million people to the county.

Barbecued Green Beans

A real crowd pleaser.

6 slices bacon, diced
1 onion, chopped
4 (1-pound) cans cut green beans, drained (fresh do not work well)
1 cup firmly packed brown sugar
1 cup catsup

Preheat oven to 250°. Cook bacon and onion together in medium-size skillet over medium heat until bacon is crisp. Remove with slotted spoon and place in ungreased 2-quart baking dish. Add green beans.

Mix brown sugar and catsup in medium-size bowl. Fold into green beans. Bake, covered, at 250° for 3 hours. Serves 6-8.

Winners

Amish-Style Baked Beans

1 can kidney beans
1 can butter beans
1 can pork and beans
4 slices bacon
2 small onions, chopped
1 cup brown sugar
1 cup catsup
1 teaspoon prepared mustard

Drain beans and mix together. Fry, but don't brown bacon. Add bacon and remaining ingredients to beans. Bake 1 hour at 350°.

Taste & See

A total celebration of Scottish heritage and pageantry, the Columbus Scottish Festival is held each August in Clifty Park. Highland dancing, pipe band music, and athletic competition perpetuate the customs and culture of the native land.

Tortilla-Black Bean Casserole

This recipe uses low-fat dairy products to make this prize-winning Tex-Mex favorite more healthful.

2 cups chopped onion
1½ cups chopped green pepper
1 (14½-ounce) can tomatoes, cut up
¾ cup picante sauce
2 cloves garlic, minced
2 teaspoons ground cumin
1 (15-ounce) can black beans or red kidney beans, drained
12 (6-inch) corn tortillas
2 cups shredded fat-free Monterey Jack cheese

In a large skillet combine onion, green pepper, undrained tomatoes, picante sauce, garlic, and cumin. Bring to boiling; reduce heat. Simmer, uncovered, for 10 minutes. Stir in beans.

In a 13x9x2-inch baking dish, spread ⅓ of the bean mixture over bottom. Top with ½ of the tortillas, overlapping as necessary, and ½ of the cheese. Add another ⅓ of the bean mixture, then remaining tortillas and bean mixture. Cover and bake in a 350° oven for 30-35 minutes or until heated through. Sprinkle with remaining cheese. Let stand for 10 minutes. Cut into squares to serve. Makes 10-12 side-dish servings or 6-8 main-dish servings.

Nutrition Analysis Per Serving: Calories 165; Fat 1.8g; Cal from fat 1096; Chol 3.3mg; Sod 330mg.

The Heart of Cooking

Corn Casserole

1 stick margarine, melted
2 eggs, slightly beaten
8 ounces sour cream
1 (16-ounce) can creamed corn
1 (16-ounce) can whole kernel corn, (DO NOT DRAIN)
1 box Jiffy corn bread mix

Mix margarine, eggs, and sour cream. Add corns and corn bread mix (dry). Pour into 9x13-inch pan (lightly greased). Bake at 350° for 45 minutes, uncovered.

Cooking with the Warriors

Broccoli-Corn Bake

1 (16-ounce) can cream-style corn
1 (10-ounce) package frozen chopped broccoli, cooked and drained
1 egg, beaten
1 tablespoon butter, melted
¾ cup crumbled Ritz crackers
2 tablespoons butter
2 teaspoons dehydrated onion
Salt and pepper to taste

Preheat oven to 350°. Combine corn, broccoli, egg, ½ cup Ritz crackers, 2 tablespoons butter, and dehydrated onion in large bowl and mix together thoroughly. Season with salt and pepper. Pour in a l-quart baking dish. Combine remaining ingredients in a small bowl and sprinkle evenly over top. Bake until golden, about 35-40 minutes.

Recipes from Jan's Cake & Candy Crafts

Cream Cheese and Corn

¼ cup milk
1 (3-ounce) package cream cheese
1 tablespoon butter
½ teaspoon salt
⅛ teaspoon pepper
3 cups frozen corn, cooked and drained

Combine milk, cream cheese, butter, salt, and pepper in saucepan. Cook over low heat, stirring constantly until cheese melts and is blended. Add drained corn and warm.

Note: 2 (12-ounce) cans of whole kernel corn may be used in place of frozen corn.

Home Cooking II

Mama Rose's Roasted Peppers

6 large green peppers
1 teaspoon oregano
¼ cup oil
1 toe minced garlic
¼ teaspoon salt

Heat charcoal in grill until coals are white. Lay peppers on grill. Then when outer skin becomes charred. When completely blackened, remove from grill and put into large, brown paper grocery bag. Roll top down to close securely.

Meanwhile, mix remaining ingredients together.

When peppers are cool enough to handle, remove from bag and peel charred skin from them. Cut in half, remove core and seeds, and slice peppers lengthwise into bowl. Pour dressing over peppers, toss lightly, cover and refrigerate.

Note: These are delicious on top of sandwiches, such as roast beef or salami, or delicious just served with hard crusted Italian bread.

Our Italian Family Cookbook

Stuffed Green Peppers

These were known as "Baked Mangoes" in 1914, when the Cosmos Society of the Bradley Methodist Church ran this recipe for them in a cookbook: "Fill green mangoes with well seasoned hamburg steak. Place in pan with 1 cup boiling water. Serve with cream gravy."

4 tablespoons (½ stick) butter
2 medium onions, chopped
1 pound ground round or ground chuck beef
4 large ripe tomatoes, cored and chopped
1 teaspoon salt
¼ teaspoon ground black pepper
2 cups fresh bread crumbs
10 medium green peppers, tops cut off and ribs and seeds removed from interiors
⅔ cup dry bread crumbs

In large skillet on stove top, melt butter at medium-high heat. Add onions and cook until wilted, then add ground beef and cook until meat is brown through and onions are soft. Add tomatoes, salt and pepper; allow to simmer about 10 minutes. Add the fresh bread crumbs.

Meanwhile, parboil the green peppers in pot of boiling water about 3 minutes each. When cool enough to handle, stuff each pepper with the beef-tomato filling. Space evenly in greased 13x9x2-inch baking dish. Sprinkle tops with the dried bread crumbs. Bake at 350° for 40-45 minutes, until peppers are tender and hot through. Makes 10 peppers.

Note: To freeze for later, set the stuffed peppers individually in muffin cups and freeze separately overnight. Then, wrap each pepper individually in plastic wrap and put several (as much as you need for a meal) in plastic freezer bags. Before baking frozen peppers, space in greased baking dish and allow to stand at room temperature about 30 minutes before baking.

The James Whitcomb Riley Cookbook

Gourmet Cabbage Casserole

1 medium cabbage
4 tablespoons butter
4 tablespoons flour
½ teaspoon salt
½ teaspoon pepper
2 cups milk

Cut cabbage into small wedges and cook until tender; drain and place in a 9x13-inch casserole. Melt butter in saucepan; blend in flour, salt, and pepper. Cook over low heat stirring until smooth and bubbly. Stir in milk and continue cooking, stirring constantly, until mixture comes to a boil. Continue cooking one additional minute. Spread sauce over cabbage. Bake 375°for 20 minutes.

TOPPING:
½ green pepper, chopped
½ onion, chopped
⅔ cup Cheddar cheese, shredded
½ cup mayonnaise
3 tablespoons chill sauce

Mix green pepper, onion, cheese, mayonnaise, and chili sauce. Spread over top of casserole and bake at 4000 an additional 20 minutes. Serves 8.

More Hoosier Cooking

Cabbage Lasagne

1 pound lean ground beef
1 cup onion, chopped
½ cup green pepper, chopped
1 medium cabbage
½ teaspoon oregano
1 tea spoon salt
⅛ teaspoon pepper
1 (18-ounce) can tomato paste
8 ounces Mozzarella cheese, sliced

Sauté ground beef, onion, and pepper until meat is brown. Boil cabbage until tender. Save 2 cups of the liquid from cabbage and drain off excess. Combine 2 cups of the reserved cabbage liquid, oregano, salt, pepper, and tomato paste; simmer over low heat for 4 minutes. Add meat, onion, and green pepper to tomato mixture. Pour ½ of this mixture into a 9x13-inch pan. Layer cabbage, then remaining tomato mixture. Top with slices of cheese to cover. Bake at 400° until cheese is browned, 30-40 minutes. Serves 8.

Yields 281 calories per serving.

Taste & See

Red Cabbage

4 slices bacon, diced
1 medium head red cabbage, shredded
1 apple, chopped
5 tablespoons vinegar
¾ cup onions, chopped
1 teaspoon salt
¼ teaspoon pepper
3 tablespoons sugar
½ cup water
½ cup grape jelly

Stir and fry bacon until brown. Add shredded red cabbage to bacon and drippings. Add other ingredients as listed. Stir. Heat to boil. Simmer for ½ hour or more. Serves 6-8.

Guten Appetit

Sweet Onion Casserole

- ½ cup long-grain rice, uncooked
- 7-8 cups coarsely-chopped sweet onions
- ¼ cup melted butter
- 1 cup grated Swiss cheese
- ⅔ cup half-and-half
- 1 teaspoon salt

Cook rice in 5 cups boiling water for 5 minutes. Drain; set aside. Cook onions in butter in a large skillet until limp, but not browned. Combine all ingredients. Mix well and pour into a greased 2-quart casserole. Bake at 350° for 1 hour. Yields 8-10 servings.

Great served with pork tenderloin!

Specialties of Indianapolis II

Vidalia Onion Pie

- 1 cup saltine crackers, crushed
- 5 tablespoons butter, melted
- 2½ cups thinly sliced Vidalia onions
- 2 tablespoons oil
- 2 eggs
- ¾ cup milk
- Salt and pepper
- ¼ cup grated Cheddar cheese

Combine crackers and butter and press into 8-inch pie pan. Bake at 350° for 8-10 minutes. Sauté onions in oil until tender; put in the pie shell. Mix remaining ingredients except cheese and pour over onions. Top with Cheddar cheese. Bake 350°for 45 minutes. Serves 8.

Champions: Favorite Foods of Indy Car Racing

The world's largest living sign is in Bendix Woods County Park in New Carlisle. Back in the early '20s, Studebaker engineers planted two varieties of pine trees on a half mile of land that was then owned by the company. The trees spell out colossally "Studebaker."

Fresh Tomato Pie

2 tablespoons butter
2 large onions, thinly sliced
12 slices bacon, divided
2 cups fresh soft bread crumbs, divided
3-4 fresh ripe tomatoes, thinly sliced
2 cups grated Cheddar cheese
3 eggs
½ teaspoon salt
⅛ teaspoon pepper

Butter a 9-inch pie plate. Melt butter in a medium-size skillet over medium heat. Sauté onions for 3-5 minutes. Set aside.

Cook 9 slices of the bacon; drain and crumble. Reserve 3 slices. Place 1 cup of the bread crumbs in the prepared pie plate. Place ingredients in layers as follows: tomatoes, onions, cheese, and bacon. Repeat layers until all ingredients are used. The pie will be mounded but cooks down.

Beat eggs well; add salt and pepper. Pour over pie. Sprinkle with remaining 1 cup bread crumbs. Drape remaining bacon slices over top of pie. (Cook the other 3 slices of bacon halfway in the microwave to get rid of some of the grease before putting them on top of the pie.) Bake at 350° for 35-40 minutes. Garnish with parsley and serve.

Hopewell's Hoosier Harvest II

Parmesan Potato Rounds

⅓ cup butter or margarine, melted
¼ cup flour
¼ cup grated Parmesan cheese
Salt and pepper to taste
6 medium baking potatoes, each sliced into 4 rounds
Italian seasoning to taste

Pour butter into a 15½x10½-inch baking dish. In a plastic bag, combine flour, cheese, salt, and pepper. Shake a few potato slices at a time in the bag to coat with flour mixture. Place potatoes in a single layer over butter. Bake at 375° for 30 minutes. Turn slices and sprinkle with Italian seasoning. Bake 30 minutes more or until tender. Yield: 6 servings.

Hopewell's Hoosier Harvest II

Crunch-Topped Sweet Potato Casserole

2 (16-ounce) cans sweet potatoes, undrained
¼ cup melted butter
1 cup sugar
½ teaspoon salt
2 eggs, well beaten
½ cup milk
½ teaspoon vanilla
1 cup firmly packed brown sugar
¼ cup butter
⅓ cup flour
2 teaspoons cinnamon
1 cup chopped nuts

In a saucepan, heat undrained potatoes to the boiling point. Drain. Mash potatoes with butter. Add next 5 ingredients and blend well. Turn into a 9-inch square glass baking dish.

For topping: In a saucepan, combine brown sugar, butter, flour, and cinnamon. Heat gently over medium heat. Remove from stove and stir in nuts. Spread over sweet potatoes. Bake at 350° for 40 minutes. Can be made ahead. Serves 10-12.

Nutbread and Nostalgia

Stuffed Baked Potatoes

Everyone loves these stuffed potatoes.

3 large baking potatoes (oblong in shape)
1 stick butter, divided
1½ cup green onions, chopped
½ cup half-and-half cream
½ cup sour cream
1 teaspoon salt
½ teaspoon white pepper (or black if white is unavailable)
1 cup grated sharp Cheddar cheese
4-5 teaspoons butter
Paprika for garnish

Scrub potatoes. Rub skins with vegetable oil. Place potatoes in a shallow pan. Bake in a 400° oven for about an hour. Set aside to cool enough to handle.

Carefully cut potatoes in half lengthwise. Scoop out potato pulp into a large bowl—be careful not to damage the shells. Melt ½ stick butter and sauté green onions. To the potato pulp, add other ½ of butter, the half-and-half cream, sour cream, salt, pepper, the sautéed onions, and the Cheddar cheese. Whip the mixture with electric mixer until smooth. If mixture is too dry, add a bit more cream or sour cream.

Stuff the potato shell halves with the mixture. At this point, wrap potatoes and freeze, if desired. When ready to use, thaw potatoes. Melt 4 or 5 teaspoons butter and drizzle a little over each potato. Sprinkle with paprika. Bake in a 350°oven for 30 minutes, or until potatoes are heated through. Serves 6.

Christmas Thyme at Oak Hill Farm

Peru is known as "The Circus City." The International Circus Hall of Fame is located there. Since 1958, Peru has been presenting the Circus City Festival, the finest youth-oriented program in our nation.

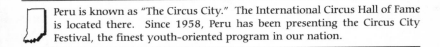

Ratatouille Monterey

A meal in itself.

6 slices bacon, cut into 1-inch pieces
1 large onion, sliced
1 (6-ounce) can tomato paste
1½ teaspoons salt
1 teaspoon dried thyme
1 large clove garlic, minced
2 tablespoons all-purpose flour
1½ pounds garden fresh tomatoes and their juice*
1 eggplant (about 1¼ pounds), peeled and cut into ½-inch slices
½ pound zucchini, cut into ½-inch slices
1 green pepper, cut into strips
1 pound Monterey Jack cheese, sliced

Preheat oven to 400°. Fry bacon and onion in large skillet over medium heat, stirring often until cooked. Stir in tomato paste, salt, thyme, garlic, and flour. Add peeled, cut-up tomatoes and their juice. Simmer tomato mixture until thickened. Lightly cover bottom of 9x13-inch baking dish with ½ cup of tomato mixture. Layer eggplant, zucchini, and green pepper in dish. Spread tomato mixture on top. Cover with cheese. Bake at 400° for 50 minutes. Serves 6-8.

*May substitute 1 (28-ounce) can whole peeled tomatoes.

Winners

Asparagus Casserole

½ stick butter
½ pound Velveeta cheese
1 can cream of mushroom soup
1 small can Carnation milk
36 Ritz crackers, crushed
1 (16-ounce) can asparagus
4 boiled eggs

Melt butter and cheese. Add mushroom soup and milk over low heat. Stir until thickened. Put cracker crumbs in 2-quart casserole. Drain asparagus and pour over crumbs. Slice eggs and layer eggs and sauce. Be sure sauce is on top layer. Bake 20 minutes at 400°.

Our Favorite Recipes II

Hash Brown Potato Casserole

2 pounds frozen hash brown potatoes
1 tablespoon salt
¼ cup melted butter
½ cup chopped onions
¼ teaspoon pepper
2 cans cream of chicken soup
1 can milk
1 pint sour cream
1½-2 pounds browned hamburger

Mix all ingredients and put into a 9x13-inch buttered dish. Bake at 350° for 1 hour.

Jasper County Extension Homemakers Cookbook

Sue's Carrot Casserole

1 pound carrots
¼ cup carrot liquid
2 tablespoons grated onion
¾ tablespoon horseradish
½ cup mayonnaise
½ teaspoon salt
½ teaspoon pepper
½ cup seasoned bread crumbs
¼ cup melted butter

Scrape carrots and cut on the diagonal, making slices about ¼-inch thick. Cook in salted water until tender-crisp. Drain, reserving ¼ cup cooking liquid. Mix onion, horseradish, mayonnaise, salt, pepper, and carrot liquid. Combine with carrots in a buttered casserole. Mix the bread crumbs with the melted butter and spread over the carrots. Bake at 375° for 15-20 minutes, or until bubbling. Serves 6.

A Taste of Fishers

Carrot Casserole

2 pounds carrots
1 cup Swiss cheese crackers (crumbled)
2 eggs, beaten
½ cup diced green onions
3 tablespoons sugar
½ cup milk
⅔ cup melted butter
1 teaspoon salt

Cut up carrots. Cook until tender; drain and mash. Add all other ingredients. Pour into a 2-quart casserole and bake uncovered at 350° for 45 minutes. Enjoy! Yield: 8 servings.

For Crying Out Loud...Let's Eat!

The University of Notre Dame in South Bend, home of the Fighting Irish, boasts such famous landmarks as the Sacred Heart Basilica, Snite Museum, the Grotto, and of course, the Golden Dome.

Marigold Cauliflower

Marigolds are such bright and cheerful flowers, and as well as being good to look at, they can also be good to eat. They have a subtle spicy flavor which can transform this favorite dish into something special.

1¼ cups butter
1½ cups white flour
1¼ cups milk
Salt and pepper
1⅓ cups grated cheese
6 heads pot (edible) marigolds
1 medium cauliflower, lightly cooked

Make a white sauce (butter, flour, milk, salt and pepper) in the usual manner. Carefully wash the flowers in cold running water and shake to dry. Reheat the sauce and stir in the cheese, but do not allow to boil. Remove from heat and gently stir in the marigold petals. Stir carefully. Place the lightly cooked cauliflower into a serving dish and pour the sauce over the top.

Cooking with Herbs

Stuffed Morels

Morels have a wild, wonderful flavor that can never be separated completely in my mind from the context of greenly veiled woods and wet dripping leaves, from the fragrance of Mother's kitchen, or from the memories of old Mooley Cow and Dad's battered felt hat.

8-10 large morels
2 cups bread crumbs (from firm white bread)
½ cup chopped cooked chicken
⅓ cup melted butter
2 tablespoons finely chopped onion
Juice of ½ lemon
1 teaspoon salt
¼ teaspoon pepper
½ cup light cream

Cut the morels in half lengthwise; rinse them in cold water, and soak for a few minutes in a mixture of 1 quart water and 1 teaspoon salt. Drain the morels well and dry on paper towels.

In a bowl combine the bread crumbs, chicken, butter, onion, lemon juice, salt, and pepper. If there are additional morels, chop them finely and mix them with the stuffing. Loosely fill the morel halves with the stuffing, join the halves together, and tie them with string. Put the stuffed morels in a buttered casserole and pour the cream over them. Bake in a hot oven (400°) for about 25 minutes.

Note: The morel halves can also be stuffed and baked open-faced, substituting a mixture of ½ cup chicken broth and 2 tablespoons white wine for the cream. Bake them in a hot oven (400°) for 18-20 minutes.

The Wild Flavor

Exploring Southern Indiana's caves is one of the coolest activities around since caves' temperatures stay in the 50s year round. Discovered by two school children in 1881, Marengo Cave, a National Landmark, is the most highly decorated cave known in the Interior Lowlands. Squire Boone Caverns near Corydon, discovered by Squire Boone and his brother Daniel in 1790, offers a "water symphony" from an underground waterfall. Wyandotte Caves in Crawford County has a variety of wet formations and prehistoric flint quarries.

Scalloped Pineapple

Warm, fragrant fruit dish to serve with ham or pork.

½ cup softened butter
1 cup sugar
2 eggs, well beaten
1 (20-ounce) can crushed pineapple, undrained
3 cups firmly packed bread cubes
1 cup miniature marshmallows

Mix butter and sugar, beating until well blended. Add eggs; mix. Add undrained pineapple, bread cubes, and marshmallows. Bake, uncovered, at 350° for 45 minutes in a greased 1½-quart casserole. Serves 6-8.

Nutbread and Nostalgia

Pineapple and Cheese Delight

1½ cups sugar
6 tablespoons flour
2 (20-ounce) cans pineapple chunks
1½ cups reserved juice
1 cup shredded Longhorn or Cheddar cheese
1 cup dry bread crumbs

Mix sugar and flour together. Add to pineapple and reserved juice and place in baking dish. Add cheese and mix thoroughly. Top with crumbs. Cover and bake at 350° until thick; about 30 minutes. Remove cover and brown crumbs for additional 2-3 minutes.

Recipes from Jan's Cake & Candy Crafts

POULTRY

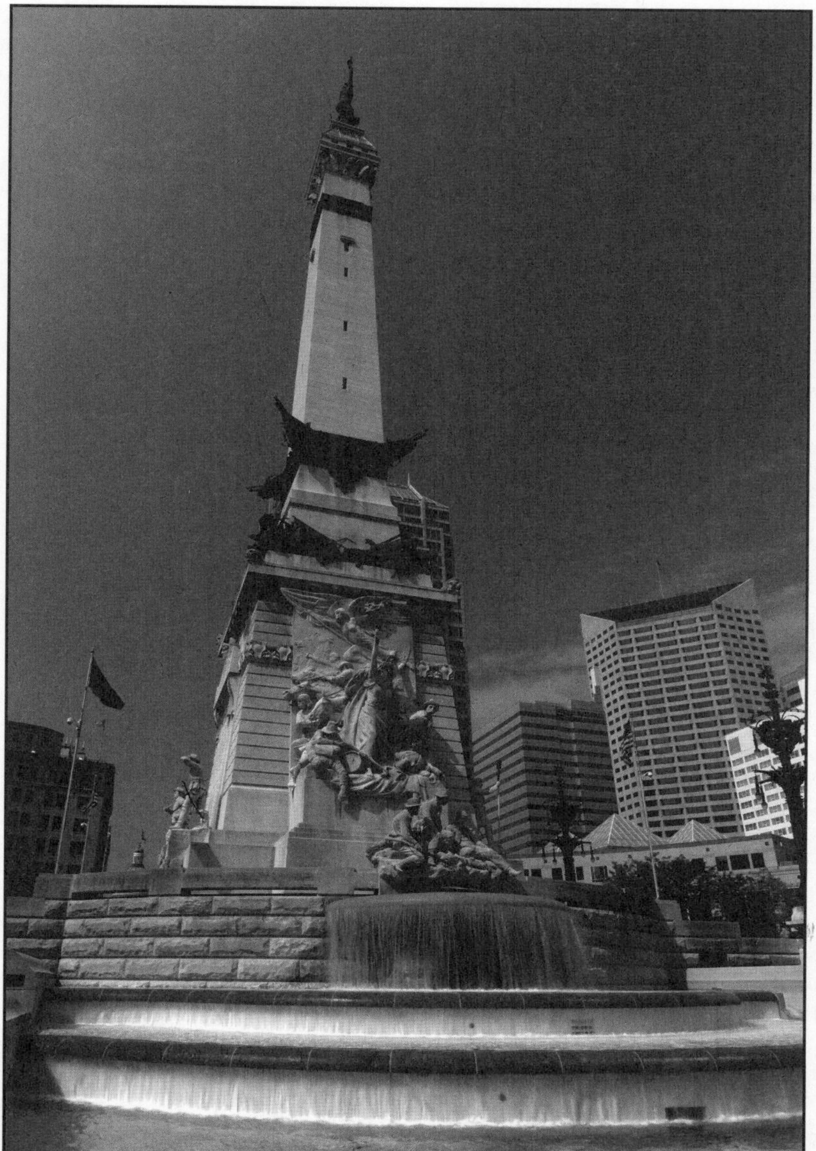

The Indiana Soldiers' & Sailors' Monument in Indianapolis is the only Civil War monument in America dedicated to ordinary soldiers and sailors. Recognized as one of the world's outstanding monuments, it cost $598,318 to build in 1902; today it would cost more than $500 million.

Tasty Baked Chicken Breasts

Tasty! Low in calories!

6 chicken breast halves, skinned and boned
2 well-beaten eggs or ½ cup Eggbeaters
1 cup Italian-seasoned bread crumbs, purchased or homemade
½ pound fresh mushrooms, sautéed
2 (4x6-inch each) slices low-fat Muenster or Monterey Jack cheese
½ cup chicken broth
Juice of 1 lemon

Submerge chicken breasts in eggs. Refrigerate 2-3 hours. Roll in bread crumbs. Spray skillet with cooking spray or use a little oil. Brown breasts. Place in 13x9-inch baking dish and cover with sautéed mushrooms. Divide cheese into six portions and place on top of chicken and mushrooms. Bake in 350° oven for 30 minutes, basting every 10 minutes with combination of chicken broth and lemon juice. Yield: 6 servings.

The Guild Cookbook IV

Crispy Herb Baked Chicken

⅔ cup Idaho "Spuds" potato flakes
¼ cup grated Parmesan cheese
2 teaspoons dried parsley flakes
¼ teaspoon garlic salt
⅛ teaspoon paprika
Dash of pepper
3-3½ pounds chicken, cut-up, skinned, rinsed and patted dry
⅓ cup butter or margarine, melted

Heat oven to 375°. Grease or line with foil a 15x10x1-inch baking pan or 13x9-inch pan. In medium bowl, combine dry ingredients. Stir until well mixed. Dip chicken pieces into margarine. Roll in potato flake mixture to coat. Place in greased pan. Bake at 375° for 45-60 minutes or until chicken is tender and golden brown. Makes 4-5 servings.

Amish Country Cookbook III

Orange Breast of Chicken

¼ cup flour
¼ teaspoon salt
1 teaspoon monosodium glutamate (MSG)
2 whole broiler-fryer chicken breasts, boned, halved
¼ cup corn oil
1 (6-ounce) can frozen orange juice concentrate, thawed
1 juice can water
3 teaspoons brown sugar
½ teaspoon nutmeg
¼ teaspoon oregano

Mix together flour, salt, and MSG, and coat chicken with mixture; shake off excess. Heat oil over medium heat, add chicken and brown on all sides. Meanwhile, in a saucepan, stir together over low heat, orange juice, water, brown sugar, nutmeg, and oregano. Bring to a boil and pour over chicken. Cover and simmer, turning several times, about 1 hour or until chicken is tender. Serve with rice, pouring remaining sauce over chicken and rice.

Love Cookin'

Crunchy Lemon Chicken

2 cups Post Natural Bran Flakes, finely crushed
½ teaspoon grated lemon peel halved
¼ teaspoon salt
1 egg white, beaten
6 boneless chicken breasts, skinned and (or about 1½ pounds)

Heat oven to 350°. Mix cereal, lemon peel and salt. Dip chicken in egg white. Coat with cereal mixture. Arrange in 13x9-inch pan which has been sprayed with no-stick cooking spray. Bake 20 minutes or until cooked through. Makes 6 servings.

Taste & See

Yogurt Marinated Chicken Broil

Excellent flavor!

2 chickens, quartered
1 teaspoon salt
½ cup lemon juice
1 cup yogurt
1 teaspoon red pepper
1 teaspoon paprika
1-2 tablespoons oil

Mix salt and lemon juice. Make small multiple slits into chicken pieces with point of sharp knife. Rub lemon and salt mixture into the chicken. Mix yogurt, red pepper, paprika, and oil together in marinating dish. Place chicken in marinade and turn frequently to allow marinade to penetrate meat for several hours. May be broiled in broiler pan in oven 30-45 minutes, or over charcoal. Turn frequently to prevent burning. Brush with marinade as chicken is turned. Yield: 8 servings.

Note: May use cubes of beef instead of chicken. Place beef on skewers and broil.

The Guild Cookbook III

Curry Chicken Delight

4 whole chicken breasts, skinned, boned and halved lengthwise
⅓ cup flour
4 slices bacon, cooked and crumbled
¼ cup honey
2 tablespoons mustard
½ teaspoon salt
½ teaspoon curry powder

Rinse chicken; pat dry. Coat with flour. Brown chicken in bacon drippings about 10 minutes. Transfer chicken to 8x8x2-inch baking dish. Bake at 350°, uncovered, about 30 minutes. Combine honey, mustard, salt, and curry powder; drizzle over chicken. Bake, uncovered, 15 minutes longer. Top with crumbled bacon. Serve with cooked rice.

Indiana's Finest Recipes

Golfer's Chicken

4 chicken quarters
1 envelope Lipton's Dry Onion Soup Mix
1 (8-ounce) bottle red Russian dressing
1 (8-ounce) jar apricot jam

Combine dry soup, Russian dressing and jam. Mix well until there are no lumps. Wash chicken and pat dry. Slightly overlap in flat Pyrex dish. Spoon and spread 1 tablespoon (or more) of sauce on each piece. Bake at 225° for 4-5 hours or however long your game takes. Be careful to place well below heating element if using an electric oven.

This can be done in 1 hour at 375° if not playing golf. Sauce keeps in refrigerator for months. Yield: 4 servings.

For Crying Out Loud...Let's Eat!

Easy Chicken

4 chicken legs and thighs, skinned
1 (8-ounce) bottle Italian dressing

Place chicken in baking dish. Pour Italian dressing over the chicken. Bake at 350° for 30 minutes. Turn chicken over and bake another 30 minutes.

Amish Country Cookbook III

Chicken Olé

½ cup medium-hot chunky taco sauce
¼ cup Dijon-style mustard
3 tablespoons fresh lime juice
3 whole chicken breasts, boneless, skinless
1 tablespoon diet margarine(< 6g fat/ tablespoon)
6 tablespoons nonfat sour cream

Combine taco sauce, Dijon-mustard, and lime juice in a large bowl. Add chicken, turning to coat. Cover and marinate in refrigerator at least 30 minutes.

Melt margarine in large skillet over medium heat until foamy. Remove chicken from marinade; reserve marinade. Add chicken to skillet and cook about 10 minutes or until brown on both sides. Add marinade; cook about 5 minutes or until chicken is tender and marinade glazes chicken. Remove chicken to serving platter. Boil marinade over high heat 1 minute; pour over chicken. Serve with sour cream. Makes 6 servings.

Nutritional Analysis Per Serving: (4 ounce chicken breast) Calories 128; Fat 4.2g; Cal from fat 28%; Chol 46mg; Sod 469mg; Fiber .4g; Exchanges 4 meats.

The Heart of Cooking II

Stacked Chicken Dinner

This is a fun meal.

Cooked white rice
Chow mein noodles
Cooked chicken, bite-size. pieces
Hot crushed pineapple
Chopped celery
Chopped green onion
Coconut, shredded or flaked
Slivered almonds
Mozzarella cheese, shredded
Hot chicken broth, slightly thickened with cornstarch

Pass each dish in the order listed. Guests take some of all the foods they like, stacking them one on top of the other, but *waiting to eat until all dishes have been passed.* Each person will have a dinner tailored to his or her own liking and the result is an amazing combination of flavors that is absolutely delicious.

The Cookery Collection

Parmesan Oven-Fried Chicken

½ cup bread crumbs
2 tablespoons parsley
¼ teaspoon pepper
⅓ cup grated Parmesan cheese
¼ teaspoon garlic
6 chicken breast halves, skinned and boneless
¼ cup French salad dressing

Combine all ingredients, except chicken and dressing, in a bag large enough to shake chicken breasts in. Dip clean breasts into salad dressing and shake in mixture in bag. Place in a 9x13-inch pan. Bake 1 hour at 350°, uncovered.

A Taste of Fishers

The nation's first gasoline pump was installed in Fort Wayne on September 5, 1885.

Mexicali Chicken

Can do one day ahead.

10 chicken breast halves
1½-2 jars green chill salsa, mild
1 bunch green onions, chopped
1½ teaspoons salt
1 (3-ounce) package cream cheese, cubed small
1 (15-ounce) can chili without beans
Approximately ¾ cup medium-size black olives, whole
8 ounces grated Cheddar cheese
8 ounces grated Monterey Jack cheese

Boil chicken breasts for 45 minutes. Remove bones. Cool and cut into large chunks. In large bowl, combine with salsa, onions, and salt. Place in ungreased 9x13-inch baking dish. Top with cream cheese cubes. Spread chili carefully over all. Place desired amount of olives over chili. Mix together grated cheeses and sprinkle over top. Bake 30 minutes at 350°. Yield: 6-8 servings.

Hint: Be sure to cube the cream cheese in small pieces. May be made using 1 bottle of mild salsa and 1 bottle of hot salsa. These are good served with flour tortillas. Recipe may be made the night before and refrigerated.

For Crying Out Loud...Let's Eat!

Company Chicken

6 chicken breasts
1 can cream of mushroom soup
1 (3-ounce) can of mushrooms, sliced
1 cup sour cream
½ cup sherry cooking wine

Place chicken breasts skin-side-up in baking dish. Combine remaining ingredients and pour over chicken (including mushroom liquid). Sprinkle generously with paprika. Bake 1-1½ hours at 350°. Makes 6 servings.

The Guild Cookbook I

Chicken Waikiki

Chicken with a Hula-skirt!

2 chicken legs
2 whole chicken breasts, split
½ cup flour
⅓ cup oil
1 teaspoon salt (optional)
¼ teaspoon pepper

Coat chicken with flour. Heat oil in a large skillet. Add chicken and brown. Remove to shallow pan, skin-side-up. Sprinkle with salt and pepper. Preheat oven to 350°.

SAUCE:
1 large can sliced pineapple
1 cup sugar
2 tablespoons cornstarch
¾ cup cider vinegar
1 tablespoon soy sauce
¼ teaspoon ginger
1 chicken bouillon cube
1 large green pepper, cut into ¼-inch circles

Drain pineapple into 2-cup measuring cup and add water to make 1¼ cups liquid. Set pineapple aside to use during baking. In medium saucepan, combine pineapple juice, sugar, cornstarch, vinegar, soy sauce, ginger, and bouillon cube. Bring to a boil, stirring constantly. Boil 2 minutes. Pour over chicken. Bake, uncovered, 45 minutes; basting every 10 minutes. Add pineapple and green pepper slices. Bake 15 minutes longer. Yield: 4 servings.

Cookin' to Beat the Band

Chicken Spectacular

3 cups cooked chicken (1 whole chicken)
1 box wild rice, prepared
1 small onion, chopped
1 small can water chestnuts, drained and chopped
1 (16-ounce) can French style green beans, drained
1 cup mayonnaise
1 can cream of celery soup

Combine chicken and cooked rice. Add onion, chestnuts, and green beans. Add mayonnaise and soup; mix well. Bake 30-40 minutes at 350° or until browned and bubbly.

Country Cooking

Chicken Casserole

1 whole (3-pound) chicken
1 (15-ounce) box Uncle Ben's Rice with seasoning
1 cup chopped celery
1 can water chestnuts, sliced
1 can cream of chicken soup
¾ cup mayonnaise
Potato chips
Sliced almonds

Boil chicken (save broth), remove from bone, and cut into bite-size pieces. Cook rice in chicken broth. Mix all ingredients, except potato chips and almonds, together well. Put into greased casserole. Top with crushed potato chips and sliced almonds. Bake at 350° for 50-60 minutes.

Our Favorite Recipes

The magnificent Valparaiso University Chapel of the Resurrection rise 140 feet into the sky. It is one of the largest university chapels in the world.

Overnight Chicken Casserole

5 chicken breasts or 1 boned stewed chicken, diced
2 cups chicken broth
1 (7-ounce) package elbow macaroni, uncooked
1 can cream of mushroom soup
1 can cream of celery soup
¼ pound diced Velveeta, or shredded sharp cheese
3 hard boiled eggs, diced
1 (4-ounce) package slivered almonds
Onion salt or flakes to taste

Mix together and pour into a 9x13-inch casserole. Store covered in the refrigerator overnight. Bake uncovered for 1 hour at 350°. Serves 12.

Mincemeat and Memories

Hot Chicken Salad

4 ounces slivered almonds
1 tablespoon margarine, melted
3½ cups chicken, cooked and diced
½ cup lemon juice
Lemon and pepper seasoning salt
1 cup real mayonnaise
2 cups grated cheese
1½ cups celery, diced
½ cup onions, finely chopped (or equivalent amount dried onion soaked in lemon juice)
Chopped hard boiled eggs, to taste
Chopped salad olives or olives to taste
Potato chips

Brown almonds in the melted margarine (can put in the oven for about 15-20 minutes at 350°). Toss chicken and other ingredients together (except potato chips). Place in 2-quart casserole. Bake in 350° oven 20-30 minutes until hot through. Before serving, sprinkle crushed potato chips over the top.

Cooking with the Warriors

Savory Crescent Chicken Squares

1 (3-ounce) package cream cheese, softened
3 tablespoons butter
2 cups cooked chicken, cubed
¼ teaspoon salt
⅛ teaspoon pepper
2 tablespoons milk
1 tablespoon chopped pimento
1 (8-ounce) can Pillsbury refrigerated crescent rolls
¾ cup seasoned croutons, crushed

Preheat oven to 350°. Blend cream cheese and 2 tablespoons butter until smooth. Add the next 5 ingredients, mix well. Separate crescent dough into 4 rectangles. Firmly press perforations to seal. Spoon ½ cup meat mixture into center of each rectangle. Bring 4 corners of dough to top center of chicken mixture, twist slightly, and seal edges. Brush top with reserved 1 tablespoon butter and dip in crouton crumbs. Bake on ungreased cookie sheet 20-25 minutes until golden brown.

MUSHROOM SAUCE:
1 can mushroom soup
½-1 cup milk

Heat together and serve with chicken squares.

Amish Country Cookbook I

The quiet, yet powerful influence of the Amish and Mennonite cultures can be felt while traveling the back roads of LaGrange County. Whitewashed farmsteads dot the rural landscape, horse-drawn buggies line the roadways, and farmers work the fields with teams of large, but gentle draft horses.

Chicken Pie

Double recipe for dough for biscuits
1 chicken, cooked
6 potatoes
2 cups peas
Salt and pepper
Light cream
Marjoram
Parsley
2 eggs

Line the sides but not the bottom of a 3-quart baking pan with part of the biscuit dough. Put in a layer of cooked chicken free of skin and bones. Cover with a layer of raw potatoes, peeled and sliced very thin. Sprinkle on some of the peas with salt and pepper. Lay a few very thin strips of half the remaining dough. Repeat layers until pan is 3/4 filled. Sprinkle light cream with chopped marjoram and parsley. Mix eggs and cream and pour over. Put on a thick crust, making a slit for steam. Bake in a moderate (350°) oven until golden brown (about 45 minutes).

The Conner Prairie Cookbook

Oven Fried Chicken

1 frying-size chicken
1/3 cup plain flour
1 teaspoon salt
Dash of pepper
1 egg
2 tablespoons water
3/4 cup corn flake crumbs
1/4 cup grated Parmesan cheese
1/4 cup soft margarine, melted

Coat chicken with combined flour and seasoning. Dip chicken in combined egg and water; coat with combined crumbs and cheese. Place in 9x13-inch baking pan, drizzle margarine over chicken. Bake at 375° for 1 hour or until tender.

Our Favorite Recipes II

Chicken Lasagna

1 can cream of mushroom soup
1 can cream of chicken soup
1 cup Parmesan cheese
1 cup sour cream
1 small onion, chopped
¼ -½ teaspoon garlic powder
Pepper to taste
2 -3 cups cooked, diced chicken
8 ounces lasagna noodles, cooked and drained
2 cups Cheddar cheese

Mix together soups, Parmesan cheese, sour cream, onion, garlic powder, pepper, and chicken. Spread ¼ of the mixture in the bottom of a 13x9-inch pan. Alternate layers of noodles, chicken mixture, and shredded cheese 3 times, ending with cheese. Bake at 350° for 40-45 minutes or until heated through. Let stand 10 minutes before cutting.

Hopewell's Hoosier Harvest II

Chicken Broccoli Lasagna Rolls

- **12 curly lasagna noodles (8 ounces)**
- **3 tablespoons butter or margarine**
- **1 small onion, chopped**
- **3 tablespoons flour**
- **1 (14-ounce) can chicken broth**
- **1 cup half-and-half**
- **1½ cups (6 ounces) shredded Monterey Jack cheese**
- **¼ teaspoon salt**

FILLING:

- **3 cups chopped, cooked chicken**
- **2 (10-ounce) packages frozen chopped broccoli, thawed and drained**
- **2 large eggs, lightly beaten**
- **1 (10½-ounce) jar chopped pimientos, drained**
- **¾ cup fresh bread crumbs**
- **¼ cup minced parsley**
- **¼ teaspoon ground red pepper**
- **¼ tea spoon salt**
- **⅛ teaspoon ground nutmeg**

Cook noodles as package directs. Drain; lay flat. Make sauce in medium saucepan over medium-high heat; melt butter, add onion; sauté until tender, about 3 minutes. Whisk in flour until blended; whisk in broth and cook 1 minute or until bubbly. Remove pan from heat; whisk in half-and-half until blended. Bring to boiling, stirring until thickened. Boil 1 minute. Remove from heat; stir in cheese and salt, stirring until smooth.

In medium bowl, mix filling ingredients with ¾ cup sauce. Set aside. Pour ⅓ of remaining sauce into 2-quart shallow baking dish and set aside. Spread filling mixture over each noodle, dividing evenly. Starting from a short end, roll up noodles, jelly-roll fashion. Place rolls, curly ends down in prepared dish. (Toothpick may be used to hold roll intact.) Top with remaining sauce. Cover with aluminum foil; bake 45 minutes until heated through.

Service League's Favorites

Senator Lugar's Turkey Breast in Pita Pockets

1½ pounds turkey breast tenderloins
2 limes, juiced
1 tablespoon paprika
½ teaspoon onion salt
½ teaspoon garlic salt
½ teaspoon cayenne pepper Sauce
¼ teaspoon white pepper
½ teaspoon fennel seeds
½ teaspoon thyme
10 pitas, cut in half
1½ cups lettuce, shredded
1½ cups Avocado Salsa (recipe follows)
1½ cups Sour Cream Sauce (optional, recipe follows)

Rub turkey with juice of limes. In small bowl combine paprika, onion salt, garlic salt, cayenne pepper, white pepper, fennel seeds, and thyme. Sprinkle mixture over fillets. Cover and refrigerate for at least 1 hour.

Preheat charcoal grill for direct heat cooking. Grill turkey for 15-20 minutes, until meat thermometer reaches 170° and turkey is no longer pink in the center. Turn turkey tenderloins over halfway through grilling time. Allow turkey to stand 10 minutes. Slice into ¼-inch strips. Fill each pita half with turkey, lettuce, Avocado Salsa, and if desired, the Sour Cream Sauce. Serves 10.

AVOCADO SALSA:

1 avocado, diced
1 lime, juiced
2 tomatoes, seeded and diced
½ cup green onion, minced
½ cup green pepper, minced
½ cup fresh cilantro

In small bowl combine avocado and lime juice. Stir in tomatoes, green onion, green pepper, and cilantro. Cover and refrigerate until ready to use.

Continued

SOUR CREAM SAUCE:

- **1 cup sour cream**
- **1 teaspoon salt**
- **¼ cup green onion, minced**
- **¼ cup green chilies, minced**
- **¼ teaspoon cayenne pepper**
- **½ teaspoon black pepper**

In small bowl combine sour cream, salt, onion, chilies, cayenne pepper, and black pepper. Cover and refrigerate until ready to use.

Indiana's Finest Recipes

Almond Turkey Casserole

1 cup shredded Cheddar cheese, divided
1 tablespoon flour
3 cups chopped, cooked turkey
1½ cups sliced celery
⅔ cup slivered almonds, divided
1 cup mayonnaise
1 tablespoon lemon juice
½ teaspoon dried oregano leaves
¼ teaspoon salt
¼ teaspoon pepper
1 large can Mandarin oranges
Pastry for 2-crust (9-inch) pie

Preheat oven to 400°. Toss ¾ cup cheese with flour. Mix cheese mixture, turkey, celery, ⅓ cup almonds, mayonnaise, juice, seasonings, and oranges. Roll both pastries into one 11x15-inch rectangle on lightly floured surface. Place in a 9x13-inch baking dish; turn 1 inch beyond edge. Turn under edge; flute. Fill with turkey mixture. Top with remaining cheese and almonds. Bake 30-35 minutes. Serves 6-8.

A Taste of Fishers

SEAFOOD

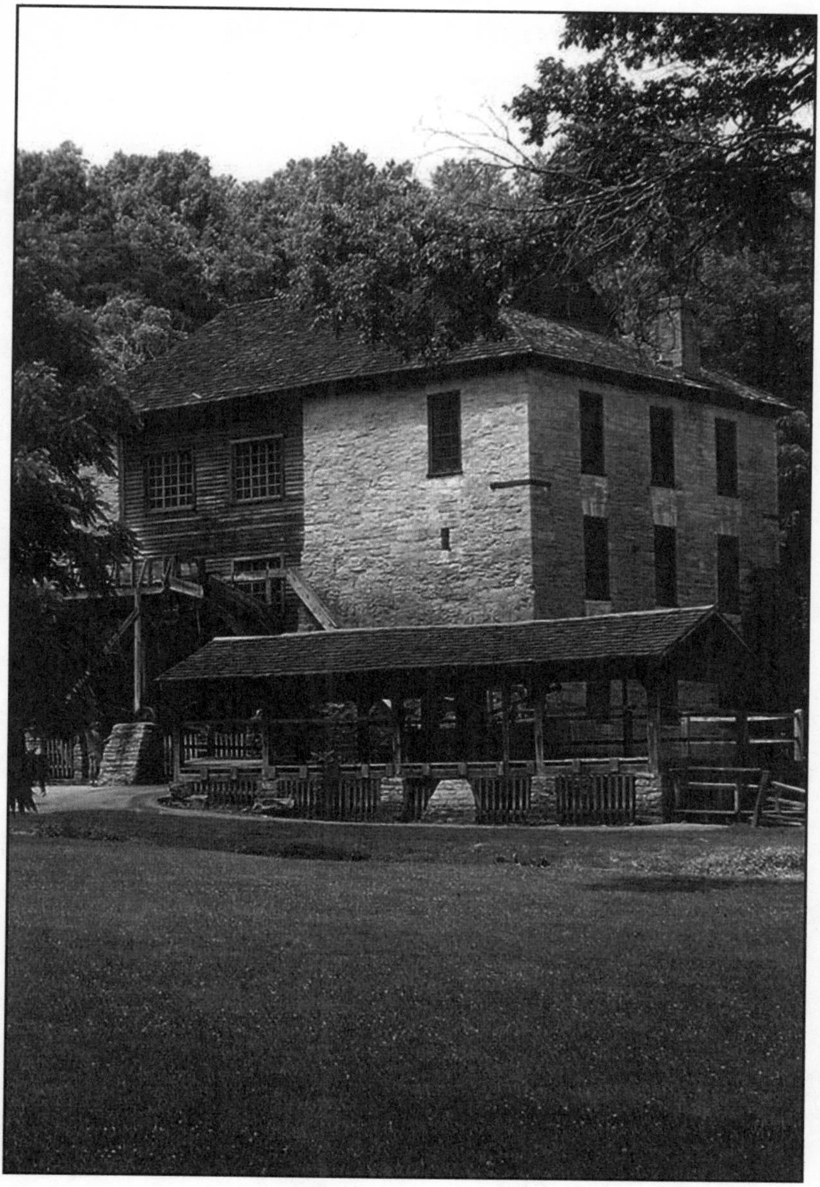

WIKIPEDIA.COM

The mill at the restored pioneer village of Spring Mill. Spring Mill State Park. Mitchell.

Grandpa Pastura's Grilled Swordfish Steaks

2 medium peeled tomatoes
4 tablespoons olive oil
4 tablespoons lemon juice
¼ teaspoon chopped marjoram
¼ teaspoon salt
⅛ teaspoon pepper
4 (6-ounce) swordfish steaks

Purée first 6 ingredients in blender or food processor. Dip fish in this mixture, then place fish steaks on grill over hot coals. Cook for 6-10 minutes on either side or until fish is done through the middle. Baste fish while cooking with additional sauce. When serving fish, serve sauce on the side,

Note: You can prepare this under the broiler if you prefer. Tuna steaks are also delicious fixed this way!

Our Italian Family Cookbook

Best Grilled Tuna

Fresh chopped garlic to taste
1 medium bunch scallions, chopped
1½ cups olive oil
½ cup Tamari (light soy) sauce
Juice of 4 limes
4 tuna steaks (the redder, the fresher)

Mix chopped garlic and scallions with olive oil, Tamari, and lime juice. Marinate tuna steaks in this for 2-3 hours in refrigerator, turning often. Grill tuna on very hot barbecue grill, basting with reserved marinade. Grill about 2-3 minutes each side for very rare, or about 4 minutes each side for medium. Serves 4.

Champions: Favorite Foods of Indy Car Racing

Grilled Fresh Tuna

4 tuna steaks, ¼-pound each
1 tablespoon honey
⅓ cup soy sauce
1 teaspoon fresh grated lemon peel
¼ cup fresh lemon juice
1 tablespoon Dijon mustard
½ cup salad oil
Lemon wedges, optional

Place tuna in shallow dish or zip-closure plastic bag. Combine honey, soy sauce, lemon peel, lemon juice, mustard, and salad oil in a small bowl. Whisk to blend. Pour marinade over fish and turn to coat well. Cover tightly. Marinate in refrigerator 1-3 hours or longer, if desired.

Preheat barbecue grill to medium-hot. Arrange tuna steaks on hot grill. Cook tuna over moderate heat about 4-6 minutes per side, basting occasionally until fish reaches desired doneness. Garnish with lemon wedges, if desired. Serves 4.

Back Home Again

Fillet of Sole with Tomatoes and Mushrooms

1 pound frozen fillet of sole, thawed
Salt and pepper
2 tablespoons butter
½ cup chopped onion
1 clove garlic, minced
1 tablespoon plus 2 teaspoons flour
½ cup each: dry white wine, milk, cream
2 medium tomatoes, peeled, seeded, diced
1 (4-ounce) can mushrooms, drained
½ teaspoon each: tarragon, thyme, basil
1 cup grated Swiss cheese

Place fillets of sole in well-buttered baking dish; season with salt and pepper. Melt butter in saucepan; add onion and garlic. Sauté until tender. Stir in flour; add wine. Slowly add milk and cream. Simmer over low heat for 3 minutes. Stir in tomatoes, mushrooms, and seasonings. Pour sauce over fish. Sprinkle with Swiss cheese. Bake at 350° for 30 minutes. To serve, lift fish carefully with slotted serving utensil. Serves 4.

Nutbread and Nostalgia

Salmon Loaf

1 (1-pound) can salmon
2 eggs, beaten
1 teaspoon lemon juice
1 cup cracker crumbs
½ cup liquid from salmon or milk
2 tablespoons celery, chopped
1 teaspoon minced onion
¼ teaspoon salt
¼ teaspoon white pepper
¼ tablespoon pimento, diced
1 tablespoon parsley, chopped

Free salmon from skin and bones. Flake salmon. Combine beaten eggs, lemon juice, and rest of ingredients. Taste and add more salt if needed. Form into loaf and place into greased pan. Bake in 350° oven until delicately browned and firm (about 1 hour). Serve with Egg Sauce.

EGG SAUCE:

4 tablespoons butter or margarine
4 tablespoons flour
2 cups milk or half-and-half
½ teaspoon salt
⅛ teaspoon white pepper
3 hard cooked eggs, diced

Simmer flour and butter 10 minutes without browning. Stir constantly. Gradually add milk, salt, and pepper. Whip smooth about 10 minutes. Add eggs.

Recipes of the Durbin

Father Edward E. Sorin, C.S.C., founded Notre Dame in 1842 with only a log cabin, but dreamed of the day L'Universite de Notre Dame du Lac would be a great Catholic university. Today Notre Dame is a beautiful 1250-acre campus on the Indiana/Michigan border, just north of South Bend, 90 miles east of Chicago. Having no fraternities, sororities, or athletic dorms, the "Notre Dame Spirit" is apparent in their 25 resident halls. Notre Dame attracts students from all 50 states and about 40 foreign countries.

Sole Stuffed with Shrimp

1½ cups finely chopped celery
½ cup finely chopped onion
3 cups (about 1 pound) small precooked shrimp
2 cups water
1 cup mayonnaise
1 cup finely crushed potato chips
Pinch of cayenne pepper
16 fresh (6-ounce) fillets of sole

Combine celery, onion, and shrimp in a saucepan with 2 cups water. Bring to a boil and simmer 1 minute. Drain. Put shrimp mixture into a bowl and combine mayonnaise, potato chips, and pepper.

Preheat oven to 350°. Place an equal amount of stuffing on 8 fillets. Cover each with a second fillet. Coat each of 8 individual baking dishes (small aluminum foil pans work well) with a little melted butter. Place a stuffed fillet in each. Pour melted butter (about ½ cup total) over fish. Sprinkle lightly with paprika. Bake for 20-25 minutes or until fish flakes with a fork. Do not overcook. Serves 8.

A Taste of Twin Pines

Haddock-Shrimp Casserole

2 pounds haddock, sole, or cod fillets
1 can cream of shrimp soup
¼ cup butter, melted
1 teaspoon grated onion
1 teaspoon Worcestershire sauce
¼ teaspoon garlic salt
1¼ cups crushed Ritz crackers (30 crackers)
1 can small shrimp

Place fillets in greased 9x13-inch baking dish. Spread with soup. Bake in 375° oven for 20 minutes. Combine butter and seasonings. Mix with cracker crumbs. Sprinkle drained shrimp and crumb mixture over fish. Bake another 10 minutes.

The Guild Cookbook II

Shrimp Gratin

2 pounds medium shrimp, peeled, deveined, rinsed and patted dry
½ cup vegetable oil
2 tablespoons chives
2 tablespoons minced parsley
1¼ teaspoons salt
¼ teaspoon dill seed
Freshly-ground pepper
½ cup toasted bread crumbs
1 large roasted, sweet, red pepper, seeded, and cut into thin strips; or 1 large pimento, cut into thin strips

Arrange shrimp in a single layer in a large, shallow dish and drizzle with oil. Sprinkle with chives, parsley, salt, dill seed, and pepper. Toss shrimp to coat evenly. Rearrange in single layer. Cover dish and refrigerate 4 hours.

About 30 minutes before serving, sprinkle bread crumbs over shrimp and toss to coat well. Divide shrimp evenly among individual gratin dishes or scallop shells. Top each serving with red pepper or pimento strips. Set aside at room temperature. Just before serving, position broiler rack as far below heat source as possible and preheat. Broil shrimp until just pink and bread crumbs are golden brown, about 5 minutes. Serve hot.

A Taste of Fishers

Seafood Fettucine

This is a pure, unadulterated pasta dish—just like you might have in a fine Italian restaurant.

About 1 pound fettuccine noodles
2 tablespoons butter
1 small onion, chopped fine
2 or 3 cloves garlic, chopped fine
1 pound fresh seafood (shrimp, scallops, crab, etc.; use one or a combination)
2 cups whipping cream
½ cup each: grated Romano and Parmesan cheese

Cook fettuccine to al dente stage (just done—*not* over cooked) in boiling salted water. Rinse well and set aside. In a heavy large sauté pan, melt butter. Sauté onion and garlic until onion is transparent. (Do not brown.) Stir all the time. Add seafood and sauté. Add whipping cream and stir until cream is warm. Add grated cheeses and heat over low heat until cheese melts and sauce thickens. You can increase heat a little, but you must stir all the time. Add cooked fettucine and lift and toss until noodles are coated with the sauce. Serve to 4 or 5 lucky people.

It's About Thyme

Kirsh's Angel Hair Pasta with Shrimp Soup

1 stick butter
½ cup green onions, diced
2 quarts chicken broth
½ package angel pasta
1 pound peeled shrimp
1 cup pea pods
Salt and pepper to taste
1 tablespoon minced parsley
½ teaspoon coriander
l hair French bread, sliced
Fresh Parmesan cheese, grated
Wine (optional)

Melt butter in large kettle. Sauté onions. Add chicken broth and bring to a boil. Add pasta, shrimp, and pea pods. Boil 7 minutes. Salt and pepper to taste and add parsley and coriander. Ladle into bowls. Place a slice of bread topped with cheese and splashed with wine on top of each bowl. Place bowls under broiler for 1 minute.

Cooking with Herbs

Seafood Supreme with Pasta

1 pound shrimp, cut up
½ cup butter, melted
2 cloves garlic, minced
½ teaspoon thyme
¼ teaspoon oregano
¾ teaspoon salt
½ teaspoon paprika
¼ teaspoon ground red pepper
⅛ teaspoon black pepper
1 pint whipping cream
1 pound angel hair pasta or thin spaghetti

Marinate shrimp overnight in all of the above ingredients, except for whipping cream and pasta. Cook pasta. Get skillet hot and cook shrimp until barely pink; add cream and remove from stove. Pour over hot pasta. Pass Parmesan cheese and freshly ground black pepper.

Hopewell's Hoosier Harvest II

Scalloped Oysters

½ cup melted butter
2 cups medium-coarse cracker crumbs
1 pint fresh oysters and oyster liquid
Pepper
Milk or cream
½ teaspoon salt
¼ teaspoon Worcestershire sauce

Pour melted butter over cracker crumbs. Toss lightly. Drain oysters. Save liquid. Butter 1 (8-inch) square pan. Spread ⅓ of the crumbs on the bottom. Cover with ½ of the oysters. Sprinkle with pepper. Add a second layer with another ⅓ of crumbs, the rest of the oysters and a little pepper. Combine oyster liquid with enough rich milk or cream to make 1 cup. Add salt and Worcestershire sauce. Pour over oysters. Top with remaining crumbs. Bake at 350° for 40 minutes. Yield: 4 servings.

For Crying Out Loud...Lets Eat!

The Indianapolis Motor Speedway is a National Historic Landmark. The Speedway was built as a combination race track and testing facility in 1909. The 500-Mile Race was first held in 1911. Today it is the world's largest one-day sporting event. The Brickyard 400, a NASCAR event, was first held in August, 1994.

MEATS

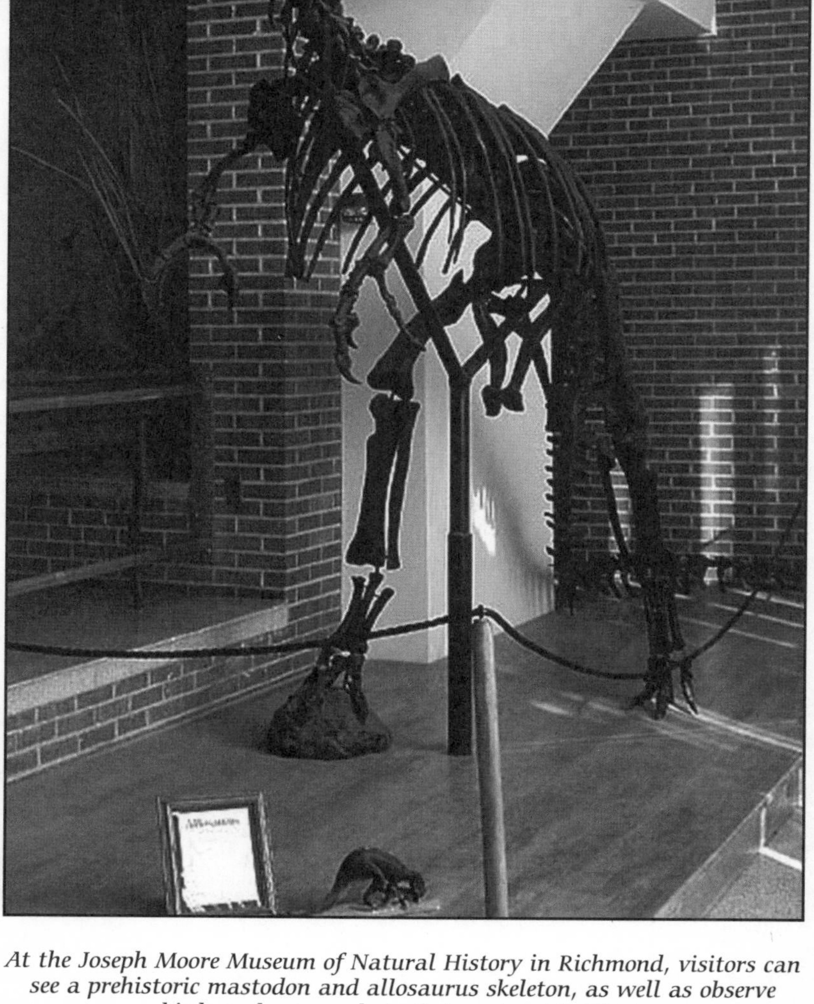

RICHMOND VISITORS BUREAU

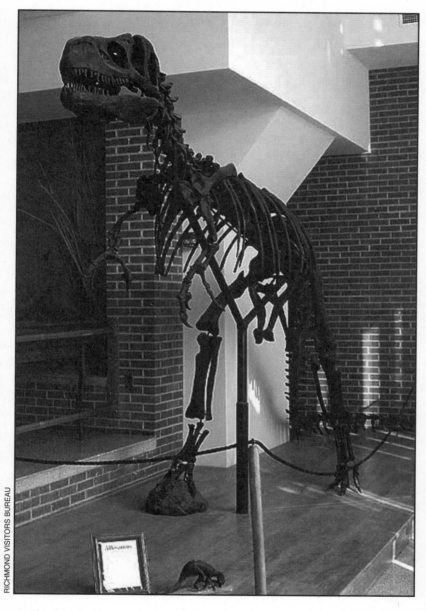

At the Joseph Moore Museum of Natural History in Richmond, visitors can see a prehistoric mastodon and allosaurus skeleton, as well as observe birds and mammals in their natural habitat.

Dad's Favorite Steak

1 top round steak, Swiss steak, or arm roast
½ cup water
¼ cup salad oil
2 tablespoons brown sugar
1 clove garlic, minced
½ cup soy sauce
¼ cup lemon juice
½ teaspoon ginger
10 drops hot sauce

Chill beef. Cut 1½-1¾ inches thick. Score both sides in diamond pattern, ⅛ inch deep.

Cook remaining ingredients for marinade slowly for 10 minutes. Chill. Place steak in plastic bag, add marinade, press out air, tie securely, and place in pan in refrigerator for 6-8 hours or overnight.

Remove steak from marinade, reserving marinade, and place on grill over ash covered coals or on a rack in broiling pan so surface meat is 4-5 inches from heat. Broil at moderate temperature, rare or medium (25-30 minutes, depending on thickness of steak and doneness desired), brushing with marinade and turning occasionally. Carve in thin slices, diagonally, against the grain.

Amish Country Cookbook III

Hong Kong Steak

Hong Kong Steak is a favorite of the more affluent Oriental families everywhere. It requires a bit of bottled oyster sauce, a popular sauce in the East. If you haven't already done so, buy a bottle and start enjoying this rare treat. It's available in Chinatown and Oriental stores; it keeps almost forever.

4 filet mignon steaks, thick-cut
4 strips bacon
1 tablespoon sweet butter
3 green onions, chopped fine
1 clove garlic, smashed
1 tablespoon soy sauce
2 tablespoons oyster sauce
1½ teaspoons sugar
1 teaspoon MSG (Accent)
3 tablespoons Sake (Japanese Rice wine) or sherry
1 teaspoon powdered ginger
1 chicken bouillon cube
½ cup boiling water
1 teaspoon cornstarch

Put the bacon around the outside of the steaks; fasten with toothpicks. Set aside on a broiler pan. Sauté the onions and garlic in the butter for 2 minutes. Stir in the soy sauce, oyster sauce, sugar, MSG, sake or sherry, ginger, bouillon cube, and boiling water. Blend well. Stir in the cornstarch, a little at a time, to blend. Cover and simmer for 5 minutes, until the sauce thickens.

Broil the steaks to the desired doneness. Slice each steak into 3 pieces and place on 4 serving dishes. Spoon the sauce over the steaks and serve hot. Serves 4. (A 1960s recipe.)

Aspic and Old Lace

The presidential campaign slogan "Tippecanoe and Tyler Too" took William Henry Harrison, first Indiana Territory Governor, and his running mate, John Tyler, to the White House in 1840. Harrison was nicknamed Tippecanoe after defeating the Shawnee Indians in 1811. He died in office after serving only thirty and one-half days as president.

Newman's Own Marinated Steak

½ cup Newman's Own Olive Oil and Vinegar Dressing
2 cloves garlic, crushed
1 large onion, cut up
Salt and pepper
1 large sirloin steak, about 1½ inches thick

Combine Newman's Own, garlic, onion, dash of salt and pepper in a shallow glass dish. Add steak; turn to coat with marinade. Refrigerate several hours, turning steak occasionally.

Just before serving, preheat broiler or grill. Drain steak; broil or grill. Slice and serve. Serves 4.

Note: Paul Newman, academy award-winning motion picture actor, has been owner of the Newman-Haas racing team since 1983.

Champions: Favorite Foods of Indy Car Racing

Swiss Steak a la Crème

2 pounds round steak
Flour
2 tablespoons vegetable oil
1 teaspoon salt
¼ teaspoon pepper
¼ teaspoon dry mustard
1 clove garlic, minced
½ cup chopped onion
¾ cup water
3 tablespoons soy sauce
2 tablespoons brown sugar
¾ cup plain yogurt

Cut meat into serving-size pieces. Pound as much flour as possible in meat with mallet. Heat oil in a 12-inch skillet. Brown steak on both sides. Add remaining ingredients. Cover pan and bake in a 300° oven, or simmer for 2 hours until tender. Thicken gravy, if desired. Flavor mellows when made the day before serving.

Specialties of Indianapolis II

Swiss Steak

½ cup flour
1 teaspoon salt
¼ teaspoon pepper
2 pounds Swiss steak (cubed round)
1 onion, sliced
1 carrot, sliced

Mix flour, salt and pepper together. Dredge steak in flour mixture and brown lightly in hot fat (2 minutes, each side). Place in baking pan. Strew onion and carrot on top of meat. Cover with gravy and bake until tender (1 hour) in 350° oven.

SWISS STEAK GRAVY:
2 tablespoons flour
2 tablespoons shortening
1 teaspoon salt
¼ teaspoon pepper
½ cup tomato juice
2½ cups stock or warm water
Few drops Kitchen Bouquet
Few drops yellow coloring

Stir flour, shortening, salt and pepper over fire until flour is lightly brown. Add remaining ingredients, stirring constantly until thickened.

Recipes of the Durbin

Company Beef

1½ pounds stew beef
1 envelope dry onion soup
1 can mushroom soup
8 ounces fresh mushrooms, sliced (optional)
1 cup ginger ale
1 small bag egg noodles (dry)

In casserole dish with lid, place beef and add onion soup, mushroom soup, mushrooms, and ginger ale. Bake covered in a 300° oven for 3 hours. (This can also be made in a crock pot set on LOW for 6 hours.) Cook egg noodles as directed on package. Drain. Serve meat over noodles. Serves 4.

Cooking with the Warriors

Spicy Beef and Asparagus

A low-caloric meal!

1 pound round steak (trim fat)
1 tablespoon cornstarch
1 tablespoon water
1 teaspoon dry sherry
½ teaspoon salt
¼ teaspoon pepper
Several dashes hot pepper sauce
¼ cup beef broth
1 tablespoon soy sauce
1 tablespoon catsup
1 teaspoon red wine vinegar
½ teaspoon sugar
2 tablespoons cooking oil
1 clove garlic, minced
¾ pound fresh asparagus, cut into 1-inch lengths, or 1 (10-ounce) package frozen asparagus, thawed
1 cup sliced cauliflower flowerets
1 small sweet red pepper, cut into narrow strips
1 small onion, cut into narrow wedges

Slice meat thinly across grain into strips. Combine cornstarch, water, sherry, salt, pepper, and hot pepper sauce. Add meat and mix well. Combine broth, soy sauce, catsup, vinegar, and sugar; set aside.

Preheat wok. Add 1 tablespoon oil; stir-fry garlic in oil for 30 seconds. Add half the meat, stir-fry 2–3 minutes until browned. Remove from skillet. Stir-fry remaining meat 2–3 minutes. Remove from skillet.

Add remaining oil if needed. Add asparagus and cauliflower; stir-fry for 4 minutes. Add red pepper and onion; stir-fry for 2 minutes. Return meat to wok. Stir in soy sauce mixture. Cook and stir until bubbly. Cover, and cook 1 minute more. Yield: 6 servings.

Cookin' to Beat the Band

Approximately fifty percent of the nation's band instruments are manufactured in Elkhart.

Wiener Schnitzel

(Breaded Veal Cutlets Vienna Style)

4 boneless veal cutlets (pork may be used)
Paprika
Salt and pepper to taste
Flour
Milk or water (1-2 tablespoons)
Bread crumbs
Butter for frying
Lemon slices

If there is a skin around meat, cut it in several places so it won't curl up while frying in the pan. Pound meat a little. Sprinkle with paprika, salt and pepper. Coat with flour. Beat egg and water (or milk) and dip cutlets in it. Coat with bread crumbs on both sides. Heat butter in fry pan and add meat. Let cook to a golden brown over medium heat, about 5 minutes on each side. Serve with lemon slices.

Guten Appetit

Sweet and Sour Pot Roast

Outstanding—this one will catch your fancy.

1 tablespoon oil
1 (4-pound) chuck roast
1 (10½-ounee) can beef bouillon
1 (16-ounce) can jellied cranberry sauce
1 (5-ounce) bottle prepared horseradish
8 carrots, peeled and cut into 2-inch pieces
2 onions, quartered

Preheat oven to 350°. Heat oil in Dutch oven and brown roast. Add bouillon, cranberry sauce, and horseradish. Cover and bake at 350° for 1½ hours. Add carrots and onions to roast. Bake an additional 1½ hours.

Reserve pan juices and pour over meat. Serve with buttered noodles, if desired. Serves 6-8.

Winners

Crockpot Barbecued Beef

1 (3 to 4-pound) roast
1 (24-ounce) bottle catsup
1/3 cup barbecue sauce
1/2 cup onion, chopped
1/4 cup brown sugar
Salt, to taste
Pepper, to taste
Chili powder, to taste

Trim all fat from roast; pat dry and place roast in crockpot. Mix all other ingredients and pour over roast. Cook on LOW for 10-12 hours. Shred with 2 forks. Easy and super good for sandwiches.

Taste & See

Meat Loaf

1 1/2 pounds ground beef
1/2 pound ground pork
3/4 cup rolled cracker crumbs
1/2 cup finely chopped onion
1 egg, beaten
1/4 teaspoon pepper
2 teaspoons salt
1 1/4 cup canned tomatoes
1 green pepper ring

Mix thoroughly all ingredients except 3/4 cup canned tomatoes and the pepper ring. Form into a cake-shaped loaf about 6 or 7 inches in diameter. Top with the 3/4 cup tomatoes and green pepper. Bake 1 hour at 350 .

Our Favorite Recipes

Stay in Bed Stew

1 pound slew meat
Salt and pepper to taste
6-8 carrots, sliced
4 medium potatoes, cubed
1 can small boiling onions. drained
1 can celery soup
2 1/2 cans water

Place meat in small roaster, or large casserole. Add salt and pepper to taste. Do not brown. Add vegetables; cover with celery soup; add water. Cover and bake for 5 hours in 275° oven. Makes 4 servings.

Hoosier Heritage Cookbook

Glazed Meatloaf

2 eggs, beaten
⅔ cup milk
2 teaspoons salt
¼ teaspoon pepper
3 slices bread, cut into small pieces
⅔ cup carrots, shredded
⅔ cup onion, chopped
1½ cups shredded Cheddar cheese
2 pounds hamburger
¼ cup brown sugar
¼ cup catsup
1 tablespoon mustard

Stir together eggs, milk, salt, pepper, and bread. Add carrots, onion, cheese, and hamburger. Mix well. Form into a loaf. Bake at 350° for 1 hour and 15 minutes. Combine brown sugar, catsup, and mustard. Spread over meatloaf and bake 15 minutes longer. About 10 servings.

Amish Country Cookbook III

Swedish Meatballs

1½ pounds hamburger
1 cup bread crumbs
2 eggs
4 tablespoons chopped onions
2 tablespoons melted butter
1½ teaspoons salt
¼ teaspoon pepper
1 tablespoon flour
⅛ teaspoon nutmeg
½ cup cream

Combine all the above ingredients. Mix well and form into bite-size balls. Brown them in a 375° oven for about 30 minutes (an ungreased 15½x10½x1-inch jelly roll pan or cookie sheet works well for this).

RED SAUCE:
½ stick butter
½ cup onion, chopped
3 small (8-ounce) cans tomato sauce
3 tablespoons cider vinegar
¾ cup brown sugar

Brown the onions in the butter. Add the other ingredients and simmer for 20 minutes. Put in the meatballs and serve warm. (A 1960s recipe.)

Aspic and Old Lace

Valpo Casserole

1 pound lean ground beef
½ teaspoon salt
¼ teaspoon pepper
Pinch of ground thyme, ground oregano, ground mustard, garlic salt
¾ cup uncooked Creamettes macaroni
¾ cup chopped green pepper
½ cup chopped onion
2 (4½-ounce) jars sliced mushrooms, drained
1 (10½-ounce) can tomato soup
1 (8-ounce) can tomato sauce
¼ cup shredded Parmesan cheese

Sauté meat with seasonings; do not brown, pour off excess fat. Cook macaroni according to package directions. In 2-quart casserole place ½ of each of the following in layers starting with beef, then onion, green pepper, mushrooms, macaroni; repeat with remainder of each. Top with tomato soup and tomato sauce. Sprinkle with cheese. Preheat oven to 325° and bake 1 hour or until green pepper is tender. Serves 4.

The Guild Cookbook I

Poppin-Fresh Barbe Cups

¾ pound hamburger
¼ cup chopped onion
½ cup barbecue sauce
1 teaspoon brown sugar
⅛ teaspoon salt
1 can refrigerator biscuits (Texas size)
¾ cup shredded Cheddar cheese

Preheat oven to 400°. Brown the hamburger and onion, drain. Add barbecue sauce, brown sugar, and salt. Separate dough into 10 biscuits. Press into bottom and sides of ungreased muffin cups. Spoon meat mixture into each cup. Sprinkle with cheese. Bake 10-12 minutes or until golden brown.

Our Favorite Recipes II

Meat 'N Biscuit Squares

The only complaint I get from family and friends is that the recipe never seems to make enough.

1 pound ground lean pork, veal, or beef
½ cup chopped onion
1 cup crumbled Bleu cheese (or grated American or Swiss cheese may also be used)
1 egg
¼ teaspoon Tabasco sauce (optional)
1½ teaspoons salt
2 tablespoons chopped parsley
Rich Biscuit Dough
1 egg yolk, beaten
1 can soup (tomato or mushroom)
½ cup milk

Heat the oven to 400°. Cook the meat and onion slowly, but do not brown. Stir while cooking to break up the meat. Take from the heat. Cool. Then mix with the cheese, egg, Tabasco sauce, salt, and parsley.

RICH BISCUIT DOUGH:
2 cups sifted flour
3 teaspoons baking powder
1 teaspoon salt
½ cup shortening or salad oil
1 egg
½ cup milk

Sift the flour, baking powder, and salt into a bowl. Cut in the shortening. Stir in the egg and milk. Round up on a lightly floured board. Knead lightly about 15 times.

Divide the biscuit dough in half. Roll or pat each half into a 9x9x1⅓-inch square pan. Spread with the meat mixture; cover with the other square of biscuit dough. Brush with the egg yolk.

Bake about 30 minutes. Serve hot in squares with tomato or mushroom sauce made from soup and milk. (A 1950s recipe.)

Aspic And Old Lace

Super Sullivan Taco

The secret to this great recipe is...the seasoned Crisco.

1 (3-pound) can of Crisco
½ teaspoon each: salt, pepper, garlic powder
1 head lettuce
1 large Bermuda onion
2 medium tomatoes
Salt, pepper, Accent, garlic
2 pounds fresh ground round steak
12 fresh corn tortillas
1 large can Rosarita Green Chili Salsa

Take ½ dozen paper towels and fold them to fit down into the loaf pan so that you can use this to drain the Crisco from the tacos once they are cooked.

Put the 3 pounds of Crisco in a 12-inch cast iron frying pan and place on stove at highest heat to preheat. Once it is melted, add ½ teaspoon each salt, pepper, and garlic powder. Stir this well so that the seasonings are well mixed. If the shortening starts smoking before you are ready to cook, turn the heat down until about 4 minutes before you start cooking.

Finely shred the lettuce by making ⅛-inch cuts across the head of lettuce and then chopping the result in half. Dice the onion and tomatoes into ¼-inch cubes. Shred the cheese.

Now we are at the heart of the preparation of the "Sullivan Super Taco". As you will see, the meat and the tortillas are cooked at the same time in Crisco that will be used over and over. After a cooking session, always pour the Crisco back into the original can after it has cooled; place the can in your refrigerator until you are ready to cook tacos again! Big Jim Sullivan's can of Crisco is about 4 years old, and over this period he has given away parts of it as a "taco starter" to friends. Each time you use it, you will have to add a hit of fresh Crisco to bring it back to the original volume. Now that you understand the basic "secret" to this recipe, we can move forward as I am sure by now your mouth is watering to the extent that you may have to wear a bib!

Continued

Take a portion of the ground beef about twice the size of a golf ball and spread it on ½ of a tortilla. It should be pressed down on the tortilla so that it is just about 3/16 or ¼-inch thick. Do this to the entire dozen tortillas. Sprinkle the meat on each tortilla liberally with salt, pepper, Accent, and garlic powder.

To cook the tortilla/meat combination, carefully fold the tortilla into a "U" shape using your thumb and 2 fingers to hold it in shape. Then carefully lower the folded tortilla into the hot Crisco. Mold it for about 10 seconds so that the bottom of the "U" is partially cooked and will hold its shape. Then lay the tortilla on its side in the Crisco. You can cook about 4 or 5 tortillas at the same time. Once the tortilla is crisp on one side, flip it over with a pair of metal cooking tongs and cook the other side. You will have to experiment a bit with timing; it will depend on the heat generated by your stove.

When the tortillas are cooked, place them in the loaf pan that has been prepared with paper towels to drain off the excess Crisco for a couple of minutes. Then carefully pull the 2 sides of the tortilla apart so that you can insert the filling. First put the cheese, followed by onion, lettuce, and then tomatoes. Your "Sullivan Super Taco" is now ready to serve. The last step is to add a tablespoon or so of the chili salsa; amount will depend on your taste.

Champions: Favorite Foods of Indy Car Racing

Tooter's Taco Casserole

CRUST:

1½ cups dry potato flakes
⅔ cup water
1 (8-ounce) carton dairy sour cream

Combine all crust ingredients and press into buttered 9x13-inch pan. Bake in preheated 350° oven for 20-25 minutes or until golden brown.

FILLING:

2 pounds ground beef
2 envelopes taco seasoning mix
1½ cups water
1½ cups (6 ounces) shredded Cheddar cheese

Brown ground beef in skillet on medium heat. Drain off fat. Stir in seasoning mix and water and bring to a boil. Reduce heat and simmer for 15 minutes, stirring occasionally. Spread filling mixture over baked crust and sprinkle with Cheddar cheese. Bake for 5 more minutes at 350°.

TOPPING:

1 cup shredded Iceberg lettuce
1 cup chopped tomato
¼-½ cup chopped black olives
2 cups slightly crushed nacho-flavored tortilla chips
Taco sauce (optional)
Sour cream (optional)

Top casserole with topping ingredients arranged in layers (or serve on the side for individual tastes). Cut into squares to serve hot. Serves 6.

Cooking with the Warriors

Larry Bird set an Indiana State University game record with nineteen rebounds in 1979 against Southern Illinois. He was named "NCAA Player of the Year" that same year. He went on to become an NBA star with the Boston Celtics.

Hot Dog!

8 hot dogs
8 cheese slices
1 (8-ounce) package crescent rolls

Split hot dogs and fill them with a folded cheese slice. Wrap this in a crescent dough roll and bake (10–13 minutes, in 375° oven).

Serve with mustard to dip them in. Yummy!

The Indiana Kid's Cookbook!

Easy Barbecued Hamburger

Prepare a salad, bring out the potato chips, and make this hot sandwich for a quick evening meal.

2½ pounds hamburger
1 cup catsup
2 cups chopped green pepper
2 onions, chopped
1 tablespoon dry mustard
3 tablespoons sugar
2 tablespoons vinegar
1 tablespoon salt

Cook first 4 ingredients together until meat is browned and vegetables are tender. Add remaining ingredients; cook ½ hour on low heat. Serve on warm hamburger buns.

Sharing Our Best

Pork Tenderloin with Scallion Mustard Sauce

The pork is beautifully enhanced by the creamy Scallion Mustard Sauce.

¼ cup soy sauce
¼ cup bourbon
2 tablespoons brown sugar
3 (1-pound) pork tenderloins

Place pork in a large zip closure bag or shallow dish. Combine soy sauce, bourbon, and sugar. Mix well. Pour marinade over pork; cover and refrigerate 2 hours or longer, turning occasionally.

Preheat oven to 325°. Remove meat from marinade; place on rack in shallow roasting pan. Roast 30 minutes or up to 1 hour, depending on degree of doneness desired. Baste several times with marinade to enhance flavor and to prevent dryness.

SCALLION MUSTARD SAUCE:
⅓ cup sour cream
⅓ cup mayonnaise
1 tablespoon finely chopped scallions
1 tablespoon dry mustard
Salt, to taste
1½ tablespoons vinegar

Combine sour cream, mayonnaise, scallions, dry mustard, salt, and vinegar. Mix well. Refrigerate until ready to serve. Carve pork into thin diagonal slices. Top with sauce to serve. Serves 5-6.

Note: This can also be cooked on an outdoor grill. Heat grill and place tenderloins on rack. Cover and cook about 20-30 minutes or to desired degree of doneness.

Back Home Again

Abraham Lincoln spent his boyhood years in Southern Indiana. The Lincoln Boyhood National Memorial and Living Historical Farm is in Lincoln City.

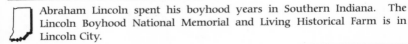

Pork Cutlets & Sour Cream Sauce

1 pork tenderloin, sliced about ½-inch thick
Salt and pepper to taste
1 teaspoon sweet or medium paprika
2 tablespoons butter
2 tablespoons oil
¼ cup finely chopped onion
½ cup dry white wine
½ cup chicken broth
½-¾ cup sour cream

Pound the meat. Sprinkle with salt, pepper, and paprika. Sauté in the butter and oil until browned and cooked. Transfer the meat to a platter. Four off the excess fat and add the onions to the skillet. Cook until wilted. Add the wine and deglaze the pan. Add the chicken broth and simmer for 5 minutes. Remove the sauce from the heat and add the sour cream. Put through a fine sieve and pour over the meat. (A 1960s recipe.)

Aspic and Old Lace

Sweet and Sour Pork with Rice

2 tablespoons cooking oil
1 pound boneless pork, cut up in 1-inch cubes
1 (15¼-ounce) can pineapple chunks
½ cup light corn syrup
¼ cup vinegar
2 tablespoons soy sauce
1 clove garlic, minced
2 tablespoons cornstarch
2 tablespoons water
½ cup red and green pepper slices

Heat cooking oil in skillet. Brown pork. Add next 5 ingredients. Bring to boil, simmer 10 minutes or until done. Mix cornstarch and water; add to pork with the peppers. Boil 2 minutes stirring constantly. Serve over rice. Serves 4.

Amish Country Cookbook I

Pork Chop Casserole

1 teaspoon salt
1 teaspoon pepper
¼ teaspoon paprika
2 cans cream of mushroom soup
1 soup can water
1 medium onion
6 large potatoes, peeled and sliced
6 center-cut pork chops
4 tablespoons butter

Combine salt, pepper, paprika, soup, and water in a 1-quart saucepan; heat just ot boil. Set aside to cool.

Separate onion into rings. layer potatoes and onions in a 2-quart casserole. Top with pork chops. Pour soup mixture over chops; dot with butter. Cover and bake at 350° for 1 hour and 30 minutes. Remove cover, allow chops to brown. Serves 6.

A Taste of Fishers

Ham Loaf

2¼ pounds ground ham
½ pound sausage
¼ cup minced onion
⅛ cup minced green pepper
1 tablespoon minced parsley
3 eggs, beaten
1 cup milk
½ teaspoon white pepper
1¼ cups dry bread crumbs

Mix together all ingredients. Shape into a loaf and bake in a 350-375° oven 30 minutes. Pour Basting Sauce over loaf and bake 30 minutes longer or until loaf is done. Makes 10-12 servings.

BASTING SAUCE:

2 tablespoons prepared mustard
6 tablespoons water
½ cup brown sugar

Stir until sugar is dissolved. Pour over ham loaf after first 30 minutes. Thicken remaining sauce with small amount of cornstarch and serve with loaf.

Recipes of the Durbin

Apricot Baked Ham

Ham is a great choice for the Christmas Eve meal, because once it goes in the oven, it practically takes care of itself until dinner time. The sugary crust makes the ham beautiful to serve.

1 (10- to 14-pound) whole ham, fully cooked, bone-in
Whole cloves
⅓ cup dry mustard
1 cup apricot jam
1 cup light brown sugar firmly packed

Trim skin and excess fat from ham. Place ham on a rack in a large roasting pan. Insert cloves in ham every inch or so. Be sure to push cloves into the ham surface as far as they'll go. Now combine the dry mustard and the jam. Spread over entire surface of the ham. Pat the brown sugar over the jam mixture. Bake uncovered at 325° for 2½-3½ hours, or until meat thermometer registers 140°. Count on 15-18 minutes per pound. The sugary crust that forms on the ham keeps the juices in. When ham os done, remove it from oven and let set for 15-20 minutes before carving it. Will serve 15 or more.

Christmas Thyme at Oak Hill Farm

Ham 'N Swiss Pie

2 cups chopped Healthy Choice smoked ham deli meat
1 cup fat-free Kraft Swiss cheese slices, chopped
⅓ cup chopped onions or green onions
1 cup egg substitute
2 cups skim milk
1 cup reduced fat Bisquick baking mix
¼ teaspoon pepper
Vegetable spray

Heat oven to 400°. Spray 9- or 10-inch pie plate with vegetable cooking spray. Sprinkle ham, cheese, and onions in pie plate. Beat remaining ingredients until smooth, 15 seconds in blender on HIGH or 1 minute with hand beater. Pour into plate. Bake until golden brown and knife inserted in center comes out clean, 35-40 minutes. Cool 5 minutes. Makes 6 servings.

Nutritional Analysis Per Serving: Calories 135; Fat 2.8g; Cal from fat 19%; Chol 2.3mg; Sod 226mg; Fiber .3g; Exchanges ½ starch, 2 meats

The Heart of Cooking II

Beef Stick

(Summer Sausage)

5 pounds ground beef
5 heaping teaspoons Morton Tenderquick Salt
2½ teaspoons salt
1 teaspoon liquid smoke
½ teaspoon sage
1 heaping teaspoon Italian seasoning
2½ teaspoons garlic salt or powder
2½ teaspoons whole mustard seed
2 teaspoons coarse pepper
½ teaspoon ground red pepper
Pinch ground cloves

Mix all ingredients together well. Refrigerate 48 hours, mixing well every day. Shape in 2-inch diameter rolls. Put on broiler pan or racks in pan. Bake 150° for 4 hours.

Hoosier Heritage Cookbook

Brain Sandwiches

About 12 ounces cleaned pork brains
3-4 heaping tablespoons all-purpose flour
1 level teaspoon baking powder
1 large egg
Salt and pepper to taste

Wash brains in pieces under cold running water, removing as much of the thin covering membrane as possible. With hands, knead brains to break up into small lumps. Combine with remaining ingredients in a large mixing howl and beat with electric mixer on medium-low speed until batter is very nearly smooth; do not over beat.

Heat about ¼ inch vegetable oil in a large skillet until bubbling hot but not smoking. Drop batter by spoonfuls (allowing about 3 tablespoons per fritter) and fry until batter bubbles and begins to look dry. Turn and fry on other side until edges are crispy and golden brown. It should take about 5-6 minutes per side. Serve on hamburger buns with sliced onion, pickle and other hamburger-type toppings and garnishments, as desired. Yield: 6-8 sandwiches.

Festival Foods and Family Favorites

Barnes' Family Mincemeat

1 large beef tongue
2 oranges
2 lemons
1 cup sugar
2 cups water
½ pound ground beef suet (optional)
5 pounds tart apples, chopped
2 pounds stewed raisins
1 pound currants
½ pound ground citron
2 ounces lemon peel
2 ounces orange peel
½ pound blanched almonds
Red and green candied cherries
Juice from oranges and lemons
3 pounds brown sugar
1 tablespoon salt
½ teaspoon mace
½ teaspoon allspice
½ teaspoon nutmeg
1 teaspoon cinnamon

Simmer beef tongue slowly until tender. Skin and trim. Grind; return to liquid when cool. Thinly peel the 2 oranges and 2 lemons. Parboil peels 3 times, changing water after each boil. Prepare simple syrup by combining 1 cup sugar with 2 cups water; add peelings and cook to a medium syrup. Add remaining ingredients. Mix thoroughly. Let stand a week before using. When baking pies, dilute with spiced sweetened vinegar or apple cider.

Mincemeat and Memories

CAKES

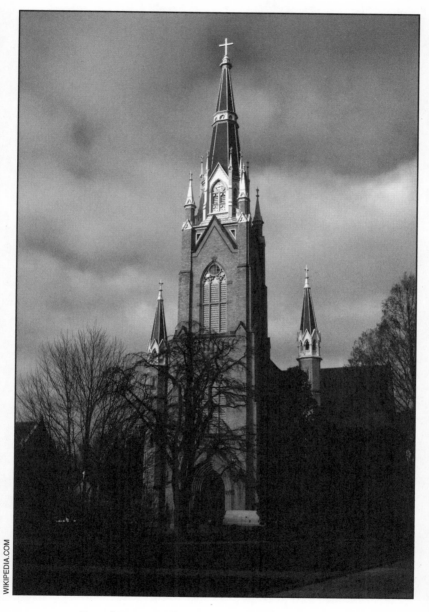

WIKIPEDIA.COM

Sacred Heart Basilica on the Notre Dame Campus. South Bend.

Apple Dump Cake

1 cup chopped nuts
1 cup apple pie filling (don't drain)
2 eggs
1 teaspoon salt
1 cup corn oil
2 cups unsifted flour
1 teaspoon vanilla
2 cups sugar
1 teaspoon baking soda
1 teaspoon cinnamon

Dump all ingredients into large bowl and stir until mixed well (stir with spoon or fork, not mixer). Put into greased 11x9x2-inch pan. Bake at 350° for 35-45 minutes. Top with icing made by mixing following ingredients:

1 (8-ounce) package cream cheese
¾ stick margarine
½ box powdered sugar
1 teaspoon vanilla

Recipes from Jan's Cake & Candy Crafts

Apple Dapple Cake

3 eggs
1½ cups salad oil
2 cups sugar
3 cups flour
1 teaspoon salt
1 teaspoon soda
2 teaspoons vanilla
3 cups peeled and chopped apples
1½ cups chopped pecans
1 cup brown sugar
¼ cup milk
1 stick margarine

Mix eggs, oil, and sugar. Blend well. Add flour, salt, and soda. Mix well. Add vanilla, apples, and nuts. Bake in 350° oven for 1 hour in an 8- or 9-inch greased tube pan. To make topping, combine brown sugar, milk, and margarine and cook 2½ minutes. Pour over cake while still hot and in the pan. Let set until cool. Remove from pan when completely cold.

Home Cooking II

Brandied Apple Cake

This cake stays moist for a long time. Great for packing in lunches or for snacks!

2 cups flour
1½ teaspoons salt
1 teaspoon nutmeg
1 teaspoon cinnamon
1 teaspoon soda
1¼ cups vegetable oil
1⅓ cups sugar
2 eggs (or 3 egg whites)
2 cups peeled chopped apples
1 cup nuts
⅓ cup brandy (apricot is good)
1 teaspoon vanilla

Sift together the dry ingredients and set aside. Mix oil and sugar in mixer bowl. Add eggs and flour mixture and beat well. Add remaining ingredients. Pour into 13x9-inch greased pan and bake in 350° oven for 35-45 minutes. Yield: 15 servings.

Note: Needs no frosting, but very good with ice cream.

The Guild Cookbook IV

Apple Cake

2 cups sugar
1½ cups cooking oil
3 well-beaten eggs
2 teaspoons vanilla
3 cups sifted flour
1 teaspoon soda
½ teaspoon baking powder
1 teaspoon salt
3 cups finely chopped apples
1 cup flaked coconut
½ cup chopped nuts (optional)

Mix sugar and oil, add eggs and mix well. Add vanilla; then add mixed dry ingredients, blending thoroughly. Then add apples, coconut, and nuts and blend well. Bake in a greased and floured 9x13-inch pan at 350° for 55 minutes. Frost as desired, or serve with whipped cream. Serves 16.

The Guild Cookbook I

Heart Center Carrot Cake

This is a delicious and virtually fat-free carrot cake.

2 cups whole wheat flour
¾ cup granulated sugar
¾ cup brown sugar, packed
2 teaspoon soda
1 teaspoon salt
1 teaspoon cinnamon
8 egg whites or 1 cup egg substitute
1 cup crushed pineapple (in its own, unsweetened juice)
4 cups grated carrots
1 cup raisins

Mix flour, sugars, soda, salt, and cinnamon and set aside. In a large bowl beat eggs. Add flour mixture slowly, beating until smooth. Mix in crushed pineapple, carrots, and raisins.

Pour into greased and floured cake pan (13x9-inch). Bake for 35 minutes in 350° oven. Serves 12.

Nutrition Analysis Per Serving: Serving size 2-inch square: Calories 160; Fat 0.4g; Cal from fat 2%; Chol 0mg; Sod 190mg.

The Heart of Cooking

Wasp's Nest Cake

1 (3-ounce) box cook and serve vanilla pudding
2 cups milk
Yellow cake mix
1 (12-ounce) package butterscotch morsels

On the stove top mix pudding with milk and bring to a boil. Dump in a box of cake mix. Stir and pour into a greased 9x13-inch pan. Sprinkle in butterscotch morsels. Bake in 350° oven for 30 minutes. Let cool; serve.

Taste and See

Before refrigeration, the ice needed for the meat packing industry in Chicago was transported by ice farmers on Cedar Lake. The ice farmers lived in boarding houses collectively called "Armourtown." Only one boarding house remains, now the Lake of the Red Cedars Museum. It features fascinating displays on the ice cutting industry and other artifacts from that period.

Mocha and Cherry Cake

2 cups granulated sugar
1¾ cups all-purpose flour
¾ cup unsweetened cocoa powder
2 teaspoons baking soda
1 teaspoon baking powder
½ teaspoon salt
½ cup egg substitute
1 cup nonfat buttermilk
1 cup strong coffee, cooled
½ cup applesauce
2 teaspoons vanilla
1 can Betty Crocker Light Fudge Icing

Preheat oven to 350°. In a very large mixing bowl, combine the 2 cups sugar, flour, cocoa powder, baking soda, baking powder, and salt. Add egg substitute, buttermilk, coffee, applesauce, and vanilla. Beat with an electric mixer on LOW speed for 30 seconds until combined, then for 2 minutes at medium speed. Spray 2 (9x1½-inch) round pans with butter-flavored spray; sprinkle with cocoa powder. Pour batter into pans. Bake for 25-30 minutes or until cakes test done. Cool on rack for 10 minutes. Remove from pans. Cool.

Split each cake horizontally to make 4 layers total.

FILLING:

2½ cups fat-free ricotta cheese
½ cup granulated sugar
⅓ cup miniature semi-sweet chocolate chips
½ cup chopped maraschino cherries, well drained

Combine ricotta cheese, ½ cup sugar, and chocolate chips. Gently stir in cherries. Place one cake layer on a serving plate. Spread ⅓ of the filling on the bottom layer of cake. Top with another cake layer. Continue layering the filling and cake, ending with cake.

Ice cake with Betty Crocker Light Fudge Icing. Makes 14-16 servings.

Nutritional Analysis Per Serving: (1/14 of cake) Calories 352; Fat 2.7g; Cal from fat 7%, Chol 2 6mg; Sod 260mg; Fiber 2g; Exchanges 4 starch.

The Heart of Cooking II

Mt. Mama Mudslide Cake

1 stick soft margarine
1 cup flour
1 cup chopped pecans
1 (8-ounce) package cream cheese
1 cup powdered sugar
1 (9-ounce) carton Cool Whip
1 (4-ounce) package chocolate instant pudding
1 (4-ounce) package vanilla instant pudding
2 cups cold milk
1 chocolate bar, grated

Combine margarine, flour, and nuts. Mix well and press into 13x9x2-inch pan. Bake 20 minutes at 350°. Let cool. Combine cream cheese and powdered sugar until fluffy. Fold in 1 cup Cool Whip. Spread over crust.

Combine pudding mixes with milk. Mix until thick and creamy. Pour over cheese layer. Top with remaining Cool Whip. Grate chocolate bar over top.

Our Favorite Recipes

Pistachio Bread

Serve this bread as a dessert with a dollop of low-fat whipped topping!

1 lite yellow cake mix
2 small packages pistachio pudding mix
½ cup chopped pecans
4 eggs or 1 cup egg substitute
¼ cup fat-free sour cream
1 cup water

Mix above ingredients well. Pour into Bundt pan or 2 loaf pans sprayed with vegetable spray. Bake 45 minutes at 325°. Yields 16 slices. (Omit nuts to reduce fat even further.)

Nutrition Analysis Per Serving: Calories 117; Fat 3.5g; Cal from fat 26%; Chol 0mg; Sod 212mg

The Heart of Cooking

Italian Cream Cake

5 eggs
½ cup margarine
½ cup vegetable shortening
2 cups sugar
1 teaspoon baking soda
1 cup buttermilk
2 cups flour, sifted twice
1 (3½-ounce) can coconut
1 cup chopped nuts
1 teaspoon vanilla extract
1 teaspoon coconut flavor extract (like Watkins)

Separate eggs and beat whites until stiff. Set aside. Mix margarine and vegetable shortening until creamy and add sugar. Add egg yolks, one at a time, beating well after each addition. Dissolve baking soda in buttermilk; add alternately with flour. Beat well. Add coconut, nuts, and extract flavors. Fold in stiffly-beaten egg whites. Pour into 3 separate greased and floured 9-inch cake pans using approximately 2 cups of batter for each pan. Bake in preheated 350° oven for 25 minutes. Spread Cream Cheese Icing between layers and on top and sides of cooled cake.

CREAM CHEESE ICING:

1 (8-ounce) package cream cheese, softened
½ cup margarine
1 (1-pound) box powdered sugar
1 teaspoon almond extract

Combine ingredients and beat well.

Indiana's Finest Recipes

Grandma Principe's Coconut Cake

2 eggs
1 cup sugar
1 tablespoon melted butter or margarine
½ cup milk
1 teaspoon baking powder
1 cup flour

Beat eggs for 10 minutes. Add sugar. Continue beating slowly. Add remaining cake ingredients. Mix until all ingredients are well blended. Pour into 13x9-inch greased and floured pan. Bake at 350° for 25 minutes. While cake is baking prepare Topping.

TOPPING:
3 tablespoons melted butter or margarine
3 tablespoons cream or evaporated milk
½ cup brown sugar
½ cup coconut
½ cup chopped pecans or walnuts

Cook over medium heat until mixture begins to boil. Carefully spread on top of hot cake (right from oven) and put under the broiler until the topping is bubbly.

Our Italian Family Cookbook

Coconut Cake

1 package yellow or white cake mix, with pudding in the mix
¼ cup oil
2 eggs
1½ cups water
1 can cream of coconut, divided
2 cups coconut, divided
1 medium-size tub of whipped topping

Mix the cake mix, oil, eggs, water, 1 cup cream of coconut, and 1 cup coconut. Bake 350° for 35 minutes in 9x13-inch pan. Punch holes in cake and pour rest of cream of coconut over cake; let cool and frost with 1 cup coconut and whipped topping. Refrigerate.

Bob Knight (Head Coach, Men's Basketball)

The IU Cookbook

Mocha Torte Cake

A family tradition—if you like coffee flavor, you'll like this.

3 eggs, well beaten
1 cup sugar
2 tablespoons coffee, strong and cold
1 cup flour
1 teaspoon baking powder
Pinch of salt
1 pint (2 cartons) cream
2 tablespoons sugar
2 tablespoons cold coffee

Add sugar and coffee to beaten eggs, beating thoroughly. Add (sifted together) flour, baking powder, and salt. Bake in 2 layers at 325° for 22 minutes or longer. When cake is cold, whip cream. Add sugar and cold coffee. Spread between layers and on sides and top of cake.

Also, make an icing, using 1 cup powdered sugar mixed with 2 tablespoons coffee and drizzle this over all whipped cream areas. It is best placed in freezer, but can be kept in refrigerator. Serve cold.

Sharing Our Best

Gooey Chocolate-Toffee Cake

1 box German chocolate pudding and cake mix
1 (16-ounce) jar butterscotch topping
1 can sweetened condensed milk
8 ounces whipping cream
4 Skor candy bars, crushed

Prepare cake mix as directed on package for 9x13-inch pan. Let cool 10-13 minutes. Poke holes evenly over entire cake with the end of a wooden spoon. Combine butterscotch topping with sweetened condensed milk. Pour evenly over top of warm cake. Refrigerate at this point to completely cool cake. Finish by icing the top of the cake with 8 ounces whipped cream. Sprinkle crushed candy bars over the top. Serves 10-12.

A Taste of Fishers

Tunnel of Fudge Cake

1½ cups margarine, softened
6 eggs
1½ cups sugar
2 cups flour
1 package dry Pillsbury frosting (double Dutch or fudge)
2 cups chopped nuts

Preheat oven to 350°. Generously grease bottom, sides and tube of 12-cup Bundt pan. In a large bowl, cream margarine; add eggs, one at a time, beating well after each. Gradually add sugar, creaming until light and fluffy. By hand, stir in flour, dry frosting mix and nuts until well blended. Pour batter into prepared pan. Bake at 350° for 60 minutes. Cool 1 hour; remove from pan.

Note: We like this without any frosting, but you can make a light glaze to drizzle over the top.

Love Cookin'

Hot Fudge Sundae Cake

1 cup flour
¾ cup sugar
2 tablespoons cocoa
2 teaspoons baking powder
¼ teaspoon salt
½ cup milk
2 tablespoons salad oil
1 teaspoon vanilla
1 cup chopped nuts (optional)
1 cup brown sugar
¼ cup cocoa
1¾ cups hottest tap water

Stir together the first 5 dry ingredients in a 9x9-inch pan. Mix milk, oil, and vanilla with a fork, then stir into dry ingredients and mix until smooth. Stir in nuts if desired. Sprinkle on brown sugar-cocoa mixture. Pour hot water over batter. DO NOT stir. Bake at 350° for 40 minutes. Let stand 15 minutes.

Hopewell's Hoosier Harvest II

Bourbon Pecan Cake

- 2 teaspoons nutmeg
- ½ cup bourbon
- 1½ cups sifted all-purpose flour, divided
- 2 cups pecans
- 1 cup raisins, finely chopped
- ½ cup butter
- 1 cup plus 2 tablespoons sugar
- 3 eggs, separated
- 1 teaspoon baking powder
- Dash salt
- Pecan halves

Preheat oven to 325°. Grease a 10-inch tube pan. Soak nutmeg in bourbon. Mix ½ cup flour with the nuts and raisins, coating thoroughly. Reserve.

Cream butter and sugar until light and fluffy. Add egg yolks, one at a time, bearing well after each addition. Beat in remaining flour, baking powder, and salt. Beat in bourbon-nutmeg mixture and continue beating until batter is well mixed. Add the nuts and raisins. Beat the egg whites until very stiff. Fold in. Spoon batter into pan. Press down firmly to squeeze out air pockets and allow to stand 10 minutes. Bake at 325° for 1¼ hours or until cake tests done. Cool in the pan, right-side-up, 1-2 hours before turning out. Continue cooling.

Note: This cake improves with age. Store in a covered container for several days, wrapped in a bourbon-soaked napkin.

The Conner Prairie Cookbook

Conner Prairie, near Indianapolis, was awarded two four-star ratings for authenticity and entertainment, has been ranked one of the Top 10 Places to Relive America's Past, and one of the 10 Best USA Summer Vacations for Families. Its history comes alive in the 1836 Village of Prairietown, the 1823 William and Elizabeth Conner home, and the hands-on Pioneer Adventure Area.

Unbeatable Sourdough Chocolate Cake

Best chocolate cake ever eaten!

1½ cups cake flour
½ cup powdered milk
1 teaspoon baking soda
½ teaspoon salt
1 cup well-ripened starter (16 hours or more) (see page 34]
1 cup strong black coffee, cooled
1 teaspoon vanilla
4 squares unsweetened chocolate
½ cup (1 stick) unsalted butter
2 cups sugar
3 large eggs, separated

Mix cake flour, powdered milk, baking soda, and salt; set aside.

Combine starter, coffee, and vanilla; set aside.

Melt chocolate in double boiler. Cream butter; add sugar and beat on HIGH until smooth and fluffy. Beat in egg yolks, one at a time. Add melted chocolate and beat on HIGH for 1 minute. Continue to beat while adding alternately the cake flour and the sourdough mixtures. Beat on HIGH until well combined and smooth. Set aside.

Beat egg whites with clean beaters until they form peaks.

Carefully fold whites into chocolate mixture. Pour into 3 (9-inch) layer cake pans which have been greased and lined with wax paper on the bottom. Bake in preheated 350° oven 30-40 minutes. Cake springs back when lightly touched in center and has shrunk away slightly from sides of pan. Let cool.

ICING:

1 (6-ounce) package chocolate chips
⅔ cup dark brown sugar, firmly packed
1 (3-ounce) package cream cheese
½ teaspoon vanilla
1 teaspoon cinnamon
⅛ teaspoon salt
1 small egg yolk
1 cup heavy cream, whipped until stiff

Continued

Melt chocolate in double boiler. Beat sugar, cream cheese, vanilla, cinnamon, and salt until creamy. Beat in egg yolk and stir in melted chocolate. Gently fold in whipped cream. Cover and refrigerate about an hour until thick. Frost between layers and on outside of cake.

The Guild Cookbook III

Pumpkin Roll

3 eggs
1 cup sugar
⅔ cup pumpkin
1 teaspoon salt
¾ cup flour
1 teaspoon soda
½ teaspoon cinnamon
1 (8-ounee) package cream cheese
1 cup powdered sugar

Beat eggs; add sugar gradually and add next 5 ingredients. Pour onto greased 10½x15½-inch jelly roll pan lined with wax paper. Bake at 350° for 15 minutes. Turn out on a tea towel sprinkled with powdered sugar. Roll up long way. Cool.

Cream together the cream cheese and powdered sugar. Unroll cake; spread with filling. Re-roll and chill.

Service League's Favorites

Chess Cake

1 yellow cake mix
1 stick margarine, melted
1 egg
2 eggs
2½ cups powdered sugar
1 (8-ounce) softened cream cheese

Mix together cake mix, margarine, and egg; pat in 9x13-inch pan. Beat remaining ingredients and pour on crust mixture. Bake at 325° for 40 minutes. (Do not open oven door while baking.)

Our Favorite Recipes II

Harvey Wallbanger's Cake

1 package yellow cake mix
1 (3¾-ounee) package instant vanilla pudding
½ cup liquid shortening
4 eggs
¼ cup vodka
¼ cup Galliano
¾ cup orange juice

Mix all ingredients together and beat for 4 minutes. Pour batter into well greased and lightly floured Bundt pan. Bake at 350° for 45-50 minutes. Dust with confectioners' sugar or frost with orange glaze, butter, cream cheese, or lemon frosting.

White Feather Farms Saturday Secrets

Blackberry Jam Cake

1 cup butter
2 cups sugar
5 eggs
3 cups flour
¼ teaspoon salt
½ teaspoon cinnamon
1½ teaspoons cloves
1½ teaspoons allspice
1 teaspoon baking soda
1 cup buttermilk
1 cup chopped dates or raisins
1 cup chopped hickory nuts or pecans
1 tablespoon flour
1 cup blackberry jam

In the large bowl of an electric mixer, cream butter, gradually add sugar, and beat until light and fluffy. Add eggs and continue beating. Sift flour with salt and spices. Dissolve baking soda in buttermilk. To the creamed mixture, add the flour mixture alternately with the buttermilk. Beat well. Toss fruit and nuts with the tablespoon of flour, and blend in. Add blackberry jam. Grease 2 (9-inch) layer-cake pans and line with 9-inch circles of wax paper. Stir batter well and pour into pans. Bake in a moderately slow oven (325°) for 40 minutes or until a toothpick inserted into the cake comes out dry. Cool the layers in the pans for 15 minutes and turn them out onto a wire rack. Ice the cake with Caramel Icing. Serves 6–8.

CARAMEL ICING:
3 cups brown sugar
1 cup evaporated milk
½ cup butter

In a saucepan, combine the brown sugar, evaporated milk, and butter. Cook until a soft ball forms when a small amount of syrup is dropped into cold water, or to 238° on a candy thermometer. Beat until creamy enough to spread over cake layers.

The Wild Flavor

In Mentone, you can see the world's largest egg. Constructed to symbolize the area being the largest egg producer in the Midwest, the 3,000-pound egg is hard to miss.

Friendship Starter

This recipe trio has a "most often requested" status.

1 cup canned pineapple chunks
1 cup sugar
2 tablespoons brandy

In large glass jar, combine pineapple chunks, sugar, and brandy, stirring well. Cover and let sit at room temperature for 2 weeks, stirring daily.

AFTER TWO WEEKS ADD:
1 cup maraschino cherries with liquid
1 cup sugar
2 tablespoons brandy

Let stand at room temperature for two weeks more, stirring daily.

AFTER SECOND TWO WEEKS ADD:
1 cup sliced canned peaches with syrup

Let stand at room temperature for 2 weeks more, stirring daily.

FINALLY, SIX WEEKS FROM STARTING TIME:
Drain the fruit, reserving the liquid. The liquid is the starter that will be used in the next step of the recipe. The fruit may be served over the top of ice cream if not used in a cake.

Festival Foods and Family Favorites

Friendship Extender

1½ cups Friendship Starter liquid
2-2½ cups sugar
1 (28-ounce) can sliced peaches with syrup

Combine in a large glass container and cover loosely; store at room temperature for 10 days, stirring daily.

AFTER 10 DAYS ADD:
1 (16-ounce) can crushed pineapple with liquid
2½ cups sugar

Store as before for 10 days, stirring daily.

Continued

AFTER 10 MORE DAYS ADD:

2½ cups sugar
1 (16-ounce) can crushed pineapple with liquid
1 (10-ounce) jar maraschino cherries with syrup

Store as before for 10 days, stirring daily. Note that 30 days have passed since you began this procedure. (This is the procedure your friends will follow when you have passed along some of your starter liquid.)

ON THE 30TH DAY:

Drain liquid from fruit and divide fruit into 3 equal portions. Divide juice into 1½-cup portions and give to friends along with this 30-day recipe and the one that follows.

Festival Foods and Family Favorites

Friendship Cake

1 box white or yellow cake, non-pudding variety
½-⅔ cup vegetable oil
1 small box instant pudding (vanilla or pineapple)
3-4 small eggs
About 2 cups drained fruit from starter mixture
1 cup chopped nuts, (optional)
1 (3½-ounce) can shredded coconut (optional)

Combine all ingredients and bake in a large greased and floured tube or Bundt cake pan for 50-60 minutes at 350°, or until cake tests done. Cake freezes well for up to 1 month and is delicious served with a dollop of whipped cream.

Many people make up to 3 cakes, reserving one for themselves and sending the others along as part of their gift of Friendship Starter and recipes.

Festival Foods and Family Favorites

7-UP Cake

1 box lemon cake mix
1 box instant lemon pudding mix
1 small can crushed pineapple, drained
½ cup cooking oil
4 eggs
10 ounces 7-UP
7 teaspoons lemon juice
¾-1 cup powdered sugar

Combine all ingredients. Bake in 9x13-inch pan at 350° for 40-45 minutes.

Combine lemon juice and powdered sugar; mix well and pour over hot cake.

Taste & See

Tiny Cheesecakes

FILLING:
3 eggs, separated
2 (8-ounce) packages softened cream cheese
¾ cup sugar
½ cup graham cracker crumbs mixed with 2 tablespoons sugar

Beat egg whites until stiff. Set aside. In a separate bowl, combine the cream cheese, egg yolks, and sugar. Beat until light and fluffy. Fold in egg whites. Generously butter mini-muffin tins (approximately 1½-inches in diameter). Coat tins well with graham cracker crumb mixture. Fill with cream cheese mixture. Bake at 350° for 15-20 minutes. Remove from oven to cool. A small depression will occur on the top.

TOPPING:
¾ cup sour cream
2 tablespoons sugar
½ teaspoon vanilla

In a small bowl, combine the sour cream, sugar, and vanilla. Place ½ teaspoon of this mixture in the depression of each mini-cake. Bake again at 400° for 5 minutes. Remove from pans while still warm. Makes 3 dozen.

Nutbread and Nostalgia

Easiest Cheesecake Ever

- 2 packages crescent rolls
- 2 (8-ounce) packages Philadelphia cream cheese
- ¾ cup sugar
- 1 egg, separated (save egg white)
- 1½ teaspoons vanilla
- 1 (20-ounce) can crushed pineapple, well drained

Beat last 5 ingredients until fluffy. Open 1 package crescent rolls at a time. Press perforations together and roll or stretch to cover bottom and halfway up the sides of 13x9-inch (Pyrex) pan. Pour in filling and cover top with other can of crescent dough. Brush egg white over top and sprinkle lightly with sugar. Bake at 350° for approximately 30–35 minutes. Cool well. May be refrigerated.

Love Cookin'

Black Forest Cheesecake

¾ cup SnackWell's chocolate sandwich cookies, crushed, or other low-fat cookies (<1g fat/cookie)
Butter-flavored cooking spray
2 (8-ounce) packages Healthy Choice fat-free cream cheese
1½ cups sugar
¾ cup egg substitute
½ cup semi-sweet chocolate morsels, melted
¼ cup unsweetened cocoa
1½ teaspoons vanilla extract
1 (8-ounce) carton nonfat sour cream
1 (21-ounce) can cherry pie filling
¾ cup Dream Whip

Preheat oven to 300°. Spread cookie crumbs on bottom of 9-inch spring-form pan coated with cooking spray; set aside.

Beat cream cheese product at HIGH with an electric mixer until fluffy; gradually add sugar, beating well. Gradually add egg substitute, mixing well. Add melted chocolate, cocoa, and vanilla, mixing until blended. Stir in fat-free sour cream. Pour into prepared pan.

Bake for 1 hour and 40 minutes. Remove from oven; run a knife around edge of pan to release sides. Let cool on wire rack; cover and chill at least 8 hours.

Remove sides of pan, and spread with cherry pie filling. Dollop each serving with 1 tablespoon of whipped topping, if desired. Makes 12 servings.

Nutritional Analysis Per Serving: (1/12 of cake) Calories 333, Fat 2.3g; Cal from fat 6%; Chol 10.2mg; Sod 481mg, Fiber 0.3g; Exchanges 4 starch, ½ fruit.

The Heart of Cooking II

Turtle Cheesecake

This cheesecake offers something for everyone—chocolate, caramel, and nuts.

1 cup graham cracker crumbs
1 cup chocolate wafer crumbs
6 tablespoons margarine, melted
1 (14-ounce) bag caramels
1 (5-ounce) can evaporated milk
1 cup chopped pecans, toasted
1 pound cream cheese, softened
½ cup sugar
1 teaspoon vanilla extract
2 eggs
Pecan halves for garnish

Preheat oven to 350°. In a small bowl, combine crumbs with margarine. Press onto bottom of 9-inch spring-form pan. Bake 10 minutes.

In a 1½-quart saucepan, melt caramels and milk over low heat. Stir until smooth. Reserve ¼–½ cup sauce for topping. Pour remainder over crust. Sprinkle pecans over caramel layer.

In a medium bowl, combine cream cheese, sugar, and vanilla. Mix at medium speed until well blended. Add eggs, one at a time. Mix well after each addition. Pour over pecans.

Place a 9x13-inch baking pan of water on center rack in oven. Increase oven temperature to 450°. When oven is ready, remove pan of water. Bake cheesecake for 10 minutes at 450°. Then reduce temperature to 250° and continue to bake for 30 minutes. At that time, turn oven off. Leave cheesecake in the closed oven for an additional 30 minutes. Do not open the oven door.

At the end of that 30 minutes, crack oven door open with a hot pad and cool cheesecake another 30 minutes. Pour remaining caramel sauce over top. Garnish with pecan halves. When completely cool, refrigerate. Yield: 10–12 servings.

Great Beginnings, Grand Finales

Chocolate Pound Cake

8 (1.5-ounce) plain Hershey candy bars
2 sticks margarine
2 cups sugar
1 cup buttermilk with ½ teaspoon soda mixed in
1 (12-ounce) can Hershey chocolate syrup
1 teaspoon vanilla
2½ cups flour
4 eggs

Melt candy bars over hot water. Add soft margarine (room temperature). Add all other ingredients. Mix and bake in tube pan at 350° for 1 hour and 15 minutes.

3 tablespoons flour
1 cup water
1 cup sugar
1 cup butter, softened
1 teaspoon vanilla

Cook flour and water until thick, then cool thoroughly. Cream sugar, butter, and vanilla together, being sure sugar is dissolved before adding flour mixture. Spread on thoroughly cooled cake. Keeps well in refrigerator.

Home Cooking II

United Church of Christ Angel Food Cake

1¼ cups flour
¾ cup sugar
2 cups egg whites
¼ teaspoon salt
1½ teaspoons cream of tartar
1¼ teaspoons vanilla
¼ teaspoon almond flavoring
1⅔ cups sugar

Sift together 3 times the flour and ¾ cup sugar. Set aside. Beat stiff foamy with electric mixer the whites and salt. Add, continuing to beat to soft peaks, cream of tartar, vanilla, and almond flavoring. Add 1⅔ cups sugar gradually with electric mixer. Fold in with wire whisk the flour/sugar mixture previously set aside. Do this gradually. Do not stir. Fold over. Do not bang whisk on bowl at any time. Pour into ungreased angel tube pan. Smooth top evenly. Place on lowest rack of oven. Bake at 350° for 20 minutes and turn, then bake 20 minutes more. Remove and invert on pop bottle for 1 hour. Remove from pan when cool. As oven temperatures vary, you may need to adjust time and temperature accordingly.

Note: For fruit flavored cake, add 1¼ boxes Jell-O per cake. Fold in after folding in flour/sugar mixture.

Country Cooking

The glaciers which swept across the Midwest 12,000 years ago never reached Southern Indiana, but their melting water carved out deep ravines and valleys. Today the natural beauty of crystal clear lakes, canyons, and rivers are a pleasant surprise for visitors.

Old Fashioned Jelly Roll

¾ cup cake flour
¾ teaspoon baking powder
¼ teaspoon salt
4 eggs
¾ cup sugar
1 teaspoon vanilla
1 cup tart red jelly

Sift flour then measure. Combine baking powder, salt, and eggs in bowl. Beat with egg beater, adding sugar gradually until mixture becomes thick and light colored. Gradually fold in flour, then vanilla. Turn into 15x10-inch pan, which has been lined with paper, then greased. Bake in hot oven (400°) 13 minutes or until done. Turn cake out on cloth or towel, dusted with powdered sugar. Quickly remove paper and cut off crisp edges of cake. Roll and wrap in cloth. Let cool about 10 minutes, unroll, spread cake with jelly, and roll again. Wrap in cloth; place on cake rack to finish cooling.

Amish Country Cookbook I

Old-Fashioned Pork Cake

1 pound fresh pork sausage
3 cups brown sugar, firmly packed
1 egg, lightly beaten
1 teaspoon baking soda
1 cup cold strong coffee
1 cup raisins
1 cup hickory nuts, walnuts, or pecans
1 teaspoon salt
3 cups sifted flour
1 teaspoon each cinnamon, nutmeg, and allspice

Mix sausage with sugar. Add the beaten egg and mix well. Add the soda to the coffee, then stir mixture into the sausage mixture. Add raisins, nuts, salt, flour, and spices, and mix well. The batter will be very stiff. Turn into a 9- or 10-inch tube pan with greased sides and a wax-paper lining on the bottom. Bake at 350° for 1 hour, or until cake shrinks from sides of pan and tests done when a cake tester is inserted in its center. Ice with Caramel Frosting.

Continued

CARAMEL FROSTING:

½ cup sugar
1 cup dark brown sugar, firmly packed
1 cup light cream
1 tablespoon butter

Combine all ingredients in a saucepan and boil to the soft-ball stage, or 234° on a candy thermometer. Cool slightly, and beat until thick enough to spread.

The Midwestern Country Cookbook

Blueberry Gingerbread

½ cup butter or margarine
½ cup sugar
1 egg
1 cup sorghum molasses
2½ cups flour
1½ teaspoons baking soda
½ teaspoon salt
1 teaspoon ginger
1 teaspoon cinnamon
1 teaspoon cloves
1 cup hot water
1½ cups fresh blueberries, damp but well drained

Cream the butter and the sugar, using an electric mixer. Add the egg and beat well. Then add the molasses and beat until well blended. Sift together the flour, baking soda, salt, and spices. Take out 2 tablespoons of the flour mixture, sprinkle it over the blueberries, and toss. Set aside while finishing the batter.

Add the sifted dry ingredients to the creamed mixture alternately with the hot water, adding about ⅙ of the dry ingredients each time, and beat until smooth after each addition. Fold in the flour-coated blueberries.

Grease a 9x13x2-inch pan and dust with flour. Pour in the batter. Bake in a moderate oven 375° for 40-45 minutes, or until a toothpick inserted in the center comes out clean. Serve hot or cold, with or without whipped cream or ice cream. Serves 12.

Note: This is an old family recipe that makes a good plain gingerbread without the blueberries.

The Wild Flavor

Boiled Penuche Frosting

Penuche (rich brown sugar flavor) was extremely popular 1890-1910 Penuche fudge was the favorite seller at Hoosier county fairs, second only to chocolate.

1 cup packed brown sugar
½ cup granulated sugar
6 tablespoons milk
2 tablespoons soft shortening
2 tablespoons butter
1 tablespoon white corn syrup
¼ teaspoon salt
1 teaspoon vanilla
½ cup chopped walnuts
1½ cups confectioners' sugar

In saucepan, place brown and granulated sugars, milk, shortening, butter, corn syrup, and salt. Bring slowly to a full rolling boil, stirring constantly, and boil briskly for 1 to 1½ minutes. Remove from heat and cool slightly. Add vanilla, nuts, and confectioners' sugar. Beat well until smooth and beginning to dull, then pour over cake to set.

The James Whitcomb Riley Cookbook

Quick Frosting

The secret to this fast frosting is using a blender to mix it!

1 (8-ounce) package fat-free cream cheese (Philadelphia Free)
1 cup powdered sugar
1 teaspoon vanilla

Place all ingredients in a blender or food processor. Blend until smooth and creamy. Completely frost cooled cake. Keep refrigerated. Frosts one cake.

Nutrition Analysis Per Serving: Calories 36; Fat 0g; Cal from fat 0%; Chol 0mg; Sod 56mg

The Heart of Cooking

Kin Hubbard's legendary cartoon character, Abe Martin (created in the early 1900s), immortalized Brown County philosophy. His quick-witted advice can be seen throughout the town of Nashville on its many park benches, and as the theme of several lodging and restaurant facilities.

COOKIES & CANDIES

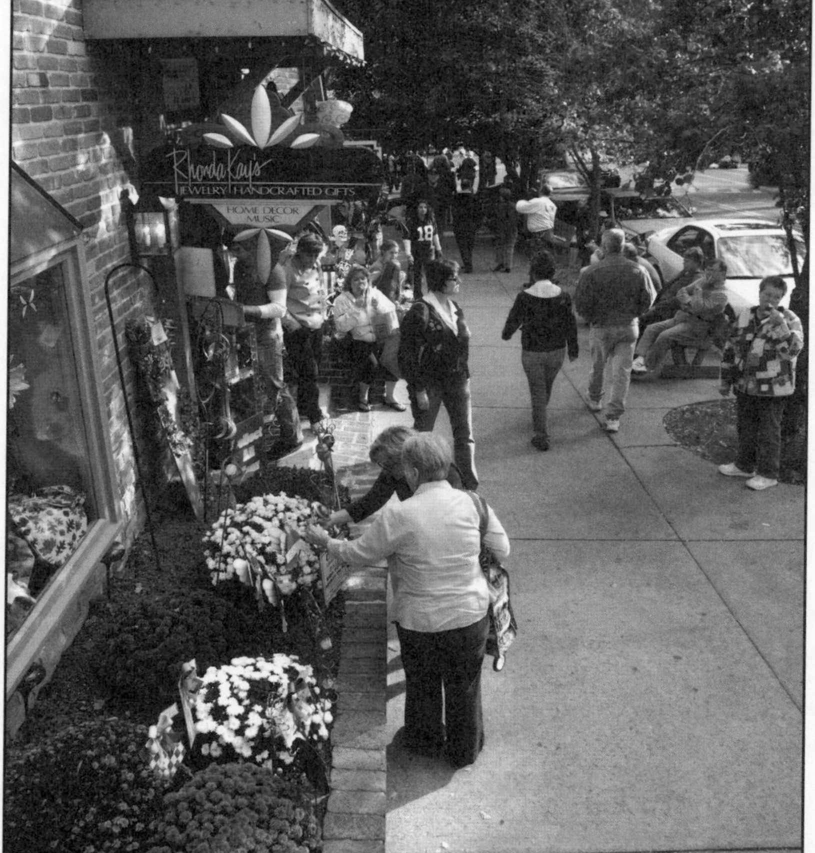

BROWN COUNTY CONVENTION AND VISITORS BUREAU

The town of Nashville has over 300 art, craft and specialty shops.

Special K Brownies

¾ cup white corn syrup
¾ cup light brown sugar
1 cup crunchy peanut butter
5 cups Special K cereal
1 (6-ounce) package butterscotch bits
1 (6-ounce) package chocolate chips

Bring syrup and sugar to boil in a large pan and remove from burner. Add peanut butter and cereal. Stir until well coated. Press into 9x13-inch buttered pan.

Over low heat, melt chips. Spread on top and let set. You may refrigerate to set topping. Cut into squares.

H. Dean Evans—EDD '66 (Former Indiana State Superintendent of Public Instruction.)

The IU Cookbook

Quickest Brownies Ever

Moist type.

1 (4-ounce) square bitter chocolate
1 cup butter or margarine
2 cups sugar
4 eggs, unbeaten
1 cup flour
1 cup nuts (optional)
1 teaspoon vanilla

Melt chocolate and butter in saucepan. Add remaining ingredients in order. Pour into greased 9x13x2-inch pan. Mixes well with a wooden spoon. Bake at 350° for 30 minutes. Cool and frost with chocolate icing or sprinkle with sifted confectioners' sugar. Yield: Approximately 24 squares.

The Guild Cookbook I

Marshmallow Brownies

¾ cup shortening or margarine
1⅓ cups sugar
3 eggs
1⅓ cups flour
½ teaspoon baking powder
2 tablespoons cocoa
⅓ teaspoon salt
1½ teaspoons vanilla
¾ cup chopped nuts
1 small bag miniature marshmallows

Mix all but marshmallows in order given. Bake at 325° for 20 minutes. Take out of oven and cover with marshmallows. Put back in oven for 3 minutes. Pour icing over top.

ICING:
¾ cup brown sugar
⅓ cup water
3 tablespoons cocoa
4 tablespoons butter
1½ teaspoons vanilla
2 cups powdered sugar

Boil first 5 ingredients for 3 minutes. Let cool. Add powdered sugar.

Amish Country Cookbook I

A No-Chocolate Brownie

Attention butterscotch lovers!

¼ cup (½ stick) butter, melted
1 cup firmly packed brown sugar
1 egg, beaten
½ teaspoon salt
¾ cup all-purpose flour
1 teaspoon baking powder
½ teaspoon vanilla
¼ cup shredded coconut
¼ cup chopped nuts

Preheat oven to 350°. Grease and flour an 8-inch square baking pan. Beat together butter and brown sugar until smooth. Add egg, salt, flour, baking powder, vanilla, coconut, and nuts; mix well. Spread in prepared pan. Bake at 350° for 20-25 minutes. Cool.

FROSTING:
¼ cup (½ stick) butter,
¼ cup firmly packed brown sugar
2 tablespoons half-and-half
½ teaspoon maple extract
¾-1 cup confectioners' sugar

Melt butter in medium-size saucepan over medium heat. Add brown sugar and cook over low heat for 3 minutes. Stir in half-and-half, mixing well. Cool slightly. Stir in maple extract. Beat in confectioners' sugar until mixture is of spreading consistency. Frost brownies. Cut into squares after icing has set. Yield: 16 (2-inch) squares.

Note: Recipe may be doubled and baked in a 9x13-inch pan.

Winners

Lemon Cheese Bars

1 box yellow cake mix
2 eggs
⅓ cup vegetable oil
1 (8-ounce) package cream cheese, softened
⅓ cup sugar
1 teaspoon lemon juice

Mix dry cake mix, 1 egg, and oil until crumbly. Reserve one cup. Pat remaining mixture in an ungreased cake pan. Bake 15 minutes at 350°. Beat cream cheese, sugar, lemon juice, and 1 egg until light and smooth. Spread over baked layer. Sprinkle with reserved crumb mixture. Bake 15 minutes longer. Cool. Cut into bars.

Amish Country Cookbook III

Lemon Squares

2 cups flour
½ cup powdered sugar
½ pound melted butter
4 eggs, beaten
2 cups sugar
4 tablespoons flour
1 teaspoon baking powder
½ teaspoon salt
4 tablespoons lemon juice

Mix first 3 ingredients and press in a large 12x18-inch pan or cookie sheet with rim. Bake at 325° for 20 minutes.

Mix beaten eggs with remaining ingredients. Spread over crust and bake for 30 minutes at 325°. Cut in squares and dust with powdered sugar.

Home Cooking

The post office in Santa Claus, Indiana, earns its stripes at Christmastime, postmarking a half-million holiday cards and roughly 10,000 letters from children across the country. (Santa's zip is 47579, in case your kids ask.)

Fabulous Pecan Bars

Wherever and whenever you want to serve (or give) about the best cookie ever, do consider this recipe.

CRUST:

½ cup cold butter
1½ cups flour
¼ cup ice water

Use a pastry blender to cut butter into the flour. Mixture should resemble cornmeal. Add water and toss with a fork. Gather dough into a ball. Wrap in plastic wrap and refrigerate for 1 or 2 hours. Butter and flour a 9x13-inch pan. Roll dough out to about an 11x15-inch rectangle. Fit dough into the prepared pan and let it come up about 1 inch on all sides. Pierce dough with a fork. Chill while making the filling.

FILLING:

1½ cups light brown sugar, packed
1 cup butter
½ cup honey
⅓ cup sugar
1 pound pecans, chopped (but not too fine)
¼ cup whipping cream

Preheat oven to 400°. Combine brown sugar, butter, honey, and sugar in a heavy saucepan and bring to a boil over medium heat, stirring constantly. Boil until thick and dark, 3 or 4 minutes. You must stir constantly. Remove from heat. Stir in pecans and whipping cream. Pour over dough in pan. Bake for 25 minutes. Check after about 15 minutes. If the filling is browning too much, reduce oven heat to 375° and continue baking. Cool cookies in the pan. Cut into strips. Makes 5 or 6 dozen strips, depending on how large you cut them. Almost better than pecan pie!

Christmas Thyme at Oak Hill Farm

Coconut Dream Bars

½ cup butter or margarine
1 cup flour
1½ cups brown sugar
¼ teaspoon salt
1 teaspoon vanilla
2 tablespoons flour
½ teaspoon baking powder
2 eggs
½ cup chopped pecans
1½ cups shredded coconut

Cream butter, flour, and ½ cup brown sugar. Press into a buttered 13x9x2-inch pan. Bake 10 minutes at 350°.

Mix 1 cup brown sugar, salt, vanilla, flour, baking powder, and eggs. Add pecans and coconut. Spread over first mixture and bake 20 minutes in a moderate oven, 350°. Cut in squares while hot. Store in airtight containers. May be frozen.

Home Cooking II

Sour Cream Apple Squares

Perfect for brunch or dessert!

2 cups flour
2 cups firmly-packed brown sugar
½ cup soft butter
1 cup chopped walnuts
1-2 teaspoons cinnamon
1 teaspoon soda
½ teaspoon salt
1 cup dairy sour cream
1 teaspoon vanilla
1 egg
2 cups peeled, finely chopped apples (2 medium)

Preheat oven to 350°. In large bowl, combine flour, brown sugar, and butter until crumbly. Stir in nuts. Press 2¾ cups of crumb mixture into ungreased 13x9-inch pan.

To remaining mixture, add cinnamon, soda, salt, sour cream, vanilla and egg. Blend well. Stir in apples. Spoon evenly over base. Bake at 350° for 25-35 minutes until toothpick comes out clean. Cut into squares. Yield: 12-15 servings.

Cookin' to Beat the Band

Caramel Layer Choco-Squares

1 (16-ounce) package light caramels
2/3 cup evaporated milk, divided
1 package German chocolate cake mix
2/3 cup softened butter
1/2 cup chopped nuts
1 (12-ounce) package chocolate chips

In a heavy saucepan, melt caramels in 1/3 cup of milk over low heat; set aside. In a large bowl, combine remaining ingredients, except chocolate chips. Mix until dough is crumbly, but holds together. Press 1/2 the dough into a greased and floured 9x13-inch pan. Bake at 350° for 6 minutes. Remove from oven. Sprinkle chocolate chips over dough. Pour caramel mixture over chips. Top with remaining dough. Bake for 15-20 minutes. Chill. Makes 2 dozen.

Nutbread and Nostalgia

Mexican Wedding Cookies

1 cup soft butter
1/2 cup powdered sugar
2 cups flour
1 teaspoon vanilla
1/2 cup pecans, chopped

Whip butter; add sugar, then add flour, vanilla, and nuts. Roll in balls about the size of a walnut. Bake 10-15 minutes at 350°. Cool and roll in powdered sugar.

Cooking with the Warriors

Indiana limestone was formed in a shallow sea that covered the Midwest more than 300 million years ago. It can be seen throughout the US in intricate carvings, majestic columns, and stately clad buildings. A few examples: Washington National Cathedral, Empire State Building, Biltmore House, Pentagon, National Archives, Tribune Towers, Rockefeller Center, and the interior of the Lincoln Memorial.

Butterfinger Cookies

1/3 cup shortening
3/4 cup sugar
1 egg
1 1/3 cups sifted flour
1/2 teaspoon soda
1/4 teaspoon salt
2 Butterfinger candy bars, cut in small pieces

Cream shortening and sugar together. Beat in egg. Sift together dry ingredients. Sprinkle over candy bar pieces and combine with creamed mixture. Chill. Drop by spoonfuls on greased cookie sheet. Bake at 350° for about 12 minutes.

Recipes from Jan's Cake & Candy Crafts

White Chocolate Macadamia Nut Cookies

A spectacular combination of flavors!

1 pound butter, softened
2 cups sugar
2 cups firmly packed light brown sugar
¼ cup vanilla extract
5 eggs
6 cups flour
2 teaspoons baking soda
1 teaspoon salt
12 ounces white chocolate chunks
3½ ounces macadamia nuts, coarsely chopped

Preheat oven to 325°. In a very large bowl, beat together butter and sugars until light and creamy. Beat in vanilla and eggs until smooth. Combine flour, soda, and salt. Gradually beat the flour mixture into the butter mixture. Mix in chocolate chunks and nuts; batter will be very stiff.

Using a small ice cream scoop or ¼-cup measure, drop batter onto greased cookie sheets, placing 3 inches apart to allow for spreading. Bake 15 minutes or until light golden brown. Let cool on cookie sheet before removing to a wire rack. Yield: 4 dozen large cookies.

Great Beginnings, Grand Finales

Oatmeal Cookies

1 cup margarine
1 cup brown sugar, packed
1 cup granulated sugar
2 eggs
2 teaspoons vanilla
1 teaspoon salt
2½ cups oatmeal
2 cups flour
1 teaspoon baking powder
1 teaspoon baking soda

Preheat oven to 350°. Cream margarine and sugars; add eggs and vanilla. Beat well. Stir in remaining ingredients. Bake for 10-12 minutes or just until slightly golden. Makes 4 dozen.

Country Cooking

Prized Peanut Butter Crunch Cookie

1 cup butter-flavored Crisco
2 cups firmly packed brown sugar
1 cup Jif Extra Crunchy Peanut Butter
4 egg whites, slightly beaten
1 teaspoon vanilla
2 cups all-purpose flour
1 teaspoon baking soda
½ teaspoon baking powder
2 cups crisp rice cereal
1½ cups chopped peanuts
1 cup quick oats (not instant or old fashioned)
1 cup flake coconut

Heat oven to 350°. Combine butter-flavor Crisco, sugar, and peanut butter in large bowl. Beat at medium speed of electric mixer until blended. Beat in egg whites and vanilla.

Combine flour, baking soda, and baking powder. Mix into creamed mixture at LOW speed until just blended. Stir in, one at a time, rice cereal, nuts, oats, and coconut with spoon.

Drop rounded measuring tablespoonfuls of dough 2 inches apart onto ungreased baking sheet. Bake at 350° for 8-10 minutes or until set. Remove immediately to cooling rack. Makes about 4 dozen cookies.

A Taste of Twin Pines

Indiana's autumn leaves—especially in Brown County—are brilliantly resplendent because of the abundance of beautiful hardwood trees. Leaves change colors because of pigments. *Carotenoids* (think carrots) make the yellows and oranges and are present in leaves all the time, but are covered up by the green. As winter approaches and the green starts to wither and fade, the yellows and oranges become easier to see. Reds and purples come from *anthocyanins* (think cinnamon), which develop in late summer when just the right amount of sunlight, moisture, sugars, and chemicals combine to create showy fall color.

Indiana Fortune Cookies

¾ cup butter or margarine
2 cups sugar
1 teaspoon vanilla
3 eggs
1 cup sifted flour
60 intriguing fortunes written on small strips of paper

Let butter soften outside the refrigerator. In a mixing bowl put sugar and butter and blend together until fluffy. Add vanilla. Then add eggs to the mixture, one at a time. Beat well after adding each egg. Then add flour and beat thoroughly. Heat the oven to 375°. Grease the cookie sheets, then dust lightly with flour. Drop rounded teaspoons of dough at least 2 inches apart on each sheet.

Bake for 20 minutes and remove. With a wide spatula, loosen each cookie from the sheet. Place a folded fortune on each cookie. Gently fold the cookies in half with the fortune inside. Pinch edges together, then twist in the centers. Makes 60 fortune cookies.

Note: While putting a fortune inside each cookie, keep the cookie sheet warm. This will make the cookies easier to work with.

The Indiana Kid's Cookbook!

Chinese Chews

½ cup margarine
2 tablespoons white sugar
1 cup flour
2 eggs
¼ cup coconut
¾ cup nuts
1½ cups brown sugar
2 tablespoons flour
1 teaspoon vanilla

Mix together margarine, white sugar, 1 cup flour and press into 9x9-inch pan. Bake at 350° for 15 minutes.

Mix eggs, coconut, nuts, brown sugar, flour, and vanilla, and place over the above baked part. Bake again at 350° for 25 minutes.

Amish Country Cookbook I

Chocolate Chip Cookies with Snap! Crackle! Pop!

- 1¾ cups flour
- 1 teaspoon soda
- ½ teaspoon salt
- 1 cup butter
- ⅔ cup brown sugar
- 2 eggs
- 1 teaspoon vanilla
- ¾ cup sugar
- 2 cups Rice Krispies
- 1 (6-ounce) package chocolate chips

Stir together flour, soda, and salt. Set aside. Blend together butter and sugar. Add eggs, vanilla, and sugar. Mix until combined. Stir in Rice Krispies and chocolate chips. Drop onto greased cookie sheet. Bake at 350° for 10 minutes. Makes 6 dozen.

Amish Country Cookbook III

Swedish Jam Shortbread

- 1 package butter cake mix
- ½ cup finely-chopped nuts
- ¼ cup butter, softened
- 1 egg
- 1 (10-ounce) jar raspberry preserves or jam
- ½ cup powdered sugar
- 2½ teaspoons water
- ½ teaspoon almond extract

Heat oven to 350°. Grease and flour a 9x13-inch pan. In a large bowl, combine cake mix, nuts, butter, and egg at LOW speed until crumbly. Press mixture into prepared pan. Spread with preserves. Bake 20–25 minutes, or until edges are light brown.

Make glaze with remaining ingredients, mixing until smooth. If needed, add additional water, a drop at a time, for desired consistency. Drizzle over warm shortbread. Cool completely. Cut into bars. Makes 36 bars.

A Taste of Fishers

Sesame Seed Tea Cookies

These are not as sweet as most cookies. The sesame seeds give them a distinctive flavor.

½ cup butter
½ cup margarine
¾ cup sugar
¾ teaspoon vanilla
1 egg
2½ cups flour
1 teaspoon baking soda
1 teaspoon salt
1 cup sesame seeds

Cream together butter, margarine, and sugar until very light. Add vanilla and egg and beat well. Sift together flour, baking soda, and salt. Add to creamed mixture and blend well. Form dough into balls using 1 teaspoon dough each. (Dough may need to be chilled for awhile to make it easy to form into balls.) Roll and coat balls in sesame seeds. Place on cookie sheet and flatten with a fork or a smooth-bottomed glass. Bake at 350° for 8-10 minutes. Cookies should be pale in color. Allow them to cool; then they can be wrapped and frozen. Serve directly from freezer. Yield: about 10 dozen.

The Cookery Collection

Apple Orchard Easies

½ cup butter or margarine
2 cups sugar
2 tablespoons flour
¼ teaspoon salt
1 cup pared, grated, apples
3 cups quick rolled oats
1 cup chopped nuts
1 teaspoon vanilla
3 tablespoons sugar
3 teaspoons cinnamon

Melt butter in a heavy pan; stir in sugar, flour, salt, and apples. Cook to boiling; boil for 1 minute. Remove from heat; add rolled oats, nuts, and vanilla immediately. Mix thoroughly. Drop, using teaspoon, on wax paper. Cool. Roll in mixture of sugar and cinnamon. Makes 60 balls.

For Crying Out Loud...Let's Eat!

Marie Wallace's World's Best Cookies!

Once in a while a really good and different recipe comes along, and this recipe falls into that category. There are interesting additions that you certainly wouldn't expect (cornflakes?!), but the cookie is buttery and very tender—not crisp. They literally melt in your mouth!

1 cup butter, softened
1 cup sugar
1 cup light brown sugar, firmly packed
1 egg, slightly beaten
1 cup salad oil (Crisco, Wesson, Puritan, etc.)
1 cup quick rolled oats
1 cup crushed corn flakes (measure after crushing)
3½ cups flour
1 teaspoon baking soda
1 teaspoon salt
1 teaspoon vanilla
½ cup coconut
1 cup pecans, chopped rather fine
Red or green glazed cherries for decoration (optional)

Cream butter with the sugars. Add the egg and the oil. Mix well. Add oats, corn flakes, flour, soda, salt, and vanilla. Mix well. Stir in coconut and nuts. Roll into 1-inch balls of dough and place on a lightly greased cookie sheet. Flatten the balls with a fork in a crisscross pattern. Dip fork in water between cookies. If desired, place glacéd cherry half in the center of each cookie. Bake at 350° for about 10 minutes, or until light brown. Do not overbake. Makes 8-10 dozen cookies.

Christmas Thyme at Oak Hill Farm

Springerles

A Christmas specialty in German homes.

4 cups all-purpose flour
1 teaspoon baking powder
4 eggs
1 pound powdered sugar
10 drops anise oil
½ cup butter

Sift flour with baking powder in a large bowl. Beat eggs and sugar together until very thick and mixture forms a ribbon when beater is lifted out of the bowl. Beat anise oil and butter into egg and sugar mixture. Add flour mixture gradually to make a dough that can be rolled out easily. Knead briefly and form into a ball. Roll out on a board to ¼-inch thickness; mark cookies with a springerle board or roller and place on a buttered baking sheet. Let stand overnight to dry. Bake the next morning at 325° until straw-colored.

Festival Foods and Family Favorites

Pfeffernusse

Another Christmas tradition in German homes.

2 cups butter
2 eggs
2 cups honey
1 cup sugar
1 teaspoon anise or coriander seeds
1-3 teaspoons each: powdered cloves, allspice, cinnamon, white pepper and salt
1 cup finely chopped almonds

Blend butter, well-beaten eggs, honey, and sugar. Add anise seeds. Sift dry ingredients together and slowly work into butter and egg mixture. Mix until thoroughly blended, adding chopped almonds last. Cover and allow dough to stand refrigerated overnight. In the morning roll dough out into ropes ½ inch in diameter, adding just enough flour as you work, to prevent sticking. Cut ropes into ½-inch lengths. Brush with egg whites and bake in floured pans at 350° until light brown.

Festival Foods and Family Favorites

Indiana Mud Cookies

16 graham crackers
1 (14-ounce) can of sweetened condensed milk
1 (6-ounce) package of chocolate chips

On a piece of wax paper, roll the graham crackers (a few at a time) into crumbs with a rolling pin. Put the crumbs in a bowl. Add the can of condensed milk and the chocolate chips. Drop by spoonfuls onto the greased cookie sheet. Bake at 350° for about 12 minutes. When they are done, let them cool before you remove them from the pan. Serve them with ice cold milk and lots of paper napkins!

The Indiana Kid's Cookbook!

Grandma's Gingersnaps—Four Generation Special

1 cup sugar
1 cup shortening
1 teaspoon cinnamon
3 tablespoons ginger
½ teaspoon cloves
½ teaspoon allspice
½ teaspoon salt
1 cup molasses (sorghum)
1 teaspoon soda dissolved in 3 tablespoons hot water
3½ cups flour

Cream sugar and shortening together; add spices, molasses, and soda water, and mix thoroughly together. Stir in flour. Add a bit more flour if necessary so that cookies can be rolled out easily. Roll thin and cut small. Bake at 350° until crisp (about 8-12 minutes—depending on size of cookie) on a greased cookie sheet. Yield: about 6 dozen.

Note: Also delightful made with only 3 teaspoons ginger—a mild gingersnap. A quick substitute for rolling and cutting: roll dough into small balls, place on greased cookie sheet, dip glass into sugar and flatten ball into thin cookie.

The Guild Cookbook I

Snicker Buns

8 small Snicker candy bars
1 package refrigerator crescent rolls
½ stick melted butter or margarine
½ cup powdered sugar
1 tablespoon milk
¼ teaspoon almond extract

Wrap one candy bar in each triangle of dough; roll it in the melted margarine and place in a muffin pan. (Fill remaining 4 holes in pan halfway with water, for even heat distribution.) Bake at 375° for 10 minutes. Make glaze with remaining ingredients; cover while hot.

Optional: For smaller buns, use 16 Snicker snackers and cut each crescent triangle in half. Use the mini-muffin pans instead.

A Taste of Fishers

Lemon Bon Bons

1 cup butter
⅓ cup powdered sugar
¾ cup cornstarch
1¼ cups sifted flour
½ cup finely chopped pecans

Preheat oven to 350°. Cream butter and sugar until light and fluffy. Add cornstarch and flour, and mix well. Refrigerate overnight.

Shape dough into ¾-inch balls; place on wax paper that has been scattered with nuts. Use bottom of glass (dipped in flour) to flatten balls to ¼-inch thick. Using spatula, place on ungreased cookie sheet, nut-side-up. Bake 6-8 minutes at 350°. Cool and frost.

FROSTING:
1 cup powdered sugar
1 tablespoon butter
1 tablespoon lemon juice
Food coloring

Blend sugar, butter, and lemon juice until smooth. Divide and color. Swirl on top of cookie. Yield: 2-3 dozen.

Cookin' to Beat the Band

Elephant Ears

1½ cups milk
2 tablespoons sugar
1 teaspoon salt
6 tablespoons shortening
2 packages dry yeast
4 cups flour
Oil for frying
Sugar/cinnamon mixture:
½ cup sugar
1 teaspoon cinnamon

In a saucepan combine milk, sugar, salt, and shortening; heat until shortening is melted. Do not let mixture boil. Cool mixture to lukewarm. Add yeast and stir until dissolved; stir in flour 2 cups at a time. Beat after each addition until smooth. Put in a greased bowl, cover with a damp cloth and let rise until double, about 20 minutes.

Dust hands with flour, pinch off pieces of dough about the size of a golf ball. Stretch each piece into a thin 6 to 8-inch circle. Fry one at a time in oil (350°) until dough rises to the surface. Turn and fry on other side until light brown. Drain on absorbent paper and sprinkle with the sugar and cinnamon mixture.

Amish Country Cookbook II

Pecan Pick Ups

PASTRY:

3 ounces Philadelphia cream cheese
1 stick margarine
1 cup flour

Mix until smooth. Form into 24 small balls and chill. Place in small size muffin pans and press firmly around the sides and bottom to form a pastry-like shell.

FILLING:

¾ cup brown sugar
1 tablespoon butter, melted
1 egg
1 teaspoon vanilla
½ cup pecans, chopped

Mix well. Put 1 teaspoon filling in each shell and bake at 350° for 25-30 minutes.

Amish Country Cookbook II

Church Windows

For an easy, quick cookie, this is especially pretty for the holidays. Something special means making Church Windows.

1 (12-ounce) package semi-sweet chocolate chips
1 stick (½ cup) margarine
1 cup chopped walnuts or pecans
1 (10½-ounce) package colored miniature marshmallows
Powdered sugar or coconut

Melt together chocolate chips and margarine. Cool. Add chopped walnuts or pecans and marshmallows. Divide mixture in half and form 2 large logs. Roll each log in powdered sugar or in coconut. Wrap in aluminum foil and chill for 24 hours. Slice into ⅓-inch cookies. Makes approximately 3 dozen.

Sharing Our Best

Rocky Road Squares

1 (12-ounce) package semi-sweet chocolate morsels
1 (14-ounce) can Eagle Brand Sweetened Condensed Milk
2 tablespoons butter or margarine
2 cups dry roasted peanuts
1 (10½-ounce) package white miniature marshmallows

In top of double boiler, melt chocolate morsels with Eagle Brand milk and butter. Remove from heat. In large bowl, combine nuts and marshmallows. Fold in chocolate mixture. Spread in wax-paper-lined 9x13-inch pan. Chill 2 hours or until firm. Remove from pan. Peel off wax paper and cut into squares. Cover and store at room temperature. Makes about 40 squares.

Amish Country Cookbook II

Cream Caramels

2 cups white sugar
2 cups white corn syrup
Few grains of salt
1 stick butter (½ cup)
2 cups cream
1 teaspoon vanilla

Boil sugar, corn syrup, and salt rapidly to 245°. Add butter and cream gradually so that the mixture does not stop boiling at any time. Cook rapidly to firm ball stage (245°). Stir constantly because the mixture sticks easily at the last. Add flavoring and pour into buttered pan. Cut in squares and wrap in wax paper.

Amish Country Cookbook II

Indiana's only lighthouse—in Lake Michigan—is in LaPorte County.

Homemade Mint Patties

1 bag powdered sugar
1 can Eagle Brand Milk
Peppermint oil or flavoring to taste
1 (12-ounce) bag semi-sweet chocolate chips
1 (1-inch) square paraffin

Put powdered sugar in a bowl and add Eagle Brand Milk. Mix well. Add flavoring and form into a ball like pie dough. Leave in bowl and chill overnight.

Next day: Form into little balls and chill several hours. Melt chips and wax. Dip balls into chocolate and let set till firm.

Our Favorite Recipes II

Heavenly Hash

This is a traditional Christmas family favorite.

1 box Knox gelatine (4 envelopes)
½ cup cold water
1 quart milk
1½ cups sugar
1 (20-ounce) can crushed pineapple, drained
1 pint whipping cream

Put gelatine in cold water to dissolve. Add to milk and heat, but do not boil. Stir constantly until all gelatine is dissolved. Then add sugar. Let cool until it begins to thicken. Add pineapple. Whip cream and add ½ to gelatine mixture. Color pink or green. Top with remaining whipped cream. Makes a lot.

Recipes from Jan's Cake & Candy Crafts

Hutch's Buttery Cashew Brittle

2 cups granulated sugar
1 cup light corn syrup
½ cup water
1 cup butter or margarine
1 (7-ounce) jar of dry roasted cashews
1 teaspoon soda

Combine sugar, corn syrup, and water in 3-quart saucepan. Cook and stir till sugar dissolves. When syrup boils, blend in butter. Stir frequently after mixture reaches the syrup stage (230°). Add nuts when the temperature reaches soft-crack stage (280°) and stir constantly till temperature reaches the hard-crack stage (305°). Remove from heat. Quickly stir in soda, mixing thoroughly. Pour into 2 well-buttered cookie sheets, stretching it out thin by lifting and pulling to the edge of the pan using 2 forks. After it cools, turn candy over and break into pieces. Makes 2½ pounds.

Home Cooking

Virgil's Peanut Brittle

2½ pounds sugar
16 ounces white corn syrup
½ cup water
3 pounds raw peanuts
1 stick margarine
½ teaspoon pure vanilla or 1 teaspoon imitation vanilla
½ teaspoon salt
1 tablespoon soda

Combine sugar, syrup, and water in a large, heavy aluminum pan. When this mixture boils lazily, add the raw peanuts. Cook to hard crack stage (300°). Turn off heat and add margarine, vanilla, and salt. Stir until margarine melts. Add soda; beat vigorously until soda is well mixed. Quickly pour onto large, buttered surface or cookie sheets. Spread thin. Allow to cool slightly; turn over. Finish cooling. Makes 6½ pounds.

Our Best Recipes to You, Again

Turtle Shells

1 package Azteca salad shells (in dairy case at grocery)
1 (12-ounce) package caramels
½ cup canned sweetened condensed milk
1 cup (6 ounces) milk chocolate chips
1 cup (6 ounces) pecan pieces

Preheat oven to 350°. Cut shell in 8 pie-shaped wedges. Bake on ungreased baking sheets for 7-9 minutes or until light golden brown. Remove shells and place on wax paper.

Place caramels and milk in microwave-safe bowl. Microwave on MEDIUM for 3 minutes, stirring often. Spread caramels onto cooled shells; top with pecans. Microwave chocolate on MEDIUM for 3 minutes; stir and repeat 2 minutes, stirring often. Drizzle chocolate over caramel and pecans. Makes 32 candies. Delicious!!

Country Cooking

Creamy Mocha Fudge

1⅓ cups sugar
⅔ cup evaporated milk
1 (7- or 8-ounce) jar marshmallow crème
¼ cup butter
2 tablespoons instant coffee powder or granules
¼ cup coffee liqueur
1 (12-ounce) package semi-sweet chocolate chips
1 cup chopped walnuts
1 teaspoon vanilla extract

Line an 8-inch square baking pan with aluminum foil; set aside. In 2-quart saucepan, combine sugar, milk, marshmallow creme, butter, instant coffee, and coffee liqueur. Heat to boiling over medium-high heat, stirring constantly. Boil 5 minutes.

Remove from heat; stir in chocolate chips until melted. Stir in nuts and vanilla. Spread fudge into prepared pan. Refrigerate until firm. Remove fudge from pan and discard foil. Cut fudge into squares. Wrap in plastic wrap and tie with ribbons for gift-giving, if desired.

Cooking with the Warriors

Chocolate Peanut Butter Fudge

4½ cups sugar
1 (13-ounce) can evaporated milk
½ pound margarine
2 cups nuts
2 tablespoons vanilla
9 ounces each chocolate and peanut butter bits (1½ cups each)

Mix sugar and milk and boil for 8 minutes. In large bowl combine remaining ingredients. Pour hot mixture over second mixture and stir until bits are melted. Pour into buttered pan and let set until cool. Makes 5 pounds fudge.

Home Cooking II

Peanut Butter Logs

(Microwave)

Make your own candy bars with this recipe. The kids will like these for after-school snacks and you'll like them while watching television at night!

1 cup peanut butter
¼ cup margarine
1½ cups sifted powdered sugar
3 cups Rice Krispies
1 cup chopped dry roasted peanuts
1 (6-ounce) package (1 cup) semi-sweet chocolate morsels
2 tablespoons margarine

Cream together peanut butter and margarine. Stir in sifted powdered sugar and then Rice Krispies cereal. Portion dough by tablespoons and shape into little logs. Roll in 1 cup chopped dry roasted peanuts and set aside. Melt semi-sweet chocolate morsels with margarine in small saucepan over low heat, stirring constantly. (Or heat on HIGH-power in microwave in glass measure cup for 1 minute or until soft and melted. Stir to smoothness.) Drizzle over top of logs. Chill.

Sharing Our Best

PIES & OTHER DESSERTS

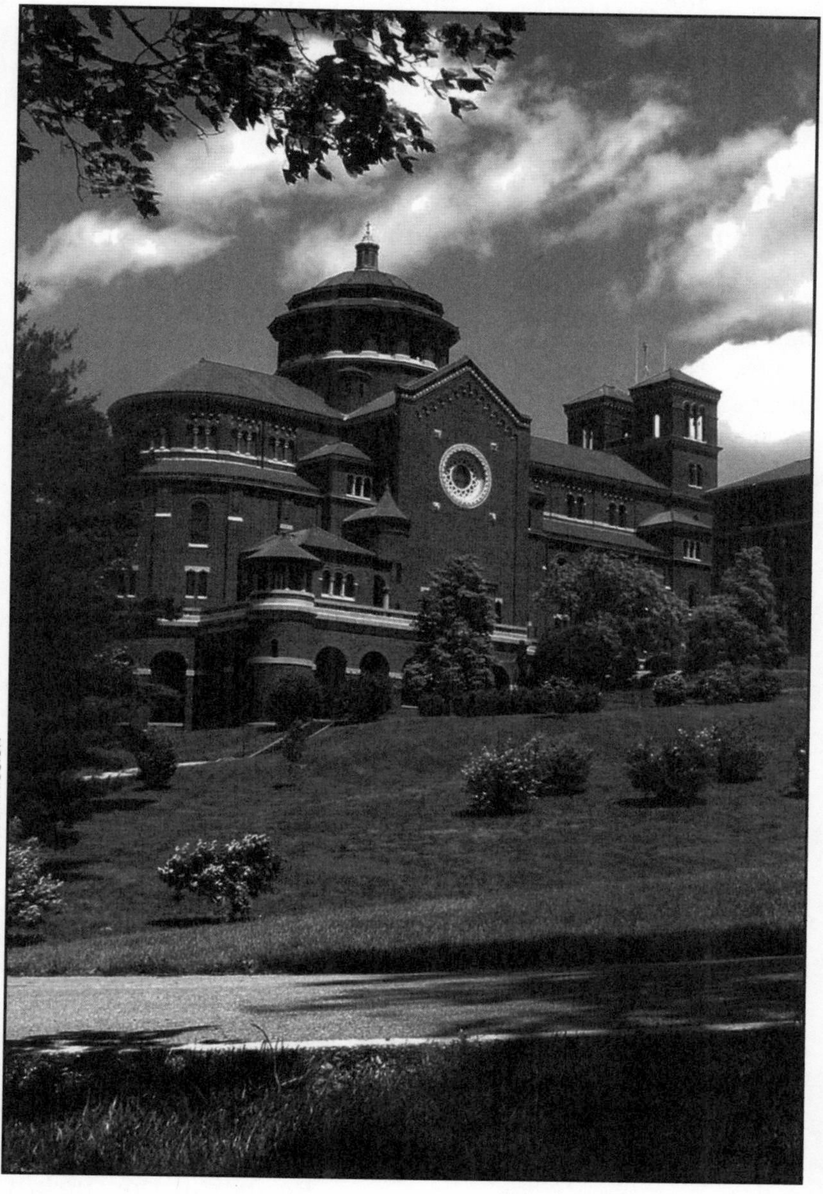

DUBOIS COUNTY VISITORS CENTER & TOURISM COMMISSION

The Monastery Immaculate Conception, located in Ferdinand, was founded in 1867, and is home to one of the nation's largest communities of Benedictine women.

Indiana Sugar Cream Pie

1 cup whipping cream
1 cup coffee cream
¾ teaspoon vanilla
½ cup flour
1 cup sugar
¼ teaspoon salt
Pastry lined 9-inch pie pan
1 tablespoon butter
½ teaspoon nutmeg

Combine heavy cream, coffee cream, and vanilla. In another bowl, combine flour, sugar, and salt. Slowly, using an electric mixer or wire whisk, add cream mixture to flour mixture until smooth. Let stand while rolling out pastry crust.

Line 9-inch pie pan with pastry; dot bottom with small pieces of the butter. Sprinkle nutmeg evenly over bottom of pie shell. Briefly beat cream mixture again before pouring into prepared pie shell. Bake at 450° for 10 minutes; stir the filling and lower heat to 325°. Bake 20-25 minutes longer. Shake the pie pan every 8-10 minutes while baking. Serves 8.

Recipe submitted by Senator and Mrs. Dan Quayle,
Former Vice-President of the United States.

Indiana's Finest Recipes

Old Fashioned Cream Pie

1 stick butter
1 cup sugar
2 cups milk (or 1 cup milk and 1 cup cream for richer filling)
¼ cup cornstarch
¼ cup milk
1 baked pie shell
Nutmeg

Heat first 3 ingredients together in top of a double boiler until very hot and butter is melted. Stir cornstarch in ¼ cup milk until smooth. Add to mixture in double boiler. Continue cooking, stirring constantly, until mixture thickens (about 5 minutes). Pour into baked pie shell. Sprinkle with nutmeg and bake at 400° about 5 minutes.

Recipes of the Durbin

Sugar Pie

1½ cups white sugar
½ cup flour
¼ teaspoon salt
1½ cups boiling water
2 tablespoons soft butter
Ground nutmeg

Mix together sugar, flour, and salt. Add boiling water and butter. Pour into unbaked 9-inch pie shell; sprinkle with nutmeg. Bake at 450° for 15 minutes, then at 350° until set.

Cooking with the Warriors

Apple Cream Pie

1½ cups sugar
4 tablespoons flour
2 cups whipping cream
Dash of salt
1 or 2 apples, cored, peeled, and sliced thin
1 (9-inch) pie shell, unbaked
1 tablespoon butter
Ground nutmeg to sprinkle on top

Combine sugar, flour, cream, and salt. Mix well, but don't beat air into it—just combine well. Add sliced apples (my favorite is Rome Beauty, but you may use any kind). Stir apples into batter. Pour into the prepared crust. Dot with butter and sprinkle nutmeg on top. Bake at 325° for 1 hour and 10-15 minutes. After this amount of time, gently shake pie—if it's still liquid in the center, bake another 10 minutes or so. If it shakes like custard, it's done. You won't believe how good this is! Another time, leave out the apples for the best old-fashioned cream pie you ever tasted!

It's About Thyme

The Indiana Extension Homemakers Association has the largest membership of homemakers in the nation, with almost 25,000 members.

Never Fail Apple Pie

6 cups sliced apples
2 tablespoons butter
½ teaspoon nutmeg
1 cup sugar
½ teaspoon cinnamon
2½ tablespoons flour
½ teaspoon salt
1 (2-crust) pie shell

Combine all of above, except pie crust. Mix well. Pour into pie shell. Use top crust, slit on top. Bake 350° for 45-55 minutes.

Cooking with the Warriors

Apple Crisp

This is by far the best apple crisp you have ever tasted! The sugar and water combine to make a wonderful "caramelly" thick sauce on the bottom with the apples.

½ cup water
½ cup sugar
1 teaspoon cinnamon
4 cups diced apples
1 cup brown sugar
1 cup flour
7 tablespoons butter

Stir water, sugar, and cinnamon together in bottom of 11x7-inch baking dish; stir in apples. Mix brown sugar, flour, and butter with fingers until crumbly and sprinkle on top. Bake in 350° oven for 35 minutes and serve warm. Yield: 8 servings.

Variation: English Apple Pie. Slice 8 medium tart apples into buttered 9-inch pie pan and sprinkle with ½ cup sugar. Mix 1 cup flour, ½ cup brown sugar, ½ cup chopped pecans (optional) and ½ cup butter together; pat on top and bake at 350° for 30 minutes.

The Guild Cookbook IV

Pineapple Pie

Whenever the occasion calls for something quick, try this good and easy Pineapple Pie.

1 (16-ounce) can crushed pineapple (in heavy syrup)
24 large marshmallows
Graham cracker crust
Cool Whip

Heat pineapple and marshmallows over low flame until marshmallows melt. Pour into graham cracker crust. Cool. Top with Cool Whip. Keep refrigerated.

Sharing Our Best

Paw Paw Pie

1½ cups peeled and diced paw paws
1 cup sugar
1 cup milk
1 egg
¼ teaspoon salt

Combine ingredients and cook over moderate heat until thickened. Pour mixture into unbaked pie shell and bake at 350° until crust is done.

The Brown County Cookbook

Apfelstrudel-Vanillesauce

Apple Strudel

2 cups flour
2 eggs
¼ cup water, lukewarm
Pinch of salt
½ teaspoon vinegar
4-5 pounds apples (tart)
⅓ cup sugar
3 tablespoons cinnamon
6 tablespoons butter, melted
4 tablespoons bread crumbs
1 cup almonds or other nuts, chopped
1½ cups raisins

Heap flour on bread board and make a depression in the center large enough to hold the beaten eggs, water, salt, and vinegar. Knead this into a firm dough which, when cut, will reveal air pockets. Set dough, covered, in a warm place.

Peel and grate apples and sprinkle with sugar and cinnamon. Dust a cloth with flour and on it, roll out dough, the thinner the better. Melt butter. Mix in bread crumbs and coat dough. Sprinkle with apples, nuts, and raisins. Roll dough over in the cloth several times to form a loaf (strudel) of several alternating layers of dough and filling. Brush finished loaf with more melted butter, put on greased baking sheet, and bake in a hot (400°) oven until crust is crisp and well browned. This may be served with Vanilla Sauce.

VANILLA SAUCE:
1 cup milk
1 teaspoon vanilla
1 tablespoon sugar
2 egg yolks
½ teaspoon cornstarch

Heat the milk and vanilla, then let cool. Blend sugar, egg yolks, and cornstarch until smooth and stir into milk. Beat in double boiler over moderate heat until mixture thickens. Remove from heat and stir until cool.

Guten Appetit

Great Fresh Strawberry Pie

I pull this recipe out every June during strawberry season. It is the best fresh strawberry pie I've ever had.

CRUST:

1½ cups flour
2 tablespoons sugar
2 tablespoons cold milk
½ teaspoon salt
½ cup Mazola corn oil (for some reason no other kind of oil will work)

Blend the ingredients together and pat by hand into a 9-inch pie pan. Bake in a 450° oven for about 10 minutes; the crust will be starting to brown. Cool the crust, then fill.

(This crust is super easy and very flaky. The taste is slightly sweet. It can be used for other 1-crust pie recipes, and is especially good when the filling is slightly tart.)

FILLING:

1 quart fresh, ripe strawberries
1 cup sugar
2 well-rounded tablespoons cornstarch
2 tablespoons white Karo syrup
1 cup water
2 tablespoons strawberry Jell-O

Clean and drain strawberries. In a saucepan, blend together the sugar and cornstarch. Slowly mix in the syrup and water, stirring well so that there are no lumps. Cook until the mixture is thick and clear.

Remove from the heat and add 2 tablespoons strawberry Jell-O dry mix. Stir until the Jell-O is dissolved. Immediately add the strawberries to the hot filling and stir in. When the filling has begun to cool, pour into the crust. Refrigerate.

Aspic and Old Lace

Vincennes, founded in 1732 as a French outpost and trading center on the banks of the Wabash River, is Indiana's oldest community and territorial capitol. The area is known for its many historic sites, parks, festivals and shops, one of which is William Henry Harrison's mansion, Grouseland.

Peaches 'N Cream Pie

¾ cup flour
½ teaspoon salt
½ cup milk
1 (3¼-ounce) package dry vanilla pudding mix (not instant)
1 teaspoon baking powder
1 egg
3 tablespoons soft margarine or butter
1 (15-20-ounce) can sliced peaches, well drained, reserve juice
1 (8-ounce) package cream cheese
3 tablespoons reserved juice
½ cup sugar
1 tablespoon sugar
½ teaspoon cinnamon

Grease and flour a deep 9-inch pie pan. Combine and beat first 7 ingredients 2 minutes at medium speed. Pour into prepared pie shell. Place peaches over batter.

Combine in small bowl and beat cream cheese, juice, and sugar 2 minutes at medium speed. Spoon over peaches to within 1 inch of edge. Combine 1 tablespoon sugar and cinnamon over cream cheese filling. Bake at 350° for 30-35 minutes. Cool. Refrigerate.

Love Cookin'

Raspberry Cream Cheese Pie

Good combination of flavors.

30 vanilla wafers, crushed
½ cup butter, melted
1 (8-ounce) package cream cheese, softened
1 cup powdered sugar
1 teaspoon vanilla extract
1 cup non-dairy whipped topping
1 (10-ounce) box frozen raspberries, drained
3-4 chocolate toffee candy bars

Preheat oven to 325°. Combine wafers and butter; pat into 9-inch pie plate. Bake 15 minutes. Turn off oven and leave crust in oven for 10 minutes; remove and cool.

Mix cream cheese, powdered sugar, vanilla, and whipped topping. Pour in raspberries. Mix and pour into crust. Crush candy bars in blender; sprinkle on top of pie. Chill 1 hour before serving. Yield: 6-8 servings.

Great Beginnings, Grand Finales

Indiana Raspberry Tart

A unique recipe combining cooked and uncooked berries with exceptional results.

PASTRY:

1 cup all-purpose flour
2 tablespoons sugar
⅛ teaspoon salt
½ cup (1 stick) butter or margarine, cold
2-3 tablespoons cold water

Preheat oven to 400°.

In medium bowl combine flour, sugar, and salt. Cut in butter until crumbly. Sprinkle water, 1 tablespoon at a time, until pastry mixture is just moist and holds together. Press pastry into the bottom and 1-inch up the side of a 9-inch spring-form pan. Set aside.

FILLING:

¼ teaspoon ground cinnamon
⅔ cup sugar
¼ cup all-purpose flour
6 cups fresh raspberries, divided
Whipping cream

Combine cinnamon, sugar and flour in small bowl. Sprinkle half the flour mixture over the bottom of pastry. Top with 4 cups raspberries. Sprinkle remaining flour mixture over raspberries.

Bake tart on lowest oven rack, 50-60 minutes, or until golden and bubbly. Remove from oven; cool on wire rack. Remove side of spring-form pan carefully after tart has completely cooled. Top with remaining 2 cups raspberries. Cut into wedges.

To serve, pour 2 tablespoons cream on individual plate; arrange a tart wedge on cream. Serves 10.

Back Home Again

Out of this World Pie

1 can cherry pie filling
¾ cup sugar
1 large can crushed pineapple, with juice
1 tablespoon cornstarch
1 teaspoon red food coloring
1 (3-ounce) box cherry Jell-O or gelatin
4 small bananas
2 baked pie shells or graham cracker crusts
Whipped topping

Combine cherry pie filling, sugar, pineapple with juice, cornstarch, and food coloring. Cook until thick. Remove from heat and add Jell-O. Allow to cool. Add sliced bananas and pour into crusts. Top with whipped topping. Makes 2 pies.

Amish Country Cookbook II

Rhubarb Cream Pie

Mmmmm good!

1 pound rhubarb, cut into 1-inch pieces
¾ cup sugar
2½ tablespoons tapioca
1 (9-inch) piecrust, unbaked
1 (8-ounce) package cream cheese
½ cup sugar
2 eggs, beaten
1 cup sour cream
2 tablespoons sugar
1 teaspoon vanilla

Cook rhubarb, sugar, and tapioca until thickened. (Red food coloring may be added, if desired.) Pour into an unbaked 9-inch pie crust. Mix well the cream cheese, sugar, and eggs. Pour over rhubarb, and bake in a 350° oven for 35 minutes, until brown and puffy. When cool, mix sour cream, sugar and vanilla together; spread over top. Cool in refrigerator until ready to serve. Serves 6-8.

Specialties of Indianapolis II

Frozen Chocolate Pecan Pie

2 cups finely-chopped pecans, toasted
1/3 cup brown sugar
5 tablespoons butter, cut into small pieces
1/4 teaspoon rum extract, plus 1 1/2 teaspoons water
6 ounces semi-sweet baking chocolate (not chocolate chips)
4 eggs, brought to room temperature
1 teaspoon vanilla
1/4 teaspoon rum extract
1 cup heavy cream*
1/2 cup additional cream
Chocolate curls/shavings

Blend pecans, brown sugar, butter, and rum extract, plus water until mixture holds together. Press into 9- or 10-inch pie pan. Freeze at least 1 hour.

Melt chocolate, then remove from heat. Whisk in eggs, vanilla, and rum extract. Blend until smooth. Cool 5 minutes. Whip heavy cream until stiff. Gently fold cream into chocolate mixture. Pour into crust and freeze. About 1 hour before serving, transfer to refrigerator.

Whip additional 1/2 cup cream. Spoon dollops of whipped cream around the edge of the pie and sprinkle with chocolate curls/shavings.

This pie can be frozen up to 3 months.

*Whipped topping, such as Cool Whip, can be substituted for cream.

The Cookery Collection

Between 1870 and 1982, the jail in Warsaw had an incredible "no escape" record—112 years! Visitors are invited to visit the Jail Museum to experience being "locked up" in the jail. Crawfordsville is the home of the unique 1882 two-story cylindrical rotating cellblock jail.

Chocolate Cream Pie

1 cup sugar
2½ tablespoons cornstarch
1 tablespoon flour
½ teaspoon salt
1¼ unsweetened chocolate squares
3 cups milk
3 egg yolks (reserve whites)
1 tablespoon butter
¾ teaspoon vanilla
1 (9-inch) pie shell, baked

Cook first 6 ingredients over moderate heat, stirring constantly, until mixture thickens and boils. Boil for 1 minute. Remove from heat.

Gradually stir in at least ½ of hot mixture into egg yolks, slightly beaten. Then blend into hot mixture in saucepan. Boil 1 minute, stirring constantly. Remove from heat. Add butter and vanilla. Pour into pie shell. Top with meringue.

3 egg whites
¼ teaspoon cream of tartar
3 heaping tablespoons powdered sugar

Beat egg whites with cream of tartar until frothy. Gradually beat in powdered sugar, a little at a time. Continue beating until stiff. Brown in 375° oven.

Home Cooking

Plantation Angel Food Pie

1 cup water
1 cup sugar
2 tablespoons cornstarch
¼ cup water
3 egg whites
1 teaspoon vanilla
1 cup whipping cream (whipped)
1 cup toasted coconut
2 cups fresh peaches or strawberries
1 (9-inch) unbaked pie shell

Mix water and sugar together and bring to a boil. Mix cornstarch with the ¼ cup water and add to boiled sugar and water. Cook slowly for 15 minutes stirring constantly. Cool. Beat egg whites until stiff and add vanilla. Fold into sugar mixture and pour into pie shell. Bake at 350° for 30 minutes until set. Cover with whipped cream and coconut.

Note: Add fresh fruit between the two layers when in season.

Hoosier Heritage Cookbook

Buttermilk Pie

1 cup sugar
3 tablespoons flour
½ teaspoon salt
3 egg yolks
2 cups buttermilk
4 tablespoons butter, melted
3 stiffly beaten egg whites
1 (9-inch) shell, unbaked
Mace or freshly grated nutmeg (optional)

Combine sugar, flour, and salt, blending well. Beat the egg yolks slightly and add the buttermilk and cooled melted butter to them. Gradually add buttermilk to the dry ingredients and blend thoroughly. Fold in egg whites. Pour pie filling into pie shell. Sprinkle mace or a grating of nutmeg on top if desired. Bake at 375° for 45 minutes, or until a silver knife inserted in the center comes out clean.

The Midwestern Country Cookbook

Sinful Sunday Pie

18 Oreo cookies, crumbled
⅓ cup melted butter
⅓ cup milk
1 cup evaporated milk
1 cup miniature marshmallows
1 (6-ounce) package chocolate chips
Dash of salt
½ gallon ice cream

Line bottom of greased 9-inch spring-form pan with crust made from crumbled Oreo cookies mixed with the butter and milk. In a saucepan, combine evaporated milk, marshmallows, chocolate chips, and salt. Cook, stirring constantly until thick. Cool slightly.

Spoon ½ of ice cream into pie shell and drizzle ½ of chocolate sauce over it. Spoon on rest of ice cream and top with remaining chocolate sauce. Chill 4 hours or overnight. Remove from freezer 15 minutes before ready to serve. Serves 6 or more.

Champions: Favorite Foods of Indy Car Racing

Pumpkin Pie Squares

1 cup sifted flour
½ cup quick Quaker Oats
½ cup brown sugar
½ cup butter
1 can pumpkin (2 cups)
1 (13½-ounce) can evaporated milk
2 eggs
¾ cup sugar
½ teaspoon salt
1 teaspoon cinnamon
½ teaspoon ground ginger
¼ teaspoon ground cloves
½ cup chopped pecans
½ cup brown sugar
2 tablespoons butter

Combine flour, Quaker Oats, ½ cup brown sugar, and ½ cup butter in mixing bowl. Mix until crumbly, using an electric mixer on LOW speed. Press into ungreased 13x9x2-inch pan. Bake at 350° for 15 minutes.

Combine pumpkin, evaporated milk, eggs, sugar, salt, and spices in mixing bowl; beat well. Pour into crust. Bake at 350° for 20 minutes.

Combine pecans, ½ cup brown sugar, and 2 tablespoons butter; sprinkle over pumpkin filling. Return to oven and bake for 15-20 minutes, or until filling is set. Cool in pan and cut in 2-inch squares.

Our Best Recipes to You, Again

Coconut Macaroon Pie

¼ cup chopped pecans
1 (8-inch) unbaked pie shell
½ cup water
¼ cup flour
1 (3½-ounce) can flaked coconut
2 eggs, slightly beaten
1½ cups sugar
¼ teaspoon salt
½ cup melted butter

Sprinkle pecans over bottom of pie shell. Combine remaining ingredients; pour into pie shell. Bake in slow oven (325°) until golden brown and almost set (about 45 minutes). Cool and serve.

Home Cooking

Rum Raisin Bread Pudding

Crunchy coconut fringe crowns a traditional rum raisin custard. To receive raves, prepare this pudding anytime for anyone.

1 cup raisins
¼ cup dark rum
5 large eggs
1 cup granulated sugar
2 tablespoons vanilla extract
2 cups milk
1 cup heavy or whipping cream
Day-old French bread, cut into ½-inch cubes to equal 6 cups (20-22 ½-inch-thick slices, about 7-8 ounces)
1 cup sweetened, shredded coconut
2 tablespoons unsalted butter, melted and cooled slightly

Generously butter a 2-quart shallow baking dish. Soak raisins in rum for at least 30 minutes. In a large bowl and with an electric mixer set on medium speed, beat together eggs, sugar, and vanilla. Reduce mixer speed to LOW and add milk and cream; continue beating until well mixed.

Place bread cubes in a separate large bowl. With a fine-mesh sieve, strain custard mixture over bread. Add raisins and rum and coconut; with a spoon, toss to combine. Let stand for 30 minutes so that the bread absorbs the liquid.

Preheat oven to 350°. Pour pudding mixture into prepared dish, distributing raisins and coconut evenly. Drizzle top with melted butter. Bake for 45-50 minutes, or until custard is set (knife inserted 1 inch from center comes out clean), pudding is puffed, and top is golden brown. Remove from oven onto a wire rack and cool for at least 10 minutes.

Spoon onto serving plates. Serve warm, at room temperature, or chilled. Let unused portions come to room temperature, cover, and refrigerate. Yield: 8 servings.

Note: If you do not have day-old bread, place fresh bread in a 300° oven until it begins to lose some of its moisture, or leave fresh bread uncovered to air-dry for several hours or overnight.

Newfangled, Old-Fashioned Bread Puddings

Persimmon Pudding

Mitchell, Indiana, has a persimmon festival each fall to celebrate the withered orange-brown fruits of a tree that grows wild throughout Southern Indiana. It is believed by many old-timers that persimmons do not ripen until they have been bitten by a frost. That's not true, but the fruits are very late to ripen and often a first frost heralds their season. Persimmon Pudding is often cited as a typical Indiana specialty.

1 cup sugar
1 cup flour
1 cup persimmon pulp
1 cup buttermilk
1 egg
1 tablespoon butter, melted
1 teaspoon baking soda
1 teaspoon salt
1 teaspoon baking powder
1 teaspoon cinnamon
1 teaspoon vanilla
½ cup chopped nuts

Combine all ingredients, mixing until smooth. Pour into a greased casserole dish; cover and bake at 350° for 1 hour.

Festival Foods and Family Favorites

Mother's Date Pudding

2 cups brown sugar
3 cups boiling water
1 tablespoon butter
1 teaspoon vanilla
1 tablespoon butter, softened
½ cup sugar
1 egg
Pinch salt
½ cup milk
2 teaspoons baking powder
1 teaspoon cinnamon
1 cup chopped dates
1 cup nut meats
1½ cups flour

Bring brown sugar, water, and 1 tablespoon butter to a boil. Simmer for 10 minutes. Remove from heat and add vanilla. Pour syrup into a 9x13-inch baking dish.

Combine remaining ingredients to make a batter. Drop by spoonfuls into hot syrup. Bake at 350° for 40 minutes.

Mincemeat and Memories

Annie's Apple Pudding

This fabulous pudding is similar to the date pudding that makes that wonderful sauce as it bakes.

1-1⅓ cups sugar (depends on tartness of apples)
⅔ cup shortening
2 eggs, beaten
6 cups apples, peeled and chopped
1 cup chopped pecans or walnuts
2 teaspoons baking soda
2 teaspoons ground cinnamon
1 teaspoon ground nutmeg
2 cups flour

Cream sugar and shortening. Add eggs, one at a time, and beat well after each addition. Fold in the chopped apples and the nuts. Sift together the baking soda, spices, and flour and add to the apple mixture. Spread the apple mixture into a greased 9x13-inch pan and pour the following sauce over the top.

SAUCE:
1½ cups brown sugar, packed
2 tablespoons flour
1 cup water
¼ cup butter
1 teaspoon vanilla

Stir together the sugar and the flour, then add remainder of ingredients in a heavy saucepan. Bring to a boil and boil gently for 3 minutes, stirring often. Pour this hot sauce over the batter. Do not stir. Bake at 325° for 1 hour. Serves 10-12.

Christmas Thyme at Oak Hill Farm

The Knobstone Trail is Indiana's longest backcountry footpath—58 miles through 40,000 acres of rugged, forested, public land in Clark, Scott, and Washington counties. It follows and was named for the Knobstone Escarpment, Indiana's most prominent geological feature, and one of the state's exceptional scenic areas.

Bailey's Irish Cream Turtle Torte

A wonderful frozen ice cream pie.

1½ cups shortbread cookie crumbs (like Keebler's Pecan Sandies)
¼ cup light brown sugar, packed
¼ teaspoon ground nutmeg
¼ cup butter, melted
1 quart butter pecan ice cream
¾ cup Bailey's Irish Cream Liqueur
1 (12-ounce) jar caramel ice cream topping
1 cup coarsely chopped pecans, toasted
1 quart chocolate ice cream
1 (12-ounce) jar fudge ice cream topping

Lightly butter sides of a 10-inch spring-form pan. Line the sides with strips of wax paper, then butter the bottom and paper-lined sides. In a bowl, combine the cookie crumbs, sugar, and nutmeg. Stir in melted butter. Pat evenly on bottom of pan and refrigerate. Spoon slightly softened butter pecan ice cream into a bowl and swirl in ½ cup of the Irish Cream. (Do not overmix.) Pack this into the chilled crust. Pour caramel topping into a small bowl and stir in 2 tablespoons of the Irish Cream. Drizzle over the butter pecan layer, then sprinkle with ¾ cup of pecans. Freeze 1 hour.

Spread slightly softened chocolate ice cream on top of frozen first layer. Pour fudge topping into another small bowl and stir in the remaining 2 tablespoons of Irish Cream. Spoon this over chocolate ice cream. Cover with foil and freeze until firm, 6 hours or overnight.

To serve, remove sides of pan. Carefully peel off wax paper. Place bottom of spring-form pan on serving plate. Garnish top with remaining ¼ cup pecans. Let torte stand for 10 minutes before slicing. If desired, serve with a dollop of whipped cream atop each serving. Serves 14-16.

It's About Thyme

Lemon Torte

Great summer dessert.

20 graham crackers, crushed
¼ cup sugar
¼ cup butter, softened
1 (8-ounce) package cream cheese
½ cup milk
1 small package vanilla instant pudding
1 small package dry Dream Whip
1⅓ cups milk
1 can lemon pie filling
1 small carton Cool Whip

Preheat oven to 350°. Mix graham crackers, sugar, and butter, and press into a 9x13-inch pan. Bake at 350° for 5–8 minutes, or until light brown. Cool.

Soften cream cheese in milk. Add pudding, Dream Whip and milk. Beat mixture well and add to cooled crust. Chill for at least ½ hour.

Spread top with pie filling. Chill again. Top with Cool Whip. Refrigerate until serving. Yield: 12–15 servings.

Cookin' to Beat the Band

Mystery Dessert

1½ cups flour
1 cup white sugar
1 teaspoon soda
1 (#303) can fruit cocktail and juice (2 cups)
½ teaspoon salt
½ teaspoon vanilla
1 egg
¾ cup brown sugar
1 cup chopped nuts

Mix all except brown sugar and nuts together and pour into buttered baking dish 8½x12½ inches. Mix brown sugar and chopped nuts. Sprinkle over top. Bake 1 hour at 325°.

Home Cooking

Amaretto Dessert

Five-star recipe.

2 cups heavy cream
1 cup sugar
½ cup finely crushed Amaretto di Saronno cookies
3 ounces semi-sweet chocolate, grated
6 egg whites
½ cup Amaretto di Saronno cookies, whole
Chocolate Whipped Cream for garnish

Beat heavy cream until thick. Gradually add sugar and cookie crumbs. Beat until stiff peaks form. Fold in chocolate. In separate bowl, beat egg whites until stiff. Gently fold in cream mixture.

Line 9x5-inch loaf pan with wax paper. Arrange whole cookies in bottom of pan. Spoon cream mixture into pan. Cover with plastic wrap. Freeze overnight until firm. Garnish with Chocolate Whipped Cream.

CHOCOLATE WHIPPED CREAM:

1 cup whipping cream
2 tablespoons powdered sugar
1 teaspoon vanilla extract
½ cup chocolate syrup

In a small mixing bowl, combine all ingredients. Beat until soft peaks form.

Great Beginnings, Grand Finales

Frozen Peanut Butter Cups

These are rich, delicious and addictive! Must be prepared and frozen several hours ahead, or overnight.

1 cup whipping cream
1 (7-7½-ounce) jar marshmallow crème
1 (3-ounce) package cream cheese, softened
½ cup chunky peanut butter

In a small bowl, with mixer at medium speed, beat whipping cream until stiff peaks form. In a large bowl, with the same beaters and with mixer now at LOW speed, beat marshmallow creme, cream cheese, and peanut butter until smooth. Use a rubber spatula and fold whipped cream into the peanut butter mixture.

Line mini-muffin pan cups with fluted paper or foil baking cups. Spoon the mousse mixture into the cups. Set uncovered pans in the freezer for 15-20 minutes (set your timer). Remove pans, wrap well, and immediately place back in freezer. Remove from freezer a few minutes before serving time.

These are wonderful to serve as a light dessert for a luncheon. One or 2 per serving with coffee is a perfect ending to a holiday (or any day!) luncheon. Makes 24.

Christmas Thyme at Oak Hill Farm

Butterfinger Dessert

2 cups crushed graham crackers
1 cup crushed soda crackers
½ cup melted margarine
2 (3½-ounce) packages instant vanilla pudding
2 cups milk
1 quart soft vanilla ice cream
1 carton Cool Whip
2 frozen crushed Butterfinger candy bars

Combine crackers with margarine. Spread ⅔ of mixture in 9x13-inch pan. Reserve ⅓ mixture for topping. Mix pudding, milk, and ice cream. Spread on top of crust. Spread the Cool Whip then combine crushed candy bars with reserved crumbs. Sprinkle on top of Cool Whip and chill in the refrigerator.

Our Favorite Recipes II

Next Best Thing to Robert Redford

This recipe is even better now that it's lower in fat!

1½ cups graham cracker crumbs
½ cup Butter Buds, reconstituted per package instructions
1 (8-ounce) package fat-free cream cheese (Philadelphia Free)
½ cup sugar (or 8 packets Equal)
1 (6-ounce) box sugar-free chocolate pudding
2¾ cups skim milk
6-8 ounces light whipped topping
2 tablespoons chopped walnuts or pecans
2 tablespoons Grapenuts

Mix graham cracker crumbs and Butter Buds together and pat into pan sprayed with butter-flavored spray. Bake 10-15 minutes at 350° until browned. Cool completely.

Mix cream cheese and sugar together on LOW speed until blended. Spread evenly over graham cracker crust. Mix pudding and milk as directed for pies and spread over cream cheese layer. Spread topping evenly over second layer.

Sprinkle nuts and Grapenuts over topping. Refrigerate and serve. Serves 16.

Nutrition Analysis Per Serving: Calories 104; Fat 2g; Cal from fat 17%; Chol 6mg; Sod 295mg.

The Heart of Cooking

Orange Compote

½ cup sugar
1 cup water
6 naval oranges, peeled and cut up
3 tablespoons grated rind
1 cup orange juice

Boil sugar and water. Add other ingredients. Store in refrigerator. This is good served as is or mixed with other fruit.

Our Best Recipes to You, Again

Fruit Pizza

1 package sugar cookie mix (or 1 roll refrigerated sugar cookie dough)
1 (8-ounce) package cream cheese
⅓ cup sugar
½ teaspoon vanilla
Sliced fruit of choice (fresh or canned)
½ cup peach or apricot preserves
2 tablespoons water

Prepare cookie mix according to directions and pat out in a 14-inch pizza pan. Bake and cool. Blend softened cream cheese, sugar, and vanilla. Spread over cookie crust. Arrange fruit over cream cheese layer (use any combination of fresh or drained canned fruit). Glaze with preserves mixed with water. Chill.

Note: If using fruits that brown (such as bananas), dip slices into lemon juice before placing on pizza to keep them fresh.

Cooking with the Warriors

Berry Nice Dessert

Gelatin desserts are cool and flavorful and this one is variable. You can have the flavor of your choice with different berry and gelatin combinations.

1 cup flour
¼ cup brown sugar
¾ cup chopped nuts
½ cup butler or margarine
30 large marshmallows
⅔ cup milk
1 cup cream
1 (6-ounce) package flavored gelatin
2 cups hot water
1 pound frozen berries

Mix first 4 ingredients together and pat lightly into 13x9x2-inch baking dish. Bake at 325° for 15 minutes. Cool.

Melt marshmallows in milk in double boiler. Cool. Whip cream and fold into marshmallow mixture. Spread onto crust.

Dissolve flavored gelatin in 2 cups hot water and mix well. Add frozen berries and mix in hot gelatin. When partially gelled, spoon on top of marshmallow layer. Refrigerate.

Sharing Our Rest

Old-Fashioned Strawberry Shortcake

2 quarts wild strawberries
2 cups flour
4 teaspoons baking powder
2 tablespoons sugar
½ teaspoon salt
⅓ cup shortening
1 egg,
½ cup milk
1 tablespoon melted butter
Additional sugar and butter
1 cup heavy cream, whipped

Sweeten strawberries to taste and set aside for at least 1 hour before the shortcake is ready.

Sift flour, baking powder, sugar, and salt together. Cut in the shortening until the mixture resembles coarse meal. Combine the egg and milk and stir into the flour mixture to form a soft dough. Turn out onto a lightly floured board and divide the dough in halves; pat each half out into a round to fit a greased 8-inch layer-cake pan. Place 1 round of dough in the pan and brush it with the melted butter; top with the second round of dough. Sprinkle the top round of dough with additional granulated sugar (about 2 tablespoons). Bake the shortcake in a very hot oven (450°) for 15-18 minutes, or until the top is lightly browned. On a large round platter, split the hot shortcake apart and re-butter the middle with additional butter, then fill the interior with a portion of the sweetened wild strawberries. Cover with the top layer of shortcake and spoon the rest of the wild strawberries and their juice over it. Cut into pie-shaped portions and serve at once, while warm, topped with whipped cream. Or pass a pitcher of rich cream to be poured over each portion. Serves 8.

The Wild Flavor

In March of 1880, Wabash became the first electrically lighted city. The crowd watched with quiet amazement as the lights began to glow on top of the city courthouse.

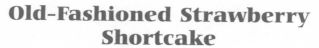

Frangelico Cream

1½ cups superfine sugar
3 egg yolks
1 teaspoon vanilla extract
1½ pounds cream cheese
2 tablespoons Frangelico liqueur
2 cups heavy cream

Beat sugar, egg yolks, and vanilla until light and pale. Beat in softened cream cheese; then Frangelico liqueur. Set aside in cool place. Whip cream until stiff in separate bowl. Fold into cheese mixture. Pour into goblets and chill. Serve plain or with fresh berries or fruit. Yield: 8–10 servings.

Variations: For liqueur cream, replace Frangelico with any fruit brandy or liqueur and garnish with corresponding fruit. For example: Kirsch with cherries, Chambord with raspberries, apricot brandy with apricots.

Great Beginnings, Grand Finales

Olsen's Chocolate Sauce

1 cup sugar
2 tablespoons cocoa
2 tablespoons butter
⅞ cup evaporated milk (Pet or Carnation)
1 teaspoon vanilla

Combine sugar and cocoa and stir over low heat about 2 minutes. DO NOT let sugar melt. Add butter and blend. Add milk stirring constantly. Increase heat and boil rapidly 1 minute, stirring. Remove from heat and add vanilla. Serve hot or cold. Serves 6–8. Good over cake or ice cream.

Home Cooking

Northern Indiana's rich history and heritage are reflected in the Amish and Mennonite cultures of Elkhart County. Designed to allow you to experience the "simple life" at your own pace, the Heritage Trail driving tour comes complete with an audio cassette, guide and map of the area and its highlights.

Jolly Jell-O

1 large package red Jell-O
1 large package green Jell-O
6 cups boiling water
1 envelope Knox gelatine
¼ cup cold water
1 cup pineapple juice, heated
1 large carton Cool Whip
2 dozen or 1½ packages graham crackers, crushed
½ cup sugar
½ cup melted margarine

Dissolve each package of Jell-O in 3 cups boiling water and chill in separate pans until firm. Soften Knox gelatine in cold water, then dissolve in hot pineapple juice. Cool. Fold pineapple mixture into Cool Whip. Cut Jell-O into squares and fold into Cool Whip mixture. Mix graham cracker crumbs, sugar, and melted margarine. Line 9x13-inch pan with ⅔ of crumb mixture. Gently spoon in Jell-O mixture and sprinkle remaining crumb mixture on top. Chill 6-12 hours. Makes 12 large servings.

Our Best Recipes to You, Again

Cinnamon Candied Apples

These are incredibly beautiful in a footed glass or crystal compote. (Cool apples and syrup before placing into a crystal bowl or compote).

1 cup sugar
2 cups water
1 cup cinnamon red hot candies
Small, firm apples, such as Jonathans

Combine the sugar, water, and red hots in a fairly large, deep saucepot. Bring to a boil and simmer until red hots are dissolved and thoroughly melted. Peel small, firm apples. Drop apples into the boiling syrup—keep syrup boiling, so just add 3 or 4 apples at a time. Cook until apples (or small, firm, peeled pears) are just tender, but not mushy. This is enough syrup to cook 6 or 8 apples.

Christmas Thyme at Oak Hill Farm

Indiana is the largest steel producer in the United States, accounting for more than 33% of the nation's steel. USX Garyworks borders the Indiana Toll Road for an awesome five-mile stretch; LTV Steel in East Chicago allows the public to tour their facilities and witness this amazing state-of-the-art process.

CONTRIBUTORS

PHOTO ©ALAN SIMONS

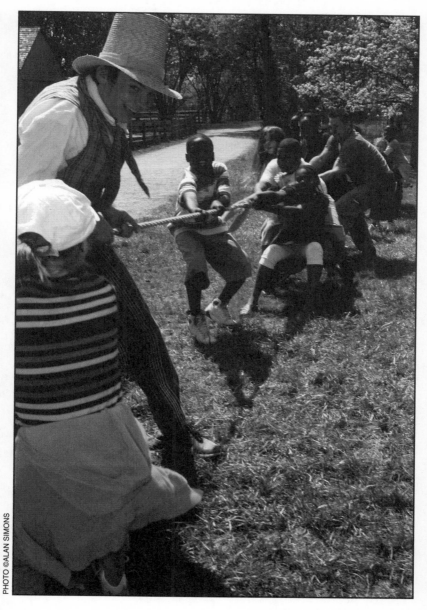

Auhtentic reproductions, costumes, and enactments bring the past to life at Conner Prairie. Fishers.

CATALOG *of* CONTRIBUTING COOKBOOKS

Fifty-seven cookbooks from all regions of Indiana have contributed recipes to this collection. The contributing cookbooks range from large Junior League editions to modest church cookbooks from small communities. Each cookbook has contributed a sampling of their most popular recipes, capturing the flavor of the state. The BEST OF THE BEST STATE COOKBOOK SERIES' goal is to Preserve America's Food Heritage. Since many of the contributing cookbooks have gone out of print, the BEST OF THE BEST COOKBOOKS serve to preserve a sampling of those wonderful family recipes that might have otherwise been lost.

AMISH COUNTRY COOKBOOK
Volumes I, II, and III
Evangel Publishing House
Nappanee, IN

ASPIC AND OLD LACE
Northern Indiana Historical Society
South Bend, IN

BACK HOME AGAIN
Junior League of Indianapolis
Indianapolis, IN

THE BROWN COUNTY COOKBOOK
by Nancy C. Ralston and Marynor Jordan
Indiana University Press
Bloomington, IN

CHAMPIONS: Favorite Foods of Indy Car Racing
Championship Auto Racing Auxiliary
Indianapolis, IN

CHRISTMAS THYME AT OAK HILL FARM and
IT'S ABOUT THYME!
by Marge Clark
Thyme Cookbooks
West Lebanon, IN

THE CONNER PRAIRIE COOKBOOK
Edited by Margaret A. Hoffman
Noblesville, IN

THE COOKERY COLLECTION
by Dorothy Nelis Nicholson
Anderson, IN

COOKIN' TO BEAT THE BAND
Tri Kappa
Elkhart, In

COOKING WITH HERBS
Columbus Herb Society
Fountaintown, IN

COOKING WITH THE WARRIORS
Whiteland Community High School
Whiteland, IN

COUNTRY COOKING
Upper Deer Creek United Church of Christ Women's Fellowship
Galveston, IN

FESTIVAL FOODS AND FAMILY FAVORITES
by Sara Anne Corrigan
Evansville, IN

FOR CRYING OUT LOUD... LET'S EAT!
The Service League of Hammond
Hammond, IN

GREAT BEGINNINGS, GRAND FINALES
Junior League of South Bend
South Bend, IN

THE GUILD COOKBOOKS
Volumes I, II, III, and IV
Valparaiso University Guild
Valparaiso, IN

GUTEN APPETIT
German-American Klub
Indianapolis, IN

THE HEART OF COOKING
Volumes I and II
The Heart Center of Fort Wayne
Fort Wayne, IN

HOME COOKING
Volumes I and II
49'ers Club of Dana
Hillsdale, IN

THE HOOSIER COOKBOOK and
MORE HOOSIER COOKING
Edited by Elaine Lumbra
Indiana University Press
Bloomington, IN

HOOSIER HERITAGE COOKBOOK
Mental Health Assn. in Hancock County
Greenfield, IN

HOPEWELL'S HOOSIER HARVEST II
Hopewell Presbyterian Church
Franklin, IN

THE IU COOKBOOK
by Terry Murray
Guild Press of Indiana
Carmel, IN

INDIANA BED & BREAKFAST ASSOCIATION COOKBOOK AND DIRECTORY
by Tracy & Phyllis Winters
Greensburg, IN

THE INDIANA KID'S COOKBOOK
Gallopade Publishing Group
Peachtree City, GA

INDIANA'S FINEST RECIPES
Beech Grove Central Elementary PTA
Beech Grove, IN

THE JAMES WHITCOMB RILEY COOKBOOK
by Dorothy June Williams and Diana Williams Hansen
Guild Press of Indiana
Carmel, IN

JASPER COUNTY EXTENSION HOMEMAKERS COOKBOOK
Jasper County Extension Homemakers
Rensselaer, IN

LOVE COOKIN'
St. Joseph's Holy Family Hall
Rockville, IN

THE MIDWESTERN COUNTRY COOKBOOK
by Marilyn Kluger
Prima Publishing
Rocklin, CA

MINCEMEAT AND MEMORIES
Tri Kappas of Anderson
Anderson, IN

NEW-FANGLED, OLD-FASHIONED BREAD PUDDINGS
by Linda Hegeman and Barbara Hayford
St. Martin's Press, Inc.
New York, NY 10010

NUTBREAD AND NOSTALGIA
The Junior League of South Bend
South Bend, IN

OUR BEST RECIPES TO YOU, AGAIN
High Street United Methodist Church
Muncie, IN

OUR FAVORITE RECIPES
Volumes I and II
English Wesleyan Women's Missionary Society
English, IN

OUR ITALIAN FAMILY COOKBOOK
by Nancy M. and C. Gary Friedman
Indianapolis, IN

RECIPES FROM JAN'S CAKE & CANDY CRAFTS AND CATERING
by Janet Travis
Anderson, IN

RECIPES OF THE DURBIN
by Mary Durbin
Homer, IN

SERVICE LEAGUE'S FAVORITES
Service League of Michigan City
Michigan City, IN

SHARING OUR BEST
Eileen Hardway
Martinsville, IL

SPECIALTIES OF INDIANAPOLIS II
Home Economists' Guild of Indianapolis
Indianapolis, IN

TASTE & SEE
Women Ministries of Sardinia Baptist
Westport, IN

A TASTE OF FISHERS
Fishers Tri Kappa
Fishers, IN

A TASTE OF TWIN PINES
Twin Pines Alumni
W. Lafayette, IN

WHITE FEATHER FARMS COOK-BOOK SATURDAY SECRETS
White Feather Farms Inc
Muncie, IN

THE WILD FLAVOR
by Marilyn Kluger
Newburgh, IN

WINNERS
Junior League of Indianapolis
Indianapolis, IN

INDEX

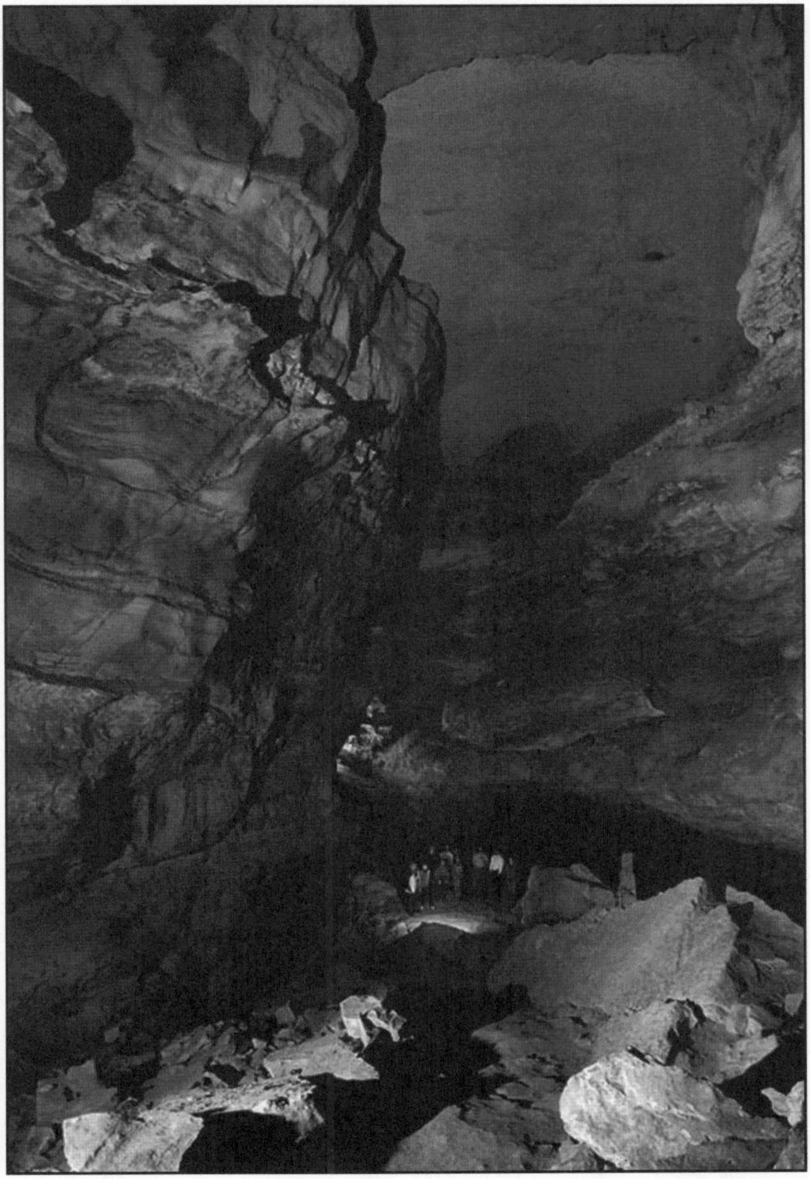

HARRISON COUNTY CVB

Marengo Cave in Marengo is Indiana's most visited show cave, and has been awing visitors with its spectacular beauty for over 120 years.

A

B

C

D

E

F

T

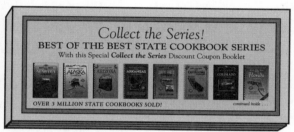

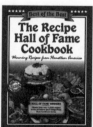

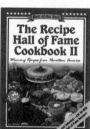

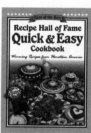

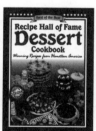

BEST OF THE BEST STATE COOKBOOK SERIES

ALABAMA
ALASKA
ARIZONA
ARKANSAS
BIG SKY
Includes Montana, Wyoming
CALIFORNIA
COLORADO
FLORIDA
GEORGIA
GREAT PLAINS
Includes North Dakota, South Dakota, Nebraska, and Kansas
HAWAII
IDAHO
ILLINOIS
INDIANA
IOWA
KENTUCKY
LOUISIANA
LOUISIANA II
MICHIGAN
MID-ATLANTIC
Includes Maryland, Delaware, New Jersey, and Washington, D.C.
MINNESOTA
MISSISSIPPI
MISSOURI
NEVADA
NEW ENGLAND
Includes Rhode Island, Connecticut, Massachusetts, Vermont, New Hampshire, and Maine
NEW MEXICO
NEW YORK
NO. CAROLINA
OHIO
OKLAHOMA
OREGON
PENNSYLVANIA
SO. CAROLINA
TENNESSEE
TEXAS
TEXAS II
UTAH
VIRGINIA
VIRGINIA II
WASHINGTON
WEST VIRGINIA
WISCONSIN

All Best of the Best Cookbooks are 6x9 inches, are comb-bound, contain over 400 recipes, and total 264–352 pages. Each contains illustrations, photographs, an index and a list of contributing cookbooks, a special feature which cookbook collectors enjoy. Scattered throughout the cookbooks are short quips that provide interesting information about each state, including historical facts and major attractions along with amusing trivia. Retail price per copy $16.95.

To order by credit card, call toll-free **1-800-343-1583**, visit **www.quailridge.com**, or use the Order Form below.

Order Form

Send check, money order, or credit card info to:
QUAIL RIDGE PRESS • P. O. Box 123 • Brandon, MS 39043

Name ____________________

Address ____________________

City ____________________

State/Zip ____________________

Phone # ____________________

Email Address ____________________

❑ Check enclosed

Charge to: ❑ Visa ❑ MC ❑ AmEx ❑ Disc

Card # ____________________

Expiration Date ____________________

Signature ____________________

Qty.	Title of Book (State) or HOF set	Total

Subtotal ________

Mississippi residents add 7% sales tax ________

Postage ($4.00 any number of books) + $4.00

TOTAL ________